... and useful reference guide that will stimulate further
... the study of cinema. For students pursuing A-levels in film, as
...ell as for beginning undergraduates, this volume condenses an encyclopedic
amount of information and a stunning array of approaches to film within a
manageable frame.'

Amy Villarejo, *Cornell University, USA*

Fifty Key American Films explores and contextualizes some of the most
important films ever made in the United States. With case studies from the
early years of cinema to the present day, this comprehensive Key Guide
provides accessible analyses from a range of theoretical perspectives.

This chronologically ordered volume includes coverage of:

- *Citizen Kane*
- *Casablanca*
- *Psycho*
- *Taxi Driver*
- *Blade Runner*
- *Pulp Fiction.*

Among a raft of well-known films, the work of some of America's best
known directors, such as Lynch, Scorsese, Coppola and Scott, is discussed.
This book is essential reading for students of film, and will be of interest to
anyone seeking to explore the impact of American cinema.

John White teaches Film, English and Media at Parkside Community College
and Anglia Ruskin University in Cambridge. He is co-author of *AS Film
Studies: The Essential Introduction* and *A2 Film Studies: The Essential Introduction*,
and co-editor of *Fifty Key British Films*, also published by Routledge.

Sabine Haenni teaches Film and American Studies at Cornell University,
New York. She is the author of *The Immigrant Scene: Ethnic Amusements in
New York 1880–1920* and has published widely on popular theatre, early
cinema and realist fiction.

ALSO AVAILABLE FROM ROUTLEDGE

Fifty Key British Films
Edited by Sarah Barrow and John White
978-0-415-43330-3

Cinema Studies: The Key Concepts (third edition)
Susan Hayward
978-0-415-36782-0

Communication, Cultural and Media Studies: The Key Concepts (third edition)
John Hartley
978-0-415-26889-9

Cultural Theory: The Key Concepts (second edition)
Edited by Andrew Edgar and Peter Sedgwick
978-0-415-28426-4

Cultural Theory: The Key Thinkers
Andrew Edgar and Peter Sedgwick
978-0-415-23281-4

Television Studies: The Key Concepts (second edition)
Neil Casey, Bernadette Casey, Justin Lewis, Ben Calvert and Liam French
978-0-415-17237-0

Fifty Contemporary Filmmakers
Edited by Yvonne Tasker
978-0-415-18974-3

Fifty Key Theatre Directors
Edited by Shomit Mitter and Maria Shevtsova
978-0-415-18732-9

The Routledge Companion to Theatre and Performance
Paul Allain and Jen Harvie
978-0-415-25721-3

FIFTY KEY AMERICAN FILMS

Edited by
John White and Sabine Haenni

Routledge
Taylor & Francis Group

LONDON AND NEW YORK

First published 2009
by Routledge
2 Park Square, Milton Park, Abingdon, Oxon, OX14 4RN

Simultaneously published in the USA and Canada
by Routledge
270 Madison Ave, New York, NY 10016

Routledge is an imprint of the Taylor & Francis Group, an informa business

Typeset in Bembo by
Taylor & Francis Books

Printed and bound in Great Britain by

A catalogu

A

ISBN 10: 0-415-77296-6 (hbk)
ISBN 10: 0-415-77297-4 (pbk)
ISBN 10: 0-203-89113-9 (ebk)

ISBN 13: 978-0-415-77296-9 (hbk)
ISBN 13: 978-0-415-77297-6 (pbk)
ISBN 13: 978-0-203-89113-1 (ebk)

CONTENTS

CHRONOLOGICAL LIST OF CONTENTS

ALPHABETICAL LIST OF CONTENTS

CONTRIBUTORS

Dave Allen began his career as an art teacher but has been involved in teaching film and media studies for over 25 years. His doctoral research had a pedagogic focus and examined links between various forms of visual teaching. He has been at the University of Portsmouth since 1988 and is currently Head of the School of Creative Arts, Film & Media.

Sarah Barrow is Senior Lecturer and Pathway Leader for Film Studies at Anglia Ruskin University, Cambridge. She has published various book chapters on British and Latin American cinema, and is preparing a book on Peruvian cinema, identity and political violence. She is a member of the Board of Management for the Cambridgeshire Film Consortium and advises on education events and resources for a number of film festivals.

Sarah Casey Benyahia is a film and media studies teacher. She is the author of *Teaching Contemporary British Cinema* (BFI, 2005), *Teaching Film and TV Documentary* (BFI, 2007) and co-author of *AS Film Studies: The Essential Introduction* and *A2 Film Studies: The Essential Introduction* (both Routledge, 2007).

Nick Davis is Assistant Professor of English and Gender Studies at Northwestern University, Illinois, where he researches and teaches in the fields of contemporary cinema, gender and sexuality studies, and twentieth-century American literature. His current book project, *The Desiring-Image*, theorizes a new model of queer cinema based on formal principles rather than identity politics, drawing heavily on Deleuzian philosophies of film and sexuality. He has published essays on Todd Haynes' *Velvet Goldmine*, John Cameron Mitchell's *Shortbus* and James Baldwin's *Blues for Mister Charlie*, and he is the author of the film reviews at www.NicksFlickPicks.com.

Terri Francis is Assistant Professor in the Film Studies Program and the Department of African American Studies at Yale University,

CT. She is currently completing a manuscript, 'The Josephine Baker Body-Museum: Blackness, Power and Cinema'. Her further research interests include film history and aesthetics in pre-independence Jamaica and home movie practices in African-American cinema.

Freddie Gaffney is Course Leader for Broadcasting at Ravensbourne College of Design and Communication. A practising screenwriter and cinematographer, he has worked in both film and television. He is Principal Examiner for WJEC AS/A Level Film Studies, and has consulted for industry lead bodies. He is co-author of *AS Film Studies: The Essential Introduction* and *A2 Film Studies: The Essential Introduction* (both Routledge, 2007).

Oliver Gaycken is Assistant Professor in the Department of English at Temple University, PA. He has published on the discovery of the ophthalmoscope, the flourishing of the popular science film in France at the turn of the 1910s, the figure of the supercriminal in Louis Feuillade's serial films and the surrealist fascination with popular scientific images. He is currently writing a book entitled *Devices of Curiosity: Cinema and the Scientific Vernacular*.

Lincoln Geraghty is Principal Lecturer in Film Studies and Subject Leader in Media Studies in the School of Creative Arts, Film and Media at the University of Portsmouth. He is author of *Living with Star Trek: American Culture and the Star Trek Universe* (IB Tauris, 2007) and *American Science Fiction Film and Television* (Berg, forthcoming) and the editor of *The Influence of Star Trek on Television, Film and Culture* (McFarland, 2007), *The Shifting Definitions of Genre: Essays on Labelling Films, Television Shows and Media*, co-edited with Mark Jancovich (McFarland, forthcoming), and *Future Visions: Key Science Fiction and Fantasy Television Texts* (Scarecrow, forthcoming).

Michael B. Gillespie is a visiting Assistant Professor in the Department of Media Studies and Film at The New School. He received his PhD in Cinema Studies from New York University. His research and teaching interests include film blackness, film noir, the Japanese New Wave, film adaptation theory and critical historiographies of visual and expressive culture. He is currently writing a book entitled *Significations of Blackness: American Cinema and the Idea of a Black Film*.

Sabine Haenni teaches Film and American Studies at Cornell University, New York. She is the author of *The Immigrant Scene:*

Ethnic Amusements in New York, 1880–1920 (University of Minnesota Press, 2008), and has published essays on popular theatre, early cinema and realist fiction in publications such as *American Literature, Cinema Journal, Theatre Research International* and *Screening Asian Americans*. She is currently working on transnational cinema in the wake of 1968 and on the relationship between cities and cinema.

Keith M. Harris is Associate Professor in the Department of English and the Department of Media and Cultural Studies at the University of California at Riverside. His areas of specialization include film, African-American and Africana Cinema, African American visual Culture, gender studies and queer theory. His recent publications include 'Boyz, Boyz, Boyz: New Black Cinema and Black Masculinity', in *The Persistence of Whiteness: Race and Contemporary Hollywood Film* (Routledge, 2007), '"Stand up, boy": Sidney Poitier, "Boy", and Filmic Black Masculinity', in *Gender and Sexuality in African Literatures and Films* (Africa World Press, 2007), *Boys, Boyz, Bois: An Ethics of Masculinity in Popular Film, Television and Video* (Routledge, 2006), and '"Untitled": D'Angelo and the visualization of the black male body', in *Wide Angle* (2004).

Adam Lowenstein is Associate Professor of English and Film Studies at the University of Pittsburgh, PA. He is the author of *Shocking Representation: Historical Trauma, National Cinema, and the Modern Horror Film* (Columbia University Press, 2005). Among his current projects is a book that considers the intersections between cinematic spectatorship, surrealism and the age of new media.

Paula J. Massood is Associate Professor of Film Studies at Brooklyn College, CUNY, and on the doctoral faculty in the Program in Theatre at The Graduate Center, CUNY. She is the author of *Black City Cinema: African American Urban Experiences in Film* (Temple, 2003) and the editor of *The Spike Lee Reader* (Temple, 2007).

Jennifer Peterson is Assistant Professor in the Film Studies Program at the University of Colorado at Boulder, CO. Her essays have appeared (or are forthcoming) in *Cinema Journal* and *Camera Obscura*, as well as the essay collections *American Cinema's Transitional Era* (University of California Press, 2004) and *Virtual Voyages: Cinema and Travel* (Duke University Press, 2006). She is currently completing work on a book entitled *Education in the*

School of Dreams: Travelogues and Nonfiction Film, to be published by Duke University Press.

Robert Shail lectures in film studies at the University of Wales, Lampeter. He has published articles and essays on film stardom, gender and British cinema history. His most recent publications include *British Directors: A Critical Guide* (Edinburgh University Press, 2007) and *Stanley Baker: A Life in Film* (University of Wales Press, 2007).

Elliot Shapiro received his PhD from the University of Rochester. He teaches in the John S. Knight Institute for Writing in the Disciplines at Cornell University, New York. At Cornell, he co-directs the Writing in the Majors Program and directs several training and development programs for faculty and graduate students. His academic writing focuses on American literature; American film; and the teaching of writing. Publications include 'Authentic Watermelon: Maxine Hong Kingston's American Novel'.

Neil Sinyard is Professor and Head of Film Studies at the University of Hull. He is the author of more than 20 books on film, including monographs of directors such as Billy Wilder, Alfred Hitchcock, Woody Allen, Steven Spielberg, Richard Lester, Nicolas Roeg and Jack Clayton. He is also co-editor of the series of monographs of British Film Makers for Manchester University Press, and of a volume of essays on 1950s British Cinema. He has been teaching Film Studies for over 30 years.

Lynda Townsend teaches film and English and in recent years has been working with the Open University and the Institute of Continuing Education at Cambridge University. She is a freelance writer on film and art, and has made contributions to *frieze* magazine. She has a particular interest in filmic representations of gender and contemporary expressions of modernity in world cinema.

Simon Ward is Head of Programming and Development at the Independent Cinema Office. His obsession with cinema began after sneaking into Romero's *Dawn of the Dead* in a Dublin fleapit at the tender age of 11. He took a degree in Film Studies at the University of Kent, and after graduating spent several years working at the London Film Festival before becoming Deputy Director of Cinema at the Institute of Contemporary Arts (ICA) in London.

Jean Welsh is Head of Media Studies and Film Studies at Hills Road Sixth Form College, Cambridge, and teaches A-levels in these subjects. She has run INSET sessions on various aspects of film and media for both the BFI and the WJEC and contributed to the *In the Picture* Film Reader on British Cinema.

Nigel Wheale includes among his publications *The Postmodern Arts* (Routledge, 1995), *Writing and Society. Literacy, Print and Politics in Britain 1590–1660* (Routledge, 1999) and *Remaking Shakespeare. Performance across Media, Genres and Cultures* (edited with Pascale Aebischer and Edward J. Esche, Palgrave, 2003). His most recent publication is *Raw Skies. New and Selected Poems* (Shearsman Books, 2005).

John White is a teacher of film, English and media currently working at Parkside Community College and Anglia Ruskin University in Cambridge. He is a co-author of *AS Film Studies: The Essential Introduction* and *A2 Film Studies: The Essential Introduction* (both Routledge, 2007) and an A-level examiner for Film Studies with the Welsh Joint Education Committee. He is a co-editor of both *Fifty Key American Films* and its companion volume, *Fifty Key British Films* (both Routledge).

Paul Young, Associate Professor of English and director of Film Studies at Vanderbilt University, is the author of *The Cinema Dreams Its Rivals: Media Fantasy Films from Radio to the Internet* (Minnesota, 2006). He has published essays and chapters on topics ranging from telegraphy in early cinema (*New Media, 1740–1915*, MIT, 2003) to film noir (*Minnesota Review*), American naturalist fiction (*Modernism/Modernity*), and Don DeLillo (*Approaches to Teaching DeLillo's* White Noise, MLA, 2006). He is currently working on a book about realism in early American film.

INTRODUCTION

This book is not an attempt to assert that the 50 films discussed here are the 'greatest' or 'best' films ever made in the United States. The suggestion is more simply that this selection of films operates to provide an initial appreciation of US cinema over the past 100 years. As an introductory survey focusing on individual texts several other '50s' would serve equally as well. There is neither effort, nor wish, to promote a particular canon of US films. The very nature of a 'canon' is that it is exclusive and this list is not designed to be that (other than in the sense that we only have room for 50 essays in this book). Nor is this list ranked in order of merit; there are two contents lists, one in date-order and the other in alphabetical order, and both of these structures leave a virtually infinite space for your own additions.

It is true, however, that compiling lists of films according to various criteria has always been a favourite pastime of both cinephiles and movie-goers. It is fun; and film, like all storytelling and art-forms, is built around different types of pleasure. Therefore, beyond the theoretical seriousness of discussions about the potential elitism, exclusivity and political manoeuvrings associated with the notion of canons, hopefully you will also simply enjoy agreeing and disagreeing with the inclusions and exclusions you find here.

What were our benchmarks for deciding on these particular 50 films? We wanted to include a spread that extended from early cinema to the present. We wanted to include a range of mainstream genres. We wanted readers to see that certain titles that have reached 'classic' status had been included and were present for their consideration, but we also wanted other films to be included that might encourage the adoption of a wider viewing experience. We wanted the selection to be useful to both students and the general reader looking for an introductory range of material.

We cannot speak for each of our contributors,[1] but for ourselves in the writing we wanted to stress that film form, narrative structure, genre, authorship and other technical approaches to film analysis only have significance within the social experience of making and viewing film; that the crucial context of film and film studies is that of producers and audiences making films and making sense of films within a social context. We wished to stress the historical and cultural, as well as the cinematic contexts. Films are clearly not created in isolation from what is happening in society during the period in which they come into being. They are products of particular societies and each is made at a particular moment in that society's history. In viewing them, for us, it is crucial to see them as determinedly exploring, purposefully commenting upon, or unwittingly reflecting issues relevant to their particular socio-historical moment, but also to see them as being continually re-framed and re-constituted by their reception at different times. Films do not exist, cut off from the world in splendid isolation within the cinema auditorium, or behind the drawn curtains of the home cinema experience or blackout facilities of the university or college screening room. In their conception, their production, their distribution, their exhibition and their reception, they take their place within the social sphere; and to be properly understood they need to be seen within this context. Although it is the case that films are re-created in every act of viewing by the individual spectator, and although any social action and historical moment can be seen and understood in a plurality of ways, still invalid and incorrect readings are possible and the validity or otherwise of any particular reading is a vital matter for discussion. Equally, every reading that has been argued clearly from the evidence of the social and historical context remains contestable. The contesting of readings is, after all, the testing of readings and this process is at the heart of both academic debate and everyday political engagement.

To finally be truthful, as our emphasis on social context suggests, as editors we cannot escape charges of 'canon building':

> That canons exist in film studies and that canon formation is involved with the political sphere is evident. Much less evident is the shifting politics, past and present, of the factors contributing to canon formation.[2]

However lacking in political 'malice aforethought' we assure you the process has been, we have ultimately chosen this list of 50 films over all other possibilities and in doing so we are displaying vested interests; but that is merely in the nature of all social exchange. What matters is that as viewers of film we should engage in this social exchange with critical awareness. As Barbara Klinger has suggested,

there are 'competing voices involved in a particular film's public signification'.[3] We should not attempt to stand apart from this creation
of 'public signification', detached from this discussion, aware of each
of these 'competing voices' but never entering into the fray; rather
we should 'get our hands dirty', become involved in discussing the
implications of these voices and through this action arrive at our own
voice and political position.

Despite our strong initial focus on the films themselves we agree
with Janet Staiger when she suggests that:

> interpreting texts or films is a historical reality determined by
> context, not an inherent or automatic act due to some essential
> human process ...

and would emphasize with her that it is at this point that the critical
debate can begin, because:

> once interpretation becomes historical rather than universal, then
> claims for privileging some interpretations can be refuted.
> Interpretations-in-history become politicized since they relate to
> historical social struggles, not to essences.[4]

In discussing her concept of a 'totalized view', Staiger talks of
achieving an approach to texts in which the discovery of meaning and
significance has been displaced from text to context. More accurately
for us, in an alert reading, context is recognized as being fully sutured
into text.

With essays of this length, the number of questions raised is always
going to be greater than the number successfully answered, but that is
as it should be. Hopefully, these short essays will encourage you to
return to, or seek out for the first time, at least some of these films
with the enthusiasm to explore further and with one or two questions
for which you are determined to seek answers. Each entry aims to be
suggestive rather than exhaustive, attempting to introduce selected
aspects of film form and thematic content in relation to the focus text,
as well as considering historical and cultural contexts. A synopsis is not
given since it is assumed the reader is familiar with plot and storyline,
or can become so very easily. Similarly, details of a film's production
history are not supplied unless this is in some way relevant to ideas at
the core of the film. There is, as we have emphasized, a strong
underlying concern throughout to place these films within social,
historical and political contexts, and not simply to analyze the 'look'

of a film. Concepts and debates relevant to film studies as an academic subject are considered within individual entries, where appropriate. So, ideas relating to genre, narrative structure, auteur theory, representation, spectatorship and performance, for example, are dealt with at various points.

In summary, this book offers brief introductions to a range of films, many of which have gained 'classic' status through critical and/or popular acclaim. The contents pages provided give both date-ordered and alphabetical listings allowing both students and the general reader to use it as a reference work, and the index of key names, institutions and topics has been designed to help with more specific research activities. The effort throughout is to offer entries that are accessible to the well-informed general reader but also sufficiently exploratory and analytical to be useful as models for students of film.

Notes

1 The central feature of a book structured around individual contributions from colleagues working in film education and the film industry is that it allows for a diversity of approaches, and is likely to absorb within itself something of this core aspect of film studies.
2 Janet Staiger, The Politics of Film Canons', *Cinema Journal*, Vol. 24, No. 3, Spring 1985, pp. 4–23.
3 Barbara Klinger, 'Film History Terminable and Interminable: Recovering the Past in Reception Studies', *Screen*, Vol. 38, No. 2, 1997, pp. 107–28.
4 Janet Staiger, *Interpreting Films: Studies in the Historical Reception of American Cinema*, Princeton, NJ, Princeton University Press, 1992, p. 18.

FIFTY KEY AMERICAN FILMS

BIRTH OF A NATION (1915)

[Production Company: D. W. Griffith Corporation/Epoch Producing Corporation. Director: D. W. Griffith. Screenplay: D. W. Griffith and Frank E. Woods, adapted from Thomas Dixon's *The Clansman*. Producer: D. W. Griffith. Cinematography: G. W. Bitzer. Cast: Henry B. Walthall (Ben Cameron), Mae Marsh (Flora, the younger sister), Miriam Cooper (Margaret, the older sister), Josephine Crowell (Mrs Cameron), Spottiswoode Aitken (Dr Cameron), Lillian Gish (Elsie Stoneman), Ralph Lewis (Austin Stoneman), Elmer Clifton (Phil Stoneman), Mary Alden (Lydia Brown), George Siegmann (Silas Lynch), Walter Long (Gus).]

Birth of a Nation is in all likelihood the most troublesome film in US history. Commemorating the 50-year anniversary of the end of the Civil War, the film was released as a major roadshow attraction. At the symbolically named Liberty Theatre on New York City's Broadway, tickets for the film cost 2 dollars, showing how far removed this kind of cinema was from the earlier nickelodeons and signalling film culture's aspiration to become part of high culture. *Birth of a Nation* was the first movie to be screened at the White House. Directed by D.W. Griffith, a major director of the silent era, who, contrary to popular legend, rarely invented new cinematic techniques but frequently refined and combined them in ways so that they effectively became associated with his name, *Birth of a Nation* has often been hailed as a cinematic masterpiece. But from the beginning critics (often the same who praised its aesthetic) and activists denounced and protested its virulent racism. Writing in *The New Republic* in 1915, Francis Hackett argued that 'this film is aggressively vicious and defamatory. It is spiritual assassination. It degrades the censors that passed it and the white race that endures it' (Lang 1994: 163). More recently, James Baldwin has called it 'an elaborate justification of mass murder' and Richard Dyer a film about 'ethnic cleansing' (Baldwin 1976: 45, Dyer 1996: 169).

Released after World War I had broken out but before the United States entered the war (a context that helps explain the references to peace), *Birth of a Nation* was the most visible and notorious Civil War film released in the teens. In 1913, an astonishing 98 Civil War films were released (Stokes 2007: 181). *Birth of a Nation* came at a time when the difference between documentary and fiction film was rather iffy, if only because the term 'documentary' would not be used before 1926 (when John Grierson applied it to Robert Flaherty's *Moana*). Arguably the line between documentary and fiction remains difficult. Time and again, the film justifies its authenticity – and authority – by inserting what it calls 'historical facsimiles' (tinted differently) and excerpts from Woodrow Wilson's *History of the American People* from 1902 (which opens Part II of the film). The status of such historical reproductions, however, is tricky, especially in scenes where the fictional characters are also present (for instance, when Mrs Cameron appeals for mercy from Lincoln, 'The Great Heart', or at Lincoln's assassination). The relationship between fiction and fact gets further complicated because Austin Stoneman was a fictionalized (and demonized) version of Thaddeus Stevens, a Member of Congress from Pennsylvania who helped draft the Reconstruction Act and the 14th Amendment to the US Constitution (which helped secure rights, such as citizenship and due process, for African Americans). Despite such obvious slippages and fictionalizations, however, Griffith and others frequently defended the film on grounds of its historical accuracy. He famously claimed that:

> The time will come, and in less than ten years ... when the children in the public schools will be taught practically everything by moving pictures. Certainly they will never be obliged to read history again.
> Imagine a public library of the near future, for instance. There will be long rows of boxes or pillars ... At each box a push button and before each box a seat ... you will merely seat yourself at a properly adjusted window, in a scientifically prepared room, press the button, and actually see what happened.
> There will be no opinions expressed. You will merely be present at the making of history.
>
> (Quoted in Lang 1994: 4)

Given the kinds of opinions that are expressed in *Birth of a Nation*, we should be grateful that Griffith was spectacularly wrong. But we should also note that today makers of controversial films still defend themselves by insisting on a film's accuracy, a strategy that often aims at closing down discussion about a film and that disregards the fact that each film by necessity presents only a limited selection of things and cannot escape adapting a particular point of view.

Within this broader historical issue, the representation of the South (a regional identity) remains problematic. The film has often been understood as trying to valorize the South, as being nostalgic for an antebellum South, a 'Plantation Idyll'. The introduction of Dr Cameron as the 'kindly master' suggests as much, especially since the camera tilts to his feet to reveal two puppies, symbolically coloured black and white, that seem perfectly content until 'hostilities' are introduced in the form of a cat. In this vision, the South is peopled by docile and subservient blacks who do not challenge their masters, let alone ask for equality (see, for instance, the many shots in which the Camerons' Mammy – in blackface – approvingly hovers in the background). But such 'a quaintly way … is to be no more', the intertitle introducing the 'Southland' announces. Richard Dyer has argued that even though the film privileges the South over the North by giving it much more screen time and a much more elaborate family structure, the South needs Northern whiteness, embodied by Elise (Lillian Gish) who is lighter and more brightly lit than Margaret (Miriam Cooper), the daughter of the South.

In this context, the film can be understood as doing a form of complex cultural work: it works to give the South a new racial, cultural, and national identity at the historical moment when it was made, the teens. Michael Rogin has taken this logic further and argued that the film displaces a number of anxieties present in US culture onto a black/white conflict. For instance, the early twentieth century saw the emergence of a 'new woman' who was no longer confined to the private sphere, but was seen in the streets, in department stores and at the movies, by herself. White slavery films from the period, such as *Traffic in Souls* (George Loane Tucker, 1913) rephrased anxieties about women's emerging public presence and (sexual) power as concerns with what might happen to unaccompanied women. By representing white women as virginal and black men as oversexualized, Rogin has argued in regard to *Birth of a Nation*, 'Griffith displaces sexuality from white men to women to blacks in order, by the subjugation and dismemberment of blacks, to reempower white men' (Lang 1994: 273). By consolidating the stereotype of the black rapist, the film also suppressed another historical truth: that especially in the antebellum South, black women were much more likely to be raped by their white masters.

By offering a sophisticated reading of the film's racism, Rogin suggests that to note the film's racism is not enough, that the more difficult task is to uncover the multiple ways in which racism can function. The turn of the century saw a decline of race relations across the board, from the systematic disenfranchisement of African Americans in Southern states to the *de facto* segregation and discussion of antimiscegenation statutes, among others, in the wake of white panic about the Great Migration of African Americans to Northern cities in Northern states. *Birth of a Nation* not only posited the antebellum

5

plantation as an ideal, it came at a time when the Ku Klux Klan was revived (and it would be used as a propaganda and recruitment tool by the Klan). The unwillingness to hire African American actors for parts and the will to keep African American extras away from white women throughout the film speaks to the film's racism at the level of production. How African American extras experienced their jobs – and whether it was more desirable than the limited kinds of other jobs available to them at the time – is a question that would deserve much more investigation.

Racism at the level of production had complex consequences on the level of representation. There are multiple ways of signifying 'blackness' in the film. It uses stereotypically exaggerated blackface derived from the minstrelsy tradition (as in the case of the Stonemans' male servant), more 'realistic' blackface (as, for instance, in the case of the faithful Mammy), as well as African American extras. There is even a moment when we are supposed to be able to distinguish between white characters in blackface and black characters played by white people in blackface. Some have read this as a moment when the film's ideology undoes itself, while others argue that the multiple uses of blackface speaks to the relative ease with which blacks were deemed recognizable. The film also distinguishes between 'faithful' African Americans (who essentially continue in the mode of the 'grateful slave') and rioting incendiaries (who are seen as incapable of any social or governmental organization). But note how even 'faithful' blacks are treated differently by the camera, made to hover in the background of shots, never getting close-ups. Camera techniques, such as framing and distance, as well as performance (think of the little kids who fall off a cart at the beginning of the first Southern sequence) are thus also mobilized to dehumanize (and infantilize) all of the black characters.

It is in the recasting of history as a (family) melodrama that the film's racism becomes most apparent. Melodrama uses strongly polarized characters (villains and heroes), and thus can be used as a segregationist vehicle. It also wants to start and end in a 'space of innocence' from which the villain has to be expelled (Williams 1991: 28). *Birth of a Nation* casts Africans as villains who have intruded onto a supposedly unproblematic space – 'The bringing of the African to America planted the first seed of disunion', an early intertitle asserts (note the absence of a subject/agent in that sentence). The expulsion of African Americans from the white cabin by the Ku Klux Klan in the role of the hero completes this melodramatic narrative arc. (The rescue sequence featuring the Klan also resonates with and seeks to repress an image of another cabin – Harriet Beecher Stowe's *Uncle*

Tom's Cabin [1852], which had sought to generate anti-slavery sentiment by capitalizing on black domesticity.) This need to expel blacks is in tension with the film's plantation ideal, maybe a reason why we never see a deportation of blacks to Africa (though there has been some speculation among critics if there was such an alternate ending). Most fundamentally, blacks are being excluded from the family melodrama: the two white, heterosexual couples at the end span North and South – giving birth to a new, distinctly white nation. In this conflation of family, race, and nation (as if these terms were interchangeable), African Americans are simultaneously deprived of family and citizenship. This use of melodrama to assert racial lines also explains that the most vilified characters in the film are mulattoes who resist the film's racially melodramatizing logic.

Nonetheless, we should keep in mind that the relationship between aesthetics and politics is always complicated and never predetermined. For a long time, critics attempted to separate the film's aesthetics from its politics, which allowed them to hail the film's narrative and visual sophistication (in terms of editing, use of close-ups, economies of scale, etc.), while condemning its content. As we have seen, however, aesthetic strategies are used to make political points. What kinds of political points are being made through an aesthetic technique, however, is often quite open. Griffith himself had used cross-cutting in *A Corner in Wheat* (1909) in order to argue against the US class system, thus making a progressive film, before using the same technique to racist ends in *Birth of a Nation*.

Birth of a Nation generated a flood of reactions, starting in 1915. In newspapers, Dixon and Griffith defended themselves against charges of racism; white film critics recognized the aesthetic importance of the film and seemed unable to deal with its content; Southern partisan journalists eagerly embraced the film; the NAACP (National Association for the Advancement of Colored People), founded in 1909, tried to stop the film from being screened, protesting the film's exhibition over 120 times between 1915 and 1972 (Gillespie and Hall 2006: 185). Censorship battles waged in many places; in Boston, for instance, the entire Gus sequence was cut, even though censors often seemed more concerned about the film's ability to incite riots than about its depiction of African Americans (ibid.: 185, 191). The year of the film's release the Supreme Court ruled that movies were not protected under the First Amendment of the US Constitution, as free speech, a ruling that would be overturned only in 1952. Nonetheless, it is important to note that this ruling had less to do with discriminatory representation and much more with anxieties about, for instance, the representation of violence and sexuality on screen. The NAACP by and large lost the censorship battles, and the Production Code, which later regulated what could be shown on screen, explicitly prohibited the representation of miscegenation.

There were also a number of cinematic reactions. Griffith himself responded by making *Intolerance* (1916), which sought to respond to charges of racism but turned away from the topic of race relations. The most powerful response came from Oscar Micheaux, a black writer and filmmaker who was a crucial director in a fledgling race film industry which in the early teens started to produce black-cast films for black audiences. In 1919, Micheaux directed *Within Our Gates,* a film that is often seen as a direct response to *Birth of a Nation*, which imagines a diasporic nation not based on race and which includes a powerful cross-cutting sequence (alternating between a lynching and a near-rape) that uses this particular cinematic technique to denounce rather than add to racism.

Today, it may seem easy to dismiss *Birth of a Nation's* racism, but we should not underestimate the longevity of the film's influence or its modes of representation. In the early 1930s, a Payne Fund study found that middle and high school students' 'favourable' opinion of African Americans dropped from 7.46 to 5.93 (on a scale of 11 to 0) after watching the film, and was unlikely to come back up (Lang 1994: 199). Authorities have often remained anxious that provocative films could incite race riots (including Spike Lee's 1989 film *Do the Right Thing*). For decades, Hollywood's white male characters made it their task to be ready to kill their women before non-white men could get to them (as in John Ford's 1939 film, *Stagecoach*), to preserve them from a 'fate worse than death', suggesting just how much the film helped shape representations of white femininity. Richard Wagner's 'Ride of the Valkyries', the music which accompanies the Klan's rescue is powerfully (and differently) used in other films, including Francis Ford Coppola's *Apocalypse Now* (1979). Structures of representation are not easy to overturn and may be unconsciously replicated. *Birth of a Nation* serves as a powerful reminder that politics cannot be disengaged from aesthetics while at the same time the relationship between politics and aesthetics remains complex and malleable.

Further reading

James Baldwin, *The Devil Finds Work*, New York, Dial Press, 1976.
Manthia Diawara, 'Black Spectatorship: Problems of Identification and Resistance', in *Black American Cinema*, New York, Routledge, 1993.

Richard Dyer, 'Into the Light: The Whiteness of the South in *Birth of a Nation'*, in Richard H. King and Helen Taylor (eds), *Dixie Debates: Perspectives on Popular Culture,* New York, New York University Press, 1996.

Michele K. Gillespie and Randal L. Hall (eds), *Thomas Dixon Jr and the Birth of Modern America*, Baton Rouge, LA: Louisiana State University Press, 2006.

Robert Lang (ed.), *The Birth of a Nation*, New Brunswick, NJ, Rutgers University Press, 1994.

Melvyn Stokes, *D. W. Griffith's* Birth of a Nation: *A History of 'The Most Controversial Motion Picture of All Time'*, New York, Oxford University Press, 2007.

Linda Williams, *Playing the Race Card: Melodramas of Black and White from Uncle Tom to O.J. Simpson,* Princeton, NJ, Princeton University Press, 1991.

SABINE HAENNI

SHERLOCK JR (1924)

[Production Company: Buster Keaton Productions. Director: Buster Keaton. Producers: Joseph M. Schenck, Buster Keaton (uncredited). Script: Jean Havez, Joe Mitchell, and Clyde Bruckman. Cinematographers: Elgin Lessley and Byron Houck. Editor: Buster Keaton (uncredited). Cast: Buster Keaton (The Boy/Sherlock Jr), Kathryn McGuire (The Girl), Ward Crane (The Rival), Joe Keaton (The Girl's Father), Erwin Connelly (Hired Man/The Butler).]

Although *Sherlock Jr* is not the only film in Buster Keaton's body of work to play with the concept of cinema, it is the film that does so most extensively. The film works with an idea that was already a commonplace by the 1920s – the concept of movies as a dream world – and makes it literal: the film's main character, a projectionist in a movie theatre, falls asleep on the job and dreams himself into the movie on the screen. Significantly, this character, played by Keaton, has no name in the frame narrative (he is introduced simply as The Boy), so that he functions as a kind of everyman character. When he dreams himself into the film, however, he becomes the masterful detective Sherlock Jr. This is one of many ways in which Keaton is able to make a comment about the effect of cinema; the film dramatizes the way spectators project themselves into movies and identify with the hero. *Sherlock Jr* presents the cinema as a particular kind of dream world: glamorous and surreal.

In portraying the cinema as a kind of nonsensical parallel universe filled with magical escapes and series of gags, *Sherlock Jr* provides a commentary on film and the modern world that was in step with the intellectual and artistic currents of the time. Indeed, Keaton's work was greatly admired by surrealist artists such as Salvador Dali and Luis Buñuel. However, Keaton was not an intentional surrealist, but a practitioner of involuntary surrealism. It is therefore more historically accurate to characterize Keaton's work as absurdist; Keaton was an intuitive modernist, not a doctrinaire one. Likewise, scholars today sometimes credit Keaton's films with providing a trenchant criticism of the modern world, even though his films are not as explicitly political as those of the other comedian/director with whom he is most frequently compared, Charlie Chaplin. But again, it is important to understand that Keaton did not set out to make a critical form of cinema; rather, his goal, like that of so many comedians, was simply to make people laugh. Of course, there is nothing very simple about that.

Sherlock Jr contains two narratives: the everyday life frame story, and the film-within-a-film, entitled 'Hearts and Pearls'. These narratives parallel each other, which allows Keaton to derive humour out of the contrast between the 'real' world and the film (within-a-film) world. Each narrative contains a mystery (the theft of a pocket watch in the frame narrative, the theft of a string of pearls in 'Hearts and Pearls'), as well as a standard melodramatic triad of characters: a hero, a villain, and an innocent girl for whom the male characters vie. Not only is The Boy transformed into a more glamorous version of himself in 'Hearts and Pearls', so are all the other characters. The Girl, who wears a humble gingham dress in the frame narrative, is dressed in a sleek black evening gown in the film-within-a-film. Likewise the villain, who wears a too-small suit in the frame narrative, is transformed into a tuxedo-wearing cad in the film-within-a-film. Even the irascible theatre manager becomes Sherlock Jr's sophisticated sidekick Gillette in 'Hearts and Pearls'. Keaton uses elements of *mise-en-scène*, particularly costume, to make his point that films make the world seem glamorous.

Mise-en-scène − which refers to the lighting, setting, costuming, and acting of figures in the scene − is an important aspect of cinema derived from the theatre. Every aspect of *mise-en-scène* can also be found in stage productions. Keaton was the child of vaudeville performers, and was raised in the world of live performance. Costumes, props, comedic and acrobatic performance − all these theatrical techniques were used to their fullest in Keaton's films, and all these techniques had been learned by him in childhood.

Keaton had been a performer in his parents' vaudeville act from the age of 5. The family act, known as 'The Three Keatons', involved Buster's father, Joe Keaton, throwing tiny Buster around the stage or into the orchestra pit while the audience roared with laughter. Buster's mother Myra had sewn a suitcase handle onto the back of his costume to make it easier to throw him around. Buster played the little straight man, never breaking into tears or cracking a smile; this was the origin of his famous unsmiling demeanour, which led to his screen nickname, 'The Great Stone Face'. Out of this experience, young Buster learned to fall without getting hurt, and he became a great acrobatic and stunt performer. Thanks to Buster's talent, the act became a huge success; for a time Buster was the most successful young comedic performer in the United States. Despite Joe Keaton's abusive behaviour (and his increasingly problematic alcoholism), Keaton always defended his father, and eventually said he owed everything to him. Buster even hired his father to play roles in several of his films; Joe Keaton plays The Girl's father in *Sherlock Jr.*

When constructing film scenes that required physical stunts, Keaton liked to use single shots or even long takes, in order to prove that the stunts were real rather than cinematic tricks. There are numerous examples of single-shot stunts in *Sherlock Jr,* from Keaton's vaulting from rooftop into car using a railroad gate, to the runaway motorcycle chase near the end of the film, in which Sherlock Jr encounters a series of obstacles: cars, felled tree logs, an incomplete bridge. Each obstacle encountered is handled in a single shot, heightening the suspense – and humour – of Keaton's miraculous escape each time.

Keaton's use of individual shots to depict stunts, along with his mastery of theatrical techniques such as costume and performance, should not lead one to think he was an uncinematic director, however, for Keaton's films – *Sherlock Jr* in particular – display virtuosic montage. When Keaton moved from vaudeville into filmmaking at the age of 21, he became just as skilled at cinematic techniques as he was in theatrical practices. Indeed, an often-told story about Keaton's early film work with Roscoe 'Fatty' Arbuckle has Keaton taking apart a camera in order to understand how it works. As *Sherlock Jr* demonstrates, Keaton's films move back and forth between theatrical moments and cinematic moments.

The film's most famous sequence, for example, derives its comedy entirely from its use of montage. In this sequence, Keaton's character, The Boy, walks up to the movie screen and enters the action of the film – all within his dream, which makes the slapstick events that follow seem plausible. He is quickly thrown back into the theatre by one of the film's actors, but then he returns and climbs into the film again. What follows is a series of quick edits as the film-within-a-film's scenes change, independent of The Boy's presence: he crouches to sit on a bench, and the scene changes to a city street, which erases the bench and topples him onto the ground. He peers over a mountain precipice, only to find himself staring down at a lion as the scene changes around him. The film creates a discontinuity between Keaton's character and its diegetic world, thus making humour out of a striking play with film form. This kind of humour could not have been executed in the theatre, and the sequence demonstrates Keaton's mastery of cinematic technology. Decades later, Keaton told interviewers that this sequence was the creative seed of the film. 'That was the reason for making the whole picture. Just that one situation: that a motion picture projectionist in a theatre goes to sleep and visualizes himself getting mixed up with the characters on the screen.'[1]

Like much of Keaton's work, *Sherlock Jr* relies heavily on prop comedy, and here again, Keaton utilizes both theatrical and cinematic techniques. One moment in particular stands out, when Sherlock Jr makes a quick escape from the villains by jumping through a window into which he has placed a mysterious hoop containing some clothing. This is one of Keaton's moments of virtuoso acrobatic performance: he runs and jumps out the window and into the costume at great speed, only to land on his feet transformed into a slow-moving old woman. This stunt is handled in a single shot, which emphasizes that it is no cinematic trick. And yet in order to render Keaton's movement from inside the villain's lair through the window and outside, a cinematic device was used: the camera was placed outside the building, and in a dissolve, the building's outer wall disappears so that the audience can see events happening both inside and outside the structure.

Another important gag comes just a moment later, as Sherlock Jr jumps through his sidekick Gillette's torso and disappears through a wall. Perhaps more than any other stunt in the film, this one seems like magic, because once again, it is handled in a single shot. But like the other gags in the film, this trick has the effect of stopping the progress of the narrative. These gags serve as moments of disruption inside the film's larger narrative.

In addition to a distinction between theatrical and cinematic qualities, then, the film also makes clear the tension between story and spectacle that defines much silent-era cinema, especially slapstick comedy. According to traditional notions of classical film narrative, the story is the most important thing, and all other elements – lighting, costume, performance – exist primarily to clarify the narrative. Anything that stops the continuous flow of the narrative – an excessively flamboyant costume, a nonsensical gag – is considered subordinate to the story, if one follows this conventional valorization of narrative. However, film scholars in recent decades have revised this assessment to emphasize the way narrative and spectacle work together in a dialectical relationship. This tension between spectacle and narrative has been called the 'pie and chase' dynamic in comedy, with the slapstick pie-throwing tradition representing the gag or spectacle element, and the comedy film's chase tradition representing narrative progression.[2] Gags such as the old woman costume or Keaton jumping through Gillette's torso stop the flow of the narrative and encourage the spectator to marvel at the magical spectacle of cinema.

There are various opinions in film studies about the meaning of this 'pie and chase' dynamic. Whereas the earliest film critics either ignored or denigrated the disruptive aspect of the gag, later scholars celebrated gags and spectacles as elements of narrative 'excess'. For these scholars, narrative was suspiciously viewed as a form of containment, narrative disruption was endorsed for its transgressive qualities, and thus slapstick came to seem like a revolutionary form of comedy. However, other scholars have since come to dispute the thesis that all anti-narrative elements are necessarily transgressive, and instead have begun to look at the ways in which non-narrative elements have been a part of so-called classical cinema from the start. From this perspective, *Sherlock Jr* is neither a masterpiece of linear storytelling nor a revolutionary exercise in gag form; rather, it is a fascinating exploration of the relationship between narrative and spectacle.

Finally, it must be mentioned that in 'Hearts and Pearls', Sherlock Jr solves the mystery and gets the girl, but in the 'real life' frame narrative, the mystery of the stolen pocket watch is solved by The Girl herself, while The Boy remains immobile, asleep on the job. Thus *Sherlock Jr* makes another point about the cinema that may not have been intentional, but which today's feminist film scholars like to point out: the cinema tends to narrate from a masculine point of view and dramatize fantasies of male heroism, when in fact it is often 'the girl in the case' who has done the work.

Notes

1 Buster Keaton, interview with John Gillett and James Blue, 'Keaton at Venice', *Sight and Sound,* Autumn/Winter 1965, p. 30.

2 Donald Crafton, 'Pie and Chase: Gag, Spectacle and Narrative in Slapstick Comedy', in Kristine Brunovska Karnick and Henry Jenkins (eds), *Classical Hollywood Comedy,* New York, Routledge, 1995, pp. 106–19.

Further reading

Tom Dardis, *Keaton: The Man Who Wouldn't Lie Down* (1979), New York, Limelight Editions, 2004.

Tom Gunning, 'Buster Keaton, or The Work of Comedy in the Age of Mechanical Reproduction', *Cineaste*, Vol. 21, No. 3, Summer 1995, pp. 14–16.

Andrew Horton (ed.), *Buster Keaton's* Sherlock Jr., Cambridge, Cambridge University Press, 1997.

Robert Knopf, *The Theater and Cinema of Buster Keaton,* Princeton, NJ, Princeton University Press, 1999.

JENNIFER PETERSON

SUNRISE (1927)

[Production Company: Fox Film Corporation. Director: F. W. Murnau. Scenario: Carl Mayer, based on the story 'Die Reise nach Tilsit' by Hermann Sudermann. Producer: William Fox. Titles: Katherine Hilliker, H. H. Caldwell. Directors of Photography: Charles Rosher, Karl Struss. Special Effects: Frank D. Williams. Editor: Harold Schuster. Art Director: Rochus Gliese. Art Department: Gordon Wiles. Musical Score: Hugo Riesenfeld. Cast: George O'Brien (the man), Janet Gaynor (the wife), Margaret Livingstone (the woman from the city).]

William Fox's production of *Sunrise*, directed by German émigré Friedrich Wilhelm Murnau, was a bid for status and power. In the mid-1920s, Fox's studio was not as prestigious as Paramount or MGM. Fox therefore launched an expansion plan that included issuing common stock; the acquisition of the Roxy, the most famous picture palace on New York City's Broadway; an interest in sound technology; and the hiring of Murnau whose German film, *The Last Laugh* (1924), had been a great critical success. Fox granted Murnau great 'financial and artistic freedom' to make a 'highly artistic picture' (Allen 1977: 335). Such a bid for artistry was not only in Fox's but also in the industry's interest, not least because it had been rocked by a number of moral scandals (such as the murder of Thomas Ince and the indictment of 'Fatty' Arbuckle). Even though Fox made a number of 'strategic errors' (Lipkin 1977: 339) in marketing the film, even though it did not do that well at the box-office and got mixed reactions, it received the Academy Award for 'Unique and Artistic Picture' during the first year of the Academy Awards' existence (the first and only time this category existed as distinct from 'Outstanding Picture').

Because *Sunrise* was a product of the influx of foreign talent into Hollywood, the film remains hybrid – suspended between a variety of influences. One might easily call it a 'Euro-American art film', a term coined by Peter Lev for much later films (such as Michelangelo Antonioni's *The Passenger* [1975] or Wim Wenders' *Paris, Texas* [1984]).[1] Part of this hybridity is stylistic. Critics have commented on the film's borrowing from German Expressionism – a cinematic style maybe most famously associated with *The Cabinet of Dr. Caligari* (Robert Wiene, 1920), where, for instance, characters' inner feelings are projected onto the set, so that the distorted landscape comes to reflect the characters' inner turmoil. In *Sunrise*, it may be above all the figure of the husband who expresses Expressionism's inner conflict. Not exclusively, but especially during the marsh sequence, George O'Brien's acting expresses his tormented psychology, a feat aided by the lead weights that the director asked him to carry in his shoes, and enhanced by eerie lighting, the tracking camera and the sinister music. As Dudley Andrew has put it, the illicit encounter with the city woman in the marsh, as well as the two trips across the lake simultaneously, borrow from the 'aesthetic of the horror tale, the mystery novel, the gothic romance' (1984: 33).

Another way of describing these competing aesthetic influences has been to point out the film's borrowing from both the cinema of Georges Méliès, the early French film pioneer famous for his investment in cinematic tricks and magic, and of the Lumière brothers, better known for their investment in recording external reality. In this context, the scene in the marsh and the visions of the city can be understood as being invested in the fantastic, while moments like the couple's exiting the church derive from an aesthetic of Realism. This conflict between the fantastic and the realistic can also be understood as a conflict between transgressive desire and social order. Robin Wood, who first pointed out this tension within the film, argues that the magic is being connected with an 'untrammelled libido' while Realism stands for 'order' (1976: 11).

In this sense, the film's conflicting visual styles also stand for conflicting thematic and contextual issues, and the most prominent among those must be that of the tension between the country and the city. Film has often been aligned with the urban experience, as editing and superimpositions so easily turn urban dwellers into 'kaleidoscope[s] gifted with consciousness' as poets like Charles Baudelaire and writers like Walter Benjamin wrote.[2] Especially in the

1920s, so-called 'city symphonies' – films like *Man with a Movie Camera* (Dziga Vertov, 1929) and *Berlin, Symphony of a Great City* (Walter Ruttmann, 1927) – used cinematic techniques to create varied, but dazzling concepts of urban consciousness. The woman's vision of the city, characterized by lights, rapid traffic, jazz, and a body consumed in out-of-control dance movements, which are created by camera movement, editing, and superimpositions, exemplifies the erotic allure of the city.

The division between the country and the city is thus deeply gendered: the City Woman is a vamp – a pleasure-loving 'vampire' bent on exploiting and destroying men – while the country girl is Madonna-like, connected to child-rearing and domesticity. The City Woman enjoys being in public, and evokes not only the vamp, but also the 'flapper', a female urban type of the Jazz Age. Flappers – most famously embodied by Clara Bow in *It* (1927; see also the entry on *The Wild One* in this volume) – cut their hair into bobs, wore short, boxy dresses and often smoked or drank alcohol. They tapped into the revolution in leisure in the early twentieth century, in which the movies participated. While in the nineteenth century a woman alone in the streets was easily understood as a 'streetwalker', women now had increasing access to public space. The years after World War I also saw a sexual revolution and new styles of dancing – in short, new ways of understanding and relating to one's body. Despite the film's demonization of the City Woman, in the end, the country girl also enjoys a good time in the city.

The film thus chronicles how the frequently gendered difference between country and city is increasingly difficult to sustain. The montage about summer vacations, which brings urban dwellers to the countryside, the easy transportation to the city, and the city's infatuation with the peasant dance and the pig suggest a traffic between country and the city that has the potential to erode the presumed differences between these locations. Even the rural couple need the city and its pleasures to find happiness. At the photographer's studio, for instance, modern technology allows them to be pictured before the background that they dreamed about. This easy traffic between city and country is in tension with the film's argument about the 'carefree and happy' country life, as suggested in an intertitle.

It is one of *Sunrise*'s distinguishing marks that these thematic tensions are always elaborated in terms of cinematic aesthetics, for instance, in terms of the conflict between silence and sound. To be sure, the film features no synchronous sound. (When it was first exhibited at the Times Square Theatre in New York City, in late September 1927, it was preceded by a Movietone newsreel of Benito Mussolini and the Vatican Choir; just days later, the premiere of *The Jazz Singer* followed, a film featuring sequences of synchronized sound narrative.) Coming at the cusp of the film industry's transition into the sound era, the film has been called a 'technological hybrid' (Allen 1977: 327), a silent film that works hard to integrate camera and sound. Noteworthy moments on the soundtrack include

> the foreboding, repetitive theme (consisting largely of two alter-nating, ominous notes) that accompanies The Man's walk through the marshes to meet his lover; the raucous jazz motif ... that conjoins the city sequence; the rippling melody (with wind sounds) that marks the episode of the couple's sail home in a storm; the church bells that ring at the exact moment The Man decides to spare his wife. ... [the] plaintive series of notes on the French horn that approximate [The Man's] cry.
>
> (Fischer 1998: 31)

Very often, these sound effects help elaborate thematic issues. For instance, after witnessing a wedding ceremony that renews their trust in each other, the couple exit the church. They obliviously walk through city traffic, imagining themselves in a rural, picturesque environment, when they are suddenly awakened by the onslaught of urban traffic. The romantic soundtrack, associated with the rural fan-tasy, is pushed into the background by an explosion of urban sound effects, though the romantic music never entirely disappears and picks up again, once the couple have safely reached the sidewalk. The soundtrack thus aurally stages the complex interaction between the urban and the rural.

Such aural tensions are amplified visually. In the same urban sequence, a simulated tracking shot of the couple walking in front of a projected screen displaying a rural space – a simulation indicating the dream-like nature of the couple's projection – is followed by a quick montage of urban shots. Tensions within the story are thus also worked out in terms of camera work and editing. Critics have noted Murnau's masterful use of the tracking shot – for instance, the shot tracking The Man through the marsh, or the shot following the trolley – a mastery for which he was well known by the time he made *Sunrise,* since the same technique had already distinguished *The Last Laugh* (1924), the German film that brought Murnau to Hollywood in the first place. The fluid tracking shot can easily be associated with late silent cinema, which had developed fairly complex camera movements, while the quick montage may be associated with early sound film, if only because it provided a way out of the conundrum that early sound cameras were less mobile than late silent models. Nonetheless, the montage had also been very much present in silent cinema, among other things because it was associated with the urban environment, maybe most famously in *The Man with a Movie Camera*. Quickly edited shots seemed a particularly apt vehicle to convey the intensity of kaleidoscopic urban stimuli and impressions. At the same time, Murnau also uses other methods to convey the frenzy of the city. For instance, at the beginning of the amusement park sequence, a quickly spinning, lit wheel visually represents urban stimulation. Elements of *mise-en-scène*, such as the complex movements of the rides in the amusement park, and photographic effects, such as superimpositions, also help stage the city. Importantly, the tracking shot is by no means absent in the city. For instance, in the amusement park sequence, a slow tracking shot brings us inside the space of amusement itself. Urbanity is thus expressed by multiple stylistic means, and a particular use of a stylistic element does not always indicate the same kind of social commentary. As in the case of the soundtrack, the interpenetration of the tracking shot and the montage in the city helps complicate – on the stylistic level – any simple opposition between the rural and the urban.

Sunrise gives us insight into such topics as individualized psychology and desire, the lure of the new (urban) leisure economy, gender regimes, the conflict between the rural and the urban, and the transition to sound cinema. In the end, the film does not merely stage conflicting views, but also complicates any simple opposition between European and American cinema, Expressionism and Realism, silence and sound, the country and the city, etc. Maybe most importantly, it explores a number of cinematic devices for social commentary while never assuming that a stylistic element always has the same social or cultural significance.

Notes

1 Peter Lev, *The Euro-American Cinema*, Austin, TX, University of Texas Press, 1993.
2 Charles Baudelaire, *The Painter of Modern Life and Other Essays*, trans. and ed. Jonathan Mayne, New York, Phaidon, 1964, p. 9; Walter Benjamin, 'Paris, Capital of the Nineteenth Century', in *Reflections*, ed. and intro. Peter Demetz, trans. Edmund Jephcott, New York, Harcourt, Brace, Jovanovich, 1978, pp. 146–62.

Further reading

Robert C. Allen, 'William Fox Presents "Sunrise"', *Quarterly Review of Film Studies*, Vol. 2, August 1977, pp. 327–38.

Dudley Andrew, 'The Turn and Return of *Sunrise*', *Film in the Aura of Art*, Princeton, NJ, Princeton University Press, 1984.

Lucy Fischer, *Sunrise: A Song of Two Humans*, London, BFI, 1998.

Sumiko Higashi, *Virgins, Vamps, and Flappers: The American Silent Movie Heroine*, Albans, Eden Press Womens' Publications, 1978.

Steven N. Lipkin, '"Sunrise": A Film Meets Its Public', *Quarterly Review of Film Studies*, Vol. 2, August 1977, pp. 339–55.

Robin Wood, 'Murnau's Midnight and Sunrise', *Film Comment*, Vol. 12, No. 3, May–June, 1976, pp. 4–19.

SABINE HAENNI

THE WILD PARTY (1929)

[Production Company: Paramount Pictures. Director: Dorothy Arzner. Screenplay: E. Lloyd Sheldon. Cinematography: Victor Milner. Music: John Leipols. Editor: Otho Lovering. Cast: Clara Bow (Stella Ames), Fredric March (James 'Gil' Gilmore), Shirley O'Hara (Helen Owens), Marceline Day (Faith Morgan).]

'Dorothy Arzner was a professional director of American movies who worked regularly for over a decade, and was a woman', David Thomson espouses in his *New Biographical Dictionary of Film*:

> She was not a great filmmaker, and her pioneering should not inflate her reputation. But she turned out some fascinating pictures and clearly was able to pursue a personal if undoctrinaire interest in the issue of women's identity. That said, one has to confess that she generally played according to the Hollywood concept of 'a woman's picture'.
>
> (2004: 33–4)

The halting cadence and serial caveats in Thomson's sketch recur frequently in accounts of Arzner's films, her artistic stature, even her persona. Judith Mayne, Arzner's most influential critic and advocate, assumes her own qualified stances in her book-length study: that Arzner was 'not a "woman" in any one-dimensional or stereotypical sense of the term'; that one cannot 'claim that Arzner's films are unqualified successes from beginning to end'; that 'there are no lesbian plots, no lesbian characters in her films; but there is constant and deliberate attention to how women dress and act and perform, as much for each other as for the male figures in their lives' (1994: 27, 1, 63). Claire Johnston, in another seminal overview of Arzner's work, invokes an improbable analogy to Leo Tolstoy, grounded in this agnostic and nearly paradoxical evaluation: 'Both are progressive artists who hold a specific and important position in history precisely because they open up an arena of contradiction in the text, but at the same time they are unable radically to change those contradictions' (1975: 8).

Was Arzner a 'great filmmaker' or not? A 'woman director' or not? A woman at all, a lesbian, a transgender, or a butch, in any communicable sense of these terms? Most centrally, do her films retain aesthetic value for contemporary viewers, or is she simply an object of symbolic import, as a rare female director in pre-war Hollywood, and of anecdotal reminiscence – as, for instance, the purported inventor of the boom mike, and a teacher to Francis Ford Coppola and many others at UCLA Film School? Underlying all of these durable questions is a notable disjuncture between the cautious, ruminative flavour of these conceptual contrasts (a woman but not a woman, attuned but inadequate to deep-structural contradictions) and the customary lightness and momentum, occasionally the outright frivolity, of Arzner's films. *Dance, Girl, Dance* (1940) has invited more scholarly attention than Arzner's other movies, probably because the patently dialectic structure of that film and its overt address toward questions of female artistry and objectification lend themselves to long-standing strains of feminist film analysis. However, as Pam Cook makes clear by revisiting Arzner's strange, insouciant, smash-hit comedy *Merrily We Go to Hell* (1932), even her less rigidly structured films often involve 'playing with formal elements to conceptualize women's position in ideology' (in Johnston 1975: 11).

As feminist film scholarship continues to evolve, and as more of Arzner's films become widely accessible, a movie like *The Wild Party* (1929) may inform Arzner's legacy just as crucially as *Dance, Girl, Dance* did for previous generations. Such a shift already loomed in 2003 and 2004, when the UCLA Film and Television Archive circulated a travelling series of restored 35mm prints of six features, none of them previously available in any commercial formats, that Arzner made at Paramount between 1929 and 1932. The brochure written to accompany this repertory series – absent more typical calling cards like *Dance, Girl, Dance*, made at RKO, or *Christopher Strong* (RKO, 1933) or *Craig's Wife* (Columbia, 1936) – celebrates the films' 'drop-dead wit, sparkling double entendres, and playful gusto' (2003: 2). If the wit sparkles even more in later films like *Honor Among Lovers* (1931) and *Merrily We Go to Hell*, *The Wild Party* still captures Arzner's sensibility in a lighter and less dogmatic mood than many of her fans, more accustomed to reading about these films than actually seeing them, are likely to expect.

The Wild Party was a sizeable hit for Arzner and for actress Clara Bow, a major star making her first appearance in a sound film. Mayne reminds us how much the Paramount bosses must have trusted Arzner to enlist her as the shepherd for Bow's transition into talking pictures. Yet what a frisky and peculiar picture *The Wild Party* is, showcasing Bow and protecting Paramount's investment without straining for 'event' status. Compare *The Wild Party* to Sam Taylor's *Coquette* (1929), the bathetic and maladroit vehicle that ushered Mary Pickford into the sound era during the same year, and *The Wild Party*'s spry energy and democratic embrace of multiple characters and subplots is all the more obvious. The film begins not with a bang or a sigh but with a giggle: Arzner's coterie of excitable co-eds titter off-screen while we behold a 'Winston '30' pennant. The film immediately proposes school pride as a recognized value while simultaneously challenging such pride with generous doses of pent-up energy and jovial iconoclasm. Making excuses for her studious roommate and best friend Helen, Stella exclaims, 'Someone's gotta work around here – we don't!' *The Wild Party* in fact keeps us guessing whether anyone else at Winston works, and whether they should, and at what. Even Helen targets her demure diligence not toward any particular course but toward winning an Alumni Prize. Driving out to a local roadhouse one ill-fated evening, Stella and the other girls chant a song called 'What's the matter with Winston? We're all right!' which is both a defensive and a self-mocking alma mater.

The Wild Party radiates ambivalence about Winston as an institution, despite the script's lyrical odes to the college's history and its stalwart foundress, further embellished with a pastoral image of the campus as a gleaming castle in a glade. The film gleans its title straight from a bitter denunciation of Stella and her cohort by James 'Gil' Gilmore (Fredric March), the new Professor of Anthropology: 'You and others like you have turned the college into a country club for four years … Life to you is just one wild party. You have no aim, all you want is cheap sensation.' In purloining his phrase, however, *The Wild Party* does not implicitly share his judgement, and we notice that Gil's invective collapses at the end of this scene. 'How could I hate you when I would have killed for you?' he asks incredulously of Stella, whom he has just saved from the armed brigands of the roadhouse, sweeping her into a tightly framed kiss before a suggestive fade-out.

To thus recapitulate, *The Wild Party*'s tenor and plot imply a fairly standard compromise between the generic maturation of the giddy heroine and her eroticized softening of the stern, judgemental professor: tempering her pride and leavening his prejudice. These typical vectors of heterosexual couple-production, however, are pervasively complicated by the emphasis Arzner places on a parallel plot about Stella and Helen, whose Alumni Prize is jeopardized when a love letter she writes is intercepted and misinterpreted. Stella exonerates Helen by claiming the letter as her own, a plot twist with its own subversive ramifications: *The Wild Party* ends not with a heroic revelation of the truth but with a malicious lie neutralized by another, more honourable lie. Moreover, Stella and Gil's joint departure from Winston in the final scene is tartly ironic and ideologically unreadable. Stella laments that she 'hasn't been such a credit to Winston' all along, while Gil abandons his lectureship after allowing several students to sweet-talk him into raising their grades. *The Wild Party* refuses to lampoon the school and yet the auspices under which Arzner ultimately unites the hetero couple, as opposed to the dotingly intimate Stella and Helen, are their shared betrayals of school values, echoed in their mutual use of 'my savage' as a term of endearment. We aren't far here from the amorous absconding of two pickpockets at the end of Ernst Lubitsch's *Trouble in Paradise* (1932).

Therefore, from the opening, non-diegetic chuckle beneath the school's insignia to Stella and Gil's final rejection of its 'civilizing' mythos, *The Wild Party* celebrates outpourings of feeling and energy that it nonetheless represents as reckless and unbecoming. Helen endangers her reputation and then her award, first by staying out all night with a boy and then by writing about it so indiscreetly. Stella, perpetually slinking in and out of doorways and windows, is repeatedly caught in compromising positions. Gil, though his dramas largely transpire offscreen, risks even greater dangers. The thugs from whom he rescued Stella later stake him out and shoot him, and he is hospitalized for a month before returning to the teaching post he will swiftly abdicate for a return into 'the jungle'.

The breathlessly scripted, fleetly edited *Wild Party* thus finds excitement, risk, and epiphany in both the school and the lawless zones that surround it: the train, the highway, the saloon, the forest, the beach, the Costume, the Malayan wilds. Finally, then, the unpredictable vitality of movement itself, often figured by the unpacking and repacking of luggage, overrides the symbolic claims of any one realm as the guiding moral value of the film. We meet Stella in the very act of dragging and opening a trunk, occasioning the first of the movie's many gazes into her suitcase, as well as an abrupt flashback sequence onboard the train that carried her to Winston. Later, after earning a poor grade on an essay for Gil's course, she packs; after testifying to the school's board of trustees, she packs; she even brings a suitcase to the formal ball at the men's college. The jazzy, heavily sequined costume sequence, described by an onscreen caption as 'the feminine equivalent of a stag', barely stays put at all; the salacious theatricality of the Hard Boiled Maidens' arrival gives way instantly to the drama of their quick expulsion, leading directly to the roadhouse sequence which itself comprises a beginning and an ending with no real middle. One could even argue that *The Wild Party* 'moves' relentlessly between silent- and sound-era aesthetics, since the occasional intertitles and the antic gesticulating of Clara Bow, who vigorously tousles her own hair when she gets angry, are drastically at odds with the more forward-looking tendencies of the direction and the soundtrack. These sophisticated touches include meaningful and plot-related shifts in musical idiom, the frequent establishment of new settings with sonic cues ahead of visual ones, and several scenes that depend upon synchronized sound for their punchlines and narrative coherence, such as a late-night public roll-call where Stella's friends attempt to conceal her absence by responding in her stead.

The Wild Party thus reprises but also self-consciously critiques numerous touchstones of Arzner's films and, not coincidentally, of so much feminist film theory, including the politics of heterosexual romance, the suggestive implications of all-female communities, and the fetishistic glamorization of female bodies. However, we reduce our sense of Arzner if, in scrutinizing *The Wild Party*'s ideas about schooling and sexuality, or in tracing the narrative braid of heteronormative desire and lesbian propinquity, we fail to underscore the vivacity and heedlessness of her characters, the velocity of Arzner's scene transitions, and the principles of itinerancy and dynamism to which this politically skittish film so proudly adheres. That academia serves as the primary locus of *The Wild Party*'s merry misgivings and nomadic wanderings offers an apt reminder that Arzner – a mainstay of college syllabi who remains largely unknown to the moviegoing public – is no one's ideological exemplar. As movies like *The Wild Party* attain greater visibility, even within her own body of work, the secret will out itself: among all of her other ambitions and achievements, Arzner just wanted to have fun.

Further reading

Directed by Dorothy Arzner, Los Angeles, UCLA Film and Television Archive, 2003.

Claire Johnston (ed.) *The Work of Dorothy Arzner: Towards a Feminist Cinema*, London, BFI, 1975.

Judith Mayne, *Directed by Dorothy Arzner*, Bloomington, IN, Indiana University Press, 1994.

David Thomson, *The New Biographical Dictionary of Film*, New York, Alfred A. Knopf, 2004.

NICK DAVIS

APPLAUSE (1929, released 1930)

[Production Company: Paramount Pictures. Director: Rouben Mamoulian. Screenplay: Garret Fort, based on the novel by Beth Brown. Cinematographer: George Folsey. Sound Recordist: Ernest Zatorsky. Editor: John Bassler. Cast: Helen Morgan (Kitty Darling), Joan Peers (April Darling), Fuller Mellish Jr (Hitch Nelson), Jack Cameron (Joe King), Henry Wadsworth (Tony), Roy Hargrave (Slim Lamont).]

It's a shame, though an understandable one, that today's viewers of the earliest sound films (those produced between 1926 and 1932) have such difficulty seeing and hearing past the leaden qualities of Hollywood's alchemic attempts to transform talking pictures into gold. The static camera set-ups, sparse editing, lugubrious pace, and unintentionally hilarious line readings of many of these films make it easy to impute incompetence to the filmmakers and low standards to their audience. Most of us would never guess that the 'silent' feature films of the preceding decade were complex and polished pieces of mass art that used to their advantage every trick of editing and cinematography imaginable, and a few more besides. The invasion of the microphone temporarily trapped camera operators in soundproof booths and forced editors to synchronize each shot to a live sound recording engraved into a gigantic, uneditable phonograph disk. Crews had to film the same shot with multiple cameras simultaneously (a bizarre and expensive process in Hollywood at the time, when the majority of movies were shot with a single camera) if they hoped to edit together shots of varying camera distances – establishing shot, two-shot, close-ups, etc. – without ruining the synchronization.

Under such conditions, even films that failed, whether critically as did *The Lights of New York* (1928) and *Tenderloin* (1928), or commercially – as did *Applause* – deserve recognition as revealing steps in Hollywood's quest to develop the sound film into a sophisticated replacement for its silent ancestor, without throwing away everything filmmakers had fought so hard to learn about telling stories with pictures over the previous three decades.

Though Hollywood followed the money then as now, the tepid box office returns of *Applause* could not obscure its experimental energy. Recognizing the nature of that energy requires that we avoid the temptation to call it 'the first Hollywood musical'. To quote a lyric from George and Ira Gershwin's *Porgy and Bess* – of which the source play *Porgy* was Rouben Mamoulian's last directorial job on Broadway before directing *Applause* – it ain't necessarily so. The musical genre's conventional approaches to music, dance, behind-the-scenes intrigue, and romance took several more years to develop. What makes *Applause* a key American film is that it successfully resisted the received idea that synched dialogue was the talkies' first duty and that photography and editing had to serve that end above all others.

Mamoulian filmed *Applause* at Paramount's Long Island studio in order to take advantage of its proximity both to the Theatre Guild, the prestigious Broadway company for which he directed *Porgy,* and to performers from the burlesque industry (including the so-called 'Beef Trust', a group of full-figured dancers whom Mamoulian invited out of retirement to perform in the film). Considering that sound recording had forced filmmakers to shoot dialogue scenes by stuffing all the actors into the frame at once and letting the camera roll until the scene ended, it's not surprising that the studios picked experienced stage directors to oversee many talking pictures, even though neither Mamoulian nor many of his colleagues had ever directed a film.

Mamoulian, the Hollywood rookie, surprised the critics by taking every opportunity to play with the possibilities of cinematography and sound mixing, at times even within lengthy dialogue takes. In one scene about 30 minutes into the film, burlesque queen Kitty Darling (Helen Morgan, later to star in James Whale's film adaptation of *Showboat* [1936]) tries to quiet her daughter April, who has just returned to New York after a decade at a convent in Wisconsin and cannot come to terms with city life or the crassness of showbiz. The key shot in this scene runs nearly five minutes and contains no fewer than five separate camera movements, beginning with a slow track-in to Kitty and April to register their facial expressions (April, played with an upper-class northeastern accent by Joan Peers, cries while her mother soothes her with word and song) and tracking out and in as the director's emphasis moves from the conversation to April's desperate rosary prayer and back again. Mamoulian later boasted that, due to the inadequacy of the standard one-microphone set-up, he mixed two separate recordings to allow Kitty's lyric, 'Close your pretty eyes', and April's prayer to be heard simultaneously. Whether or not this technique was as novel as Mamoulian claimed, it is a remarkable moment in the history of sound. As the camera excludes Kitty to centre on April begging the Virgin's protection, Kitty's song never leaves our ears. Though Mamoulian has not cut to a new shot since the scene began, he has demonstrated Kitty's maternal benevolence while also expressing April's vulnerability and the risk her mother has taken by drawing her into the tawdry world of cheap burlesque.

Lest we assume that Mamoulian shrugged off the constraints of sound single-handedly, I should make clear that technical developments in the industry by 1929 had opened up such new – or perhaps I should say old – options as camera movement to the director and his crew. Now that sound could be photographically recorded and printed directly onto 35mm film, soundtracks could be edited more easily; post-dubbing multiple tracks of dialogue, music, and effects was becoming a standard practice, as were multi-track mixing and re-recording; and smaller, lighter sound-proof 'blimps' allowed operators to pan, tilt, and roll their cameras to follow the action. None of these developments, however, led inevitably to *Applause*'s audiovisual fluidity, for the industry was still debating new standards and practices. Critics and filmmakers argued over whether synchronized sound functioned most effectively as a way to make cinema more like theatre, complete with dialogue and singing, or as a way to expand the expressiveness of silent film techniques via music and sound effects instead of dialogue. Hollywood sound technicians, many of whom came from the radio and recording industries, vigorously debated whether recording and mixing ought to strive for acoustic verisimilitude or simple intelligibility, and continued to do so into the early 1930s.

What still surprises about *Applause* is not so much the mobile framings (F. W. Murnau's 1924 German silent *The Last Laugh* [*Der Letzte Mann*] was a recognizable influence) as the consistency with which Mamoulian attempts to marry the visual possibilities of silent films with the aural possibilities of the talkies. Some of its most remarkable moments hark back to silent film by describing actions indirectly, via their consequences alone. Halfway through the film Alice is accosted by a man in the street and is rescued by another stranger, a sailor who later becomes her fiancé. But until the camera at last tilts upward to show the newly-met couple's faces, the action happens outside the frame; all we see is a high-angle shot of the actors' feet. Only the telltale sound of a punch to the jaw followed by the masher stumbling to the ground communicate the key events. By asserting cinema's power to imply, *Applause* offers an alternative to the dull literalism of all but a handful of the first dialogue pictures.

Applause certainly registered the dramatic possibilities of constructing a sound film around the backstage lives of dancers or singers, but merely to say that the film paved the way for *42nd Street* (1933) and *Singin' in the Rain* (1952) ignores how organically Mamoulian uses the technologies at his disposal to integrate plot with theme. The film's central character, the lower-tier burlesque star Kitty Darling, first appears on a poster for a show called 'The Queen of Hearts' that blows through an empty street, then gets worried to pieces by a stray dog. When coupled with shots of Kitty and her ragtag co-stars parading down the windblown avenue, these opening images cleverly foreshadow the ageing Kitty's fall from show-business grace. Hollywood musicals would later standardize certain parallels between the world of entertainment and the world outside, as when dancing and singing symbolize community, emotional bonding, and physical love. Unrestricted as yet by those generic rules, however, Mamoulian employs burlesque as a multivalent symbol of the hardscrabble city life that threatens its participants' attempts to evolve past it. In an interview, he called burlesque 'tawdry, shoddy, unworthy of a human being, woman or man' but he also registered his desire to 'show how sad it is' rather than simply mock it. As Kitty tries to raise April to be a 'lady' instead of a chorus girl, Mamoulian contrasts the vulgarity and the clunky (though appealingly frank) sexuality of burlesque to the sanctity of Kitty's motherly impulses and the purity (even prudishness) of April's ideals.

Unlike the musical numbers in such landmark films as *42nd Street*, which stop the plot in its tracks to emphasize spectacular dances, costumes, and sets, *Applause*'s numbers provide a counterpoint to Kitty's attempts to keep her boyfriend Hitch (Fuller Mellish Jr) happy and to keep her daughter out of the chorus line. The first scene in the theatre depicts Kitty passing out between dance numbers and giving birth to April as the raucous music fades. Mamoulian shoots the moments after the baby's birth from a bird's-eye angle which simultaneously emphasizes the irony of viewing women as merely bodies to leer at (the shot shows the chorines trailing past mother and child just as a similar framing will present them later, snaking down the runway toward leering fans), and invites us to understand these women as ordinary people, people who cherish family and friends but nevertheless crave the pleasures of performing and achieving stardom.

It should be clear by now that *Applause* portrays urban life and show business with deep ambivalence. In this it resembles *The Jazz Singer* (1926), the first American talking feature, but with a twist: as Jeffrey P. Smith shows, *Applause* reverses the generational terms of *The Jazz Singer* by making escape from city and stage the younger generation's goal, and in the process casts stardom as a dangerous dream for women to chase. Whereas Jacky Rabinowitz's boyhood beer hall performance in *The Jazz Singer* is clearly a necessary step toward becoming the star who holds New York in the palm of his hand by the end, the burlesque halls in *Applause* become a prison for young April; only marriage can free her to return to the trees and hymns of her Wisconsin years. And yet *The Jazz Singer* cannot demonize Jacky's Jewish heritage or the family obligations that stunt his career any more than *Applause* can afford to cast an unequivocal pall over the truly exciting city of New York, even when that same metropolis reduces the pastoral dreams of Kitty's beloved daughter to ashes. New York may at times symbolize chaos and noise, loveless sexuality, and delusions of grandeur in Mamoulian's film, but even the location shots and noises of the streets that express April's first impressions of the city give off a joyous energy reminiscent of the influential documentary *Berlin: Symphony of a Great City* (Walter Ruttmann, Germany, 1927) or the giddy delights of mass transit and Coney Island in King Vidor's fiction film *The Crowd* (1928). What we are likely to remember about *Applause*'s own great city is not the wail of the horns that torment the dying Kitty at the film's climax, but the clean lines of Art Deco and the Jazz Age that envelop April and her sailor boyfriend Tony when they sit on the Brooklyn Bridge, marvelling at the Woolworth Building and waving excitedly at a passing biplane.

This ambivalence about the modern world, which *Applause* shares with many films of the 1920s and 1930s, registers Americans' slow but general shift from suspicion of cities to curiosity and pride regarding the cultural, architectural, and business achievements that cities represented. It seems only fitting, then, that *Applause* stands so stolidly in the middle of another dichotomy between future and past – the historical split between the new sound cinema and its silent precursor – and tries so aggressively to fuse together the most exciting possibilities of both kinds of filmmaking. We could reasonably call *Applause* Mamoulian's polemic about the talkies, which could be put into words thus: talking films can and should appropriate the theatre's use of dialogue to drive plot and reveal character, but they must also take liberties with sound that stage drama cannot – liberties proper to a medium that seems magically to construct worlds out of strips of still pictures. I can't leave this point without noting the tribute Mamoulian pays to stage melodrama by employing *melos* (music) to express joy, fear, and sorrow, but with a difference both from theatrical precedent and later Hollywood melodrama in that *Applause* includes almost no music that doesn't come from the world of the film itself (no sudden interventions by invisible orchestras here!).

This decision gives the film a melodramatic impact that few films since can match, and makes me wonder what Mamoulian's 'realist' approaches to both music as performance and music as a narrative signifier might have developed into later, had other directors followed his lead. *Applause* ends with Kitty, faced with the loss of her youth, her career, and her cheating man, committing suicide in an effort to press April into marrying her sailor rather than staying to support her mother. Instead of ordering up violins for the death scene, Mamoulian allows only a raucous rendition of 'Close your pretty eyes' to seep backstage from the footlights. As the orchestra continues playing the song Kitty earlier hummed for her daughter, the camera drifts toward a tear-jerking final image of April and Tony embracing, unaware of Kitty's death. Piling irony upon irony, Tony tells April to bring her mother back to Wisconsin to live with them. As they stand before a life-sized poster of Kitty, the camera cranes up and forward to frame Kitty's frozen grin while April, now out of frame, proclaims through her tears, 'We'll always be together – all three of us.' Not for a moment does the music register the tragedy of this conclusion, in which one generation sacrifices itself to the other. Only the audience knows the selfless nature of Kitty's sacrifice. By retaining that ironic distance, the music brings the rawness of these circumstances home to the viewer-listener more forcefully than orchestral schmaltz ever could.

I don't wish to categorize *Applause* strictly as a melodrama rather than a musical, nor to downplay the artistry of the Hollywood musicals of the 1930s, 1940s, and 1950s. Certainly *Applause* resembles the heart-wrenching melodramas of the silent era like *Broken Blossoms* (1919), *Tess of the Storm Country* (1922), or *Stella Dallas* (1927) more than it does the Rogers–Astaire hit *Top Hat* (1935), Mamoulian's marvellous *Love Me Tonight* (1932), or other musical comedies that helped found a bona fide genre less than half a decade after *Applause*. I make these observations, rather, to call attention to *Applause*'s success both as a product of genre combination and as a surprisingly effortless film for its moment, a film in which sound takes its part – but only *a* part – without drowning out the cinema's spectrum of technical opportunities, its historical means of expression, or its capacity to surprise us with novel combinations of all its gifts.

My gratitude to Katherine Fusco for finding remarkable research materials for this essay.

Further reading

Alexander Bakshy, 'The Talkies Advancing', *Nation*, 30 October 1929, p. 503.
'Constantly Moving Camera Used in Filming "Applause"', *Washington Post*, 8 September 1929, p. A2.
Donald Crafton, *The Talkies: American Cinema's Transition to Sound, 1926–1931*, New York/Berkeley, Scribner/University of California Press, 1997.
Mordaunt Hall, 'Melody, Fun and Romance', *New York Times*, 13 October 1929, p. X6.
Charles O'Brien, *Cinema's Conversion to Sound: Technology and Film Style in France and the U.S.*, Bloomington, IN, Indiana University Press, 2005.
'Sime', 'Applause', *Variety*, 9 October 1929, n. p.
Jeffrey P. Smith, '"It Does Something to a Girl. I Don't Know What": The Problem of Female Sexuality in *Applause*', *Cinema Journal*, Vol. 30, No. 2, Winter 1991, pp. 47–60.

PAUL YOUNG

SCARFACE (1932)

[Production Company: The Caddo Company. Director: Howard Hawks. Screenplay: Ben Hecht, based on the novel by Armitage Trail. Producer: Howard Hughes. Cinematography: Lee Garmes, L. William O'Connell. Editor: Edward Curtiss. Art Department: Harry Oliver. Sound Department: William Snyder. Cast: Paul Muni (Tony Camonte), Ann Dvorak (Francesca Camonte), Karen Morely (Poppy), Osgood Perkins (Johnny Lovo), George Raft (Guino Rinaldo), Vince Barnett (Angelo), Inez Palange (Mrs Camonte).]

Scarface was one of the most controversial films of its era. Loosely based on the career of Al Capone, produced by eccentric millionaire businessman Howard Hughes (memorialized in Martin Scorsese's *The Aviator* [2004]), released in the midst of the Great Depression, the film brought to the screen new levels of violence, ambiguous forms of sexuality, and seemed critical of the feasibility of the 'American Dream', of the modern urban environment, even of the government.

Scarface is part of what is now recognized as the classical gangster film cycle of the early 1930s, which most famously included *The Public Enemy* (William Wellman, 1931) and *Little Caesar* (Mervyn LeRoy, 1931). This does not mean that there were no gangster films before: one of the best known, and earliest gangster films must be D. W. Griffith's short, *The Musketeers of Pig Alley* (1912), and there were feature-length gangster films throughout the 1910s and 1920s, from Maurice Tourneur's *Alias Jimmy Valentine* (1915) to Josef von Sternberg's *Underworld* (1927). However, the conversion to sound pictures in the late 1920s and the onset of the Great Depression produced unprecedented stylistic and social conditions for a (however brief) flourishing of the gangster genre.

The new sound technology opened up new ways of conveying spectacular violence. The same period also saw a flourishing of other film genres that profited greatly from sound. Musicals, such as *The Love Parade* (Ernst Lubitsch, 1929), *Applause* (Rouben Mamoulian, 1929), *Love Me Tonight* (Rouben Mamoulian, 1932), *42nd Street* (Lloyd Bacon, 1933) and *The Golddiggers of 1933* (Mervyn LeRoy, 1933) became a whole new genre. Sound was a crucial part of the film experience in horror films, such as *Frankenstein* (James Whale, 1931) and *Dracula* (Tod Browning, 1931). Maybe less obviously, the 'fast-talking dame' became a staple of comedies. The gangster film integrated a number of sound effects, from the screeching tires, to the gun blasts, to the ethnic accents and the sexually risqué dialogue. These sound effects did not always have the same kind of ideological effects, but they certainly foregrounded the experience of the talkie.

Likewise, the social commentary, implicit in many gangster films, seemed particular pertinent during an economic crisis, for as many critics have argued, the gangster film plays on old American myths. Edward Mitchell, for instance, has argued that the gangster films take up Puritanism (that we are all born into sin), Social Darwinism (that the fittest survives in a hostile social environment) and the Horatio Alger myth (that pluck and luck will lift us out of a hostile environment). It may above all have been the Horatio Alger myth – and more generally the American Dream – that was at stake in the economically difficult times of the early 1930s. In this context, the gangster represents the perversion of the American Dream, that something is

31

horribly wrong with the very idea of the American Dream: Tony Camonte and other gangsters simply want to rise in the social hierarchy. 'I got plenty. I got a house. I got an automobile. I got a nice girl', Louis Costello says with great satisfaction in the film's opening scene, right before being gunned down by Tony. In the gangster's world, the American Dream is achievable only through horrific violence. In this sense, like that *Godfather* films of the 1970s, *Scarface* presents us with an acerbic critique of US capitalism.

But the film's implicit critique of US capitalism was not the only, or even main reason for the censorship controversy it caused, for there were many. Outcry about movies' contents – and concomitant censorship concerns – had been an issue since the movies' beginnings. States and municipalities established censorship ordinances (with Chicago being the first in 1907); on Christmas Eve of 1908, the mayor of New York City ordered all the movie theatres in the city closed for fear of what was happening in and around them; in 1909, the New York Board of Motion Picture Censorship was established, quickly became the National Board of Review, but lost power by the mid-teens; in 1915, the Supreme Court determined that movies were not protected by the First Amendment (a decision that would be overturned in 1952); in 1922, the industry hired Will H. Hays as president of the newly formed Motion Pictures Producers and Distributors of America (MPPDA) in an effort to stave off censorship legislation; Hays also introduced self-regulation codes, the 'Formula' of 1924 and the 'Don'ts and Be Carefuls' of 1927, and asked studios to submit to the Hays Office questionable material. In 1930, he came up with the Motion Picture Production Code, which remained in effect until 1968 (when it was replaced by the ratings system), and in 1934 the Production Code Administration (PCA) was established in order to enforce the Code (scripts had to be approved prior to shooting, and completed films had to be cleared as well). The classical cycle of gangster films, including *Scarface*, was thus released right before self-regulation of film content became more stringent.

Begun when the debate about gangster pictures was in full swing, *Scarface* generated many objections from the MPPDA. Maybe most importantly, the film was assumed to be too closely modelled after 'Scarface Al Capone', dubbed 'Public enemy No. 1'. Capone's image was to a large extent created by the media; he was well known for his stylish flamboyance (including yellow and purple suits); he blurred the line between business and criminality by leaving the beer racket for the milk distribution business in 1930 because the latter was more profitable; and he had been indicted for tax evasion in 1931. MPPDA officials objected to Tony's 'humane and kindly qualities especially as applied to his sister', not least because the Production Code required that criminal activity 'shall never be presented in such a way as to throw sympathy with the crime as against law and justice or to inspire others with a desire for imitation' (Maltby 2001: 120). The New York censor board rejected *Scarface,* which resulted in a different ending (in which Tony was tried and executed), the revision of the brother–sister relationship, the inclusion of anti-gun propaganda, a prologue set in a juvenile court, and a change of title from *Scarface* to *Shame of a Nation* (Maltby 2001: 137–8). There was considerable back and forth between the MPPDA, the producer, and censorship boards. By March 1932, the MPPDA had agreed to an older ending (in which Tony 'only' turns cowardly). Some state censorship boards demanded more cuts, and others, as well as a substantial number of foreign censors (including Britain), rejected the film (ibid.: 139–40).

As recent scholarship has revealed, however, the explosiveness had to do not only with the film's gestures toward Al Capone – and more generally what the gangster stood for – but toward other social issues, such as the milieu of the city, the role of the government, and the connection between World War I veterans and gangsters. Hollywood's gangsters came out of American cities' immigrant tenements – in fact, *Public Enemy* starts with a brief scene set in a working-class immigrant neighborhood. In *Scarface,* the immigrant milieu is mostly confined to a domestic sphere consisting of Tony Camonte's sexualized sister and spaghetti-cooking mother, a space that might gesture toward immigrant and generational conflicts but also a space that seems irrationally contradictory and non-(re)productive. It hardly provides a social context – and explanation – for Tony. Not surprisingly, Italian American groups protested. In addition, while evidently part of the urban environment, immigrants in the film are often radically opposed to a rational, technologized urban modernity. The most famous example is certainly Angelo, Tony's illiterate assistant who spends most of the film trying to cope with the telephone. The city is characterized by technology – from telephones, to cars, to guns. Such a technological urban environment is 'complex, alienating, and overwhelming' (Schatz 1981: 84). Rationalization may be both an effect and a way of negotiating such an environment. The gangster, in the orchestration of the beer distribution business, for instance, may be said to manipulate rationalized modernity. But in the end, he proves unable to deal with the modern, rational, urban environment, as becomes most visible in Tony's childlike and misguided faith in his steel-shutters. In this context, the gangster film appears to be an anxious reaction to urban modernity, and a displacement of such anxiety onto immigrants.

And yet, immigrants were not the only demographic group that Hollywood associated with the gangster film, which can also be understood as a belated reaction to veterans returning home after World War I. As J. E. Smyth has shown, several of the post-war gangsters were (decorated) World War I veterans, suggesting that the battlefield had been moved from Europe to US cities. Capone, for one, claimed that he got his scar when fighting on the Western Front (Smyth 2004: 538). In *Public Enemy*, the gangster's more righteous brother fights in World War I and brings home grenades. Such connections between veterans and gangsters not only revised images of male US heroism, they potentially critiqued the government's handling of veterans. In this sense, the veteran–gangster connection, which was so explosive that it was suppressed in the final prints, is part of the larger scepticism towards the government that *Scarface* barely conceals: an early intertitle calls attention to the 'callous indifference of the government'. The film's attempt to put the moral burden onto the spectator – 'what are you going to do about it?' – hardly deflects that criticism.

While many of these social contexts remain on the margins of the film, the issues of sexuality and violence – issues that are still crucial to today's Hollywood – are much more apparent. The film offers few explanations for either sexuality or violence, but the two are linked from the beginning in an erotics of violence. Even before the opening shooting, a bra is among the debris left from a night's party, a bra that gestures toward a later scene when during a party, Tony's sister, Francesca, doesn't seem to be wearing one (at least as long as her dress isn't ripped). Likewise, sexual ambiguity and violence seem coupled in the gangster himself, although the connection may never be entirely clear. Tony's overprotection of his sister and his awkward advances to his boss's mistress are offset by his close connections with his male assistants, Angelo and Gino. The two sets of friends and potential interests – heterosexual and homoerotic – are linked in a disturbingly causal relationship, when Tony's sentiments for his sister prompt him to kill off his friend. Likewise, Tony discovers the pleasure of machine guns when on a lunch date with Poppy. While these incidents may suggest that Tony confuses sexuality with violence – or that his presumably 'aberrant' sexuality prompts violence – other moments reveal a more masturbatory delight in violence, such as when Tony and his gang try out the machine gun in Lovo's office, or when they massacre rival gang members by lining them up against a wall. The latter referred to the Valentine's Day Massacre of 1929, when Al Capone had members of a rival gang slaughtered in a garage on Chicago's north side. Here, the film's visual signature – an X that mimics the scar on Tony's cheek – is used most prominently, but the X is an important visual marker in the film from the beginning. In fact, finding the many visual Xs in the film – as it appears on windows, walls, doors, across characters' faces, score sheets, gowns – can be a game in its own right (see Hagemann 1984). While this points to the careful construction of the film, it also represents an early instantiation of the aestheticization of violence to which we have grown so accustomed and which may in fact limit the visceral impact violent scenes may have.

Because of censorship issues, the classical gangster film cycle was shorter than any other genre's classical moment, but its influence nonetheless cannot be underestimated. By the 1940s, the gangster film had transmogrified into Film Noir – maybe Hollywood's sleekest, and most stylish genre or mode focusing on corruption, slick, rainy city streets, disillusioned private eyes, and dangerous women. While the gangster is less prominent in Film Noir, the genre's milieu and scepticism about male heroism was indebted to the gangster cycle. As in noir, the ultimate conflict in the gangster film, as Thomas Schatz long ago argued, was in the gangster himself. In the 1970s, a new generation of filmmakers, maybe most famously Martin Scorsese and Francis Ford Coppola, rediscovered the gangster cycle, often combining it with Film Noir aesthetics, producing such classics as *Mean Streets* (Martin Scorsese, 1973), *The Godfather* (Francis Ford Coppola, 1972), and *GoodFellas* (Martin Scorsese, 1990). In 1983, *Scarface* was remade – and reimagined – by Brian De Palma. The original gangster cycle thus proved important for a new, film-literate generation of filmmakers, frequently the descendants of immigrants themselves, who continue to explore the connections between sexuality, violence and capitalism.

Further reading

E.R.. Hagemann, '*Scarface:* The Art of Hollywood, Not "The Shame of a Nation"', *Journal of Popular Culture*, Vol. 18, No. 1, Summer 1984, pp. 30–42.

Richard Maltby, 'The Spectacle of Criminality', in J. David Slocum (ed.), *Violence and American Cinema*, New York, Routledge, 2001, pp. 117–52.

Edward Mitchell, 'Apes and Essences: Some Sources of Significance in the American Gangster Film', in Barry Keith Grant (ed.), *Film Genre Reader II*, Austin, TX, University of Texas Press, 1995, pp. 203–12.

'The Production Code', in John Belton (ed.), *Movies and Mass Culture,* New Brunswick, Rutgers University Press, 1996, pp. 135–49.

Thomas Schatz, 'The Gangster Film', in *Hollywood Genres: Formulas, Filmmaking and the Hollywood System,* Philadelphia, PA, Temple University Press, 1981, pp. 81–110.

J. E. Smyth, 'Revisioning Modern American History in the Age of *Scarface* (1932)', *Historical Journal of Film, Radio and Television,* Vol. 24, No. 4, October 2004, pp. 535–63.

Robert Warshow, 'The Gangster as Tragic Hero', in *The Immediate Experience: Movies, Comics, Theatre, and Other Aspects of Popular Culture,* Garden City, NY, Doubleday, 1962, pp. 85–8.

SABINE HAENNI

FREAKS (1932)

[Production Company: Metro-Goldwyn-Mayer. Director: Tod Browning. Producers: Tod Browning, Irving Thalberg (uncredited). Screenwriters: Willis Goldbeck and Leon Gordon (uncredited). Suggested by Tod Robbins' story 'Spurs'. Cinematographer: Merritt B. Gerstad (uncredited). Editor: Basil Wrangell (uncredited). Cast: Wallace Ford (Phroso), Leila Hyams (Venus), Olga Baclanova (Cleopatra), Rosco Ates (Roscoe), Henry Victor (Hercules), Harry Earles (Hans), Daisy Earles (Frieda), Rose Dione (Madame Tetrallini), Dasy Hilton (Daisy the Siamese Twin), Violet Hilton (Violet the Siamese Twin), Schlitze (as himself, The Pinhead Girl), Josephine Joseph (Half Woman-Half Man), Johnny Eck (Johnny the Half Boy), Frances O'Connor (The Armless Girl), Peter Robinson (The Human Skeleton), Olga Roderick (The Bearded Lady), Koo Koo (The Bird Girl), Prince Randian (The Living Torso), Martha Morris (The Armless Girl), Elvira Snow (Zip the Pinhead), Jenny Lee Snow (Pip the Pinhead), Elizabeth Green (The Bird Girl), Angelo Rossitto (Angelino), Edward Brophy (Rollo Brother), Mat McHugh (Rollo Brother).]

Scorned in its own time, Tod Browning's *Freaks* eventually became one of the most important American cult films. First released in 1932, this film starring little-known actors and circus sideshow performers was an anomaly in the production roster of Metro-Goldwyn-Mayer, the studio renowned for its high production values and its slogan: 'More stars than there are in heaven'. This is a film that critiques the star system, both in its casting and in its narrative; indeed, it can be interpreted as a denunciation of our culture's obsession with appearances. The differently abled bodies of the freaks who star in the film – armless, legless, small, or exceptionally thin – serve to undermine the typical ideology of beauty promulgated by other Hollywood films. (I use the term freak without quotation marks in the spirit of defiance with which the term has been reclaimed by some in the disability community, much like the word queer has been reappropriated.) The film's very plot involves unmasking a beautiful circus star – Cleopatra, the trapeze artist and 'peacock of the air' – as a greedy, repugnant character whose exterior attractiveness is ultimately destroyed at the end, when she is turned into a 'human duck' and becomes a sideshow spectacle herself.

Director Tod Browning is renowned for his films about outsiders. Browning himself had a background in circuses, having travelled with a number of carnivals and sideshows in his youth. *Freaks* is Browning's best-known picture due to its status as a cult film, along with the early sound version of *Dracula* (1931) he made for Universal, which stars Bela Lugosi. Browning also made a number of important silent-era features with actor Lon Chaney, the legendary 'Man of a Thousand Faces', in particular *The Unholy Three* (1925) and *The Unknown* (1927). *The Unknown*, considered by many today to be Browning's masterpiece, tells the story of a circus performer (Chaney) who has his arms cut off to please the woman he loves (she fears the embrace of men), only to discover she has fallen for a strongman.

Freaks has been controversial since its release. Initially produced as a horror film, the picture was made at a time when disabled bodies were becoming viewed less as curiosities, as they had been in the old freak show tradition, and more as medical anomalies that could be 'fixed' by modern science. Freak shows had come to be looked down upon as low entertainment, and disabled people were now subjected to pity rather than gawking. Needless to say, neither approach allows the disabled person the dignity of his or her difference. What's more, despite the changing attitudes about disability in the 1930s, the film still encourages an openly voyeuristic gaze. This seemingly anachronistic gaping, coupled with the film's emphasis on the sexual desire of the freaks (Hans the circus dwarf explains that 'I am a man, with the same feelings [other men] have!'), evidently made the film distasteful for 1932 audiences. Even after substantial reediting by the studio, the film was a commercial flop, and it was quickly pulled from distribution by MGM.

Freaks then disappeared until 1947, when infamous B-picture director Dwain Esper purchased the film's distribution rights and placed it on the exploitation circuit. Esper added a lengthy prologue, which reads in part:

> Before proceeding with the showing of the following HIGHLY UNUSUAL ATTRACTION, a few words should be said about the amazing subject matter. BELIEVE IT OR NOT – STRANGE AS IT SEEMS. In ancient times anything that deviated from the normal was considered an omen of ill luck or representative of evil ... For the love of beauty is a deep seated urge which dates back to the beginning of civilization. The revulsion with which we view the abnormal, the malformed and the mutilated is the result of long conditioning by our forefathers. The majority of freaks, themselves, are endowed with normal thoughts and emotions. Their lot is truly a heart-breaking one ... Never again will such a story be filmed, as modern science and teratology is rapidly eliminating such blunders of nature from the world. With humility for the many injustices done to such people (they have no power to control their lot) we present the most startling horror story of the ABNORMAL and THE UNWANTED.

This prologue, accompanied by documentary-style orchestral music, regularly appears as part of the film today, but it must be understood as something that was added later for the film's exhibition as an exploitation feature; it was never part of Browning's original film. The prologue also highlights the film's two opposing themes: the humanization of freaks (who are 'endowed with normal thoughts and emotions') and the exploitation of freaks (who are 'blunders of nature').

After its initial commercial failure, *Freaks* was rediscovered as a cult film in the 1960s. The film's successful reissue began at the 1962 Cannes Festival Repertory, where it appeared as the official horror film entry. The film soon gained newly appreciative audiences in Europe and the US, who interpreted it quite differently than previous generations. In a new era, when the meaning of the term 'freak' had changed, audience members were more inclined to proudly fly their freak flag high. Instead of pitying the freaks or wondering how they might be fixed, these spectators were more likely to identify with their struggle against the cruel and conventional world of the 'normals'. The film played regularly in late-night movie theatres for years in the late 1960s and early 1970s, making it 'possibly the oldest of all midnight attractions'.[1]

Freaks has thus been received in widely varying reception contexts, and as such, it demonstrates the importance of audiences in shaping film meaning. From horror film flop in 1932 to cult film hit in the 1960s and after, this film has meant quite different things to different spectators in different historical moments. *Freaks* continues to inspire a wide range of responses in viewers today, from amazement to outrage. Such divergent responses are produced not only by different reception contexts outside the film, but also by the film's own inner textual ambivalence: the first two-thirds of the film work to humanize the film's freaks, but the concluding section reinscribes them as classic horror-genre monsters. The question surrounding this film today has become: is it humanizing, or is it exploitative?

For many viewers, the story of Hans's doomed love for Cleopatra pales in comparison with the film's portrayal of everyday circus life. The first section of the film introduces the viewer to a cast of sideshow characters, many of whom were circus performers of some renown. Many of the actors had worked for Ringling Bros. and Barnum & Bailey Circuses, or on Coney Island. One of the most memorable performers in the film, Prince Randian 'The Human Torso', began his long career working for P. T. Barnum in 1889, and was still working in a freak show on Times Square at the time of his death in 1934 at age 63; the film features part of his cigarette-rolling and lighting act. Perhaps the most famous of the film's sideshow performers, Daisy and Violet Hilton, were conjoined twins who had toured Europe and the United States as a Siamese Twin act from the age of 3, playing music and dancing on vaudeville. Harry and Daisy Earles, who played Hans and Frieda, were brother and sister who comprised part of a four-sibling little people act called 'the Dancing Dolls'. (Harry Earles had already starred in Browning's film *The Unholy Three*, and would later appear as one of the 'Lollipop Kids' in *The Wizard of Oz* [Victor Fleming, 1939].) Johnny Eck, 'The Half Boy', had long performed a sawing-in-half magic act with his full-bodied twin brother. Angelo Rossitto, memorable as the dwarf who passes the loving cup around the table at the wedding feast, parlayed his experience as a sideshow performer into a highly successful career in cinema, working in numerous films and television programs; he eventually became one of the founders of Little People of America. As this brief account of just some of the cast of *Freaks* begins to indicate, part of the film's appeal is the sense of realism achieved by the casting of real actors with disabilities. This realism, however, is counterbalanced by a strong dose of fantasy, as the performers' everyday life is fictionalized into a horror story.

In its opening scene, the film encourages its audience to identify with the freaks. 'But for the accident of birth, you might be even as they are', a carny talker says to the audience-within-the-film. The film's first half then contains a long sequence that serves to normalize the freaks. We see them going about their everyday business: working, playing, and, in keeping with the film's salacious tone, reproducing: 'The bearded lady's baby is born!' Much of the sequence is accompanied by swirling calliope music on the soundtrack, which sets it apart from the rest of the film.

Once this circus music background finally stops, the narrative of doomed love begins to dominate the film. The film's tone becomes progressively more carnivalesque, building up to a sensational wedding banquet scene which is preceded by the film's only intertitle, which reads, 'The Wedding Feast'. In this scene, Hans has just married Cleopatra, and the freaks decide to initiate her into their group. They begin to chant: 'Gooble gobble, gooble gobble! We accept her, we accept her! Gooble gobble, gooble gobble! One of us, one of us!' This chant filled with nonsense words sounds like a different language, and the scene has been criticized for making the freaks seem inscrutable and alien. At the same time, however, the crazy babbling quality of the chant has surprised and delighted audiences for decades, and it has become a kind of initiatory battle cry for the film's cult audience. (The Ramones' punk rock slogan 'Gabba Gabba Hey', featured in their song 'Pinhead', was famously inspired by this chant.) Despite their offer of a loving cup, Cleopatra brutally rejects the freaks' allegiance, and proceeds to humiliate Hans by dancing around with him on her shoulders. After that, she tries to murder him. If one has been siding with the freaks, the revenge that follows seems well deserved.

The macabre revenge sequence that finally comes, however, does indeed turn the freaks into monsters, undoing the humanizing work of the first portion of the film. Johnny Eck, Angelino, Schlitze, and others – even Prince Randian, carrying a knife in his mouth – march and slither through a rainstorm in the mud to attack Cleopatra and her 'normal' boyfriend, Hercules the strongman. While audiences may cheer their cause, the characters who generated so much empathy earlier have now been rendered devilish mutants, after the manner of classic horror villains. The film's humanizing has been neutralized in a blaze of sensationalism, and the film's conclusion raises the tone of voyeuristic fantasy even higher with the shocking image of Cleopatra, legless and quacking like a duck after having been deformed by her assailants. *Freaks* may be far more acceptable now than when it was first released, but it is a product of the 1930s with a sensibility that could not be reproduced today.

Note

1 J. Hoberman and Jonathan Rosenbaum, *Midnight Movies,* New York, Harper and Row, 1983, p. 295.

Further reading

Rachel Adams, *Sideshow U.S.A.: Freaks and the American Cultural Imagination,* Chicago, University of Chicago Press, 2001.

Sally Chivers, 'The Horror of Becoming "One of Us": Tod Browning's *Freaks* and Disability', in Christopher R. Smit and Anthony Enns (eds), *Screening Disability: Essays on Cinema and Disability*, Lanham, MD, University Press of America, 2001, pp. 57–64.

Oliver Gaycken, 'Tod Browning and the Monstrosity of Hollywood Style', in Christopher R. Smit and Anthony Enns (eds), *Screening Disability*, Lanham, MD, University Press of America, 2001, pp. 73–85.

Robin Larsen and Beth A. Haller, 'The Case of *Freaks:* Public Reception of Real Disability', *Journal of Popular Film and Television*, Vol. 29, No. 4, Winter 2002, pp. 164–72.

David Skal and Elias Savada, *Dark Carnival: The Secret World of Tod Browning, Master of the Macabre,* New York, Anchor Books, 1995.

JENNIFER PETERSON

GOLD DIGGERS OF 1933 (1933)

[Production Company: Warner Brothers. Director: Mervyn LeRoy. Screenwriters: David Boehm, Erwin Gelsey, Ben Markson and James Seymour. Cinematographer: Sol Polito. Editor: George Amy. Cast: Ruby Keeler (Polly Parker), Joan Blondell (Carol King), Alice MacMahon (Trixie Lorraine), Dick Powell (Brad Roberts), Ned Sparks (Barney Hopkins), Guy Kibbee (Faneul H. Peabody), Warren William (J. Lawrence Bradford), Ginger Rogers (Fay Fortune).]

Early on in Arthur Penn's classic gangster movie, *Bonnie and Clyde* (1967), Clyde Barrow (Warren Beatty), Bonnie Parker (Faye Dunaway) and their driver, C. W. Moss (Michael J.Pollard), hide out in a cinema after a botched getaway from a robbery has resulted in the fatal shooting of a bank employee. As Clyde remonstrates with Moss, Bonnie tries to watch the film which is *Gold Diggers of 1933*. 'We're in the money' sings a chorus-girl (Ginger Rogers) from the screen, in a costume of gold coins. The cheeriness of the song sharply counterpoints the mood of the three bank robbers; and the sentiments of the song also mock the situation of three people whose life of crime is their means of survival in Depression-hit America.

The cinematic reference is useful for Penn's purposes both for establishing the period and varying the mood, but it is interesting that the ironic intent in the later film is not that different from the original. Audiences of the early 1930s in America were often impoverished and went to the cinema to forget their troubles, so the song would function as extreme wish-fulfilment. Moreover, the song is ironic in the narrative itself, because as soon as it is over, the showgirls, far from being in the money, will be out of a job. This oscillation between escapism and realism will be one of the most interesting and original aspects of the film.

Gold Diggers of 1933 had been filmed in 45 days, following hard on the heels of another backstage Warner Brothers musical, *42nd Street* (1933), which had unexpectedly been a huge hit and which had prompted the studio to try to emulate its success with another musical in a similar style. The *Gold Diggers* formula by that time was well established, dating from the premiere of Avery Hopwood's play in 1919, which in turn had been filmed as a 1923 silent movie and then as a spectacular Technicolor sound film entitled *Gold Diggers of Broadway* in 1929, which was a huge box-office success. The early musicals of the sound era soon lost their novelty value because of their dull visual presentation, but the Warner Brothers' films revitalized the genre, partly through the glamour and panache of the musical numbers and partly through the grittiness of their social observation.

The film's plot could not be simpler. Three showgirls, Polly (Ruby Keeler), Carol (Joan Blondell) and Trixie (Alice MacMahon) are now out of work and looking to their producer Barney (Ned Sparks) to find a sponsor for their new show. Polly is in love with a young song-writer, Brad (Dick Powell), who lives in the apartment opposite. What she does not know is that Brad is a member of one of the wealthiest families in Boston. When Barney hears his songs and longs to put them in a show, Brad offers to put up $15,000 to help get the show produced. However, when the family hears of this, his brother, Lawrence (Warren William), and the family lawyer, Peabody (Guy Kibbee), visit Brad, determined both to discourage the romance with the show-girl and his sponsorship of the show. Carol and Trixie get to work on the brother and the lawyer, and their amorous ploys help to ensure that all is resolved happily.

Gold Diggers of 1933 did not simply cash in on the success of *42nd Street* but represented something of an advance on the earlier film in terms of both romance and comedy. There are some knowing in-jokes, as, for example, when the producer hears Brad's songs and enthuses that, by comparison, 'Warren and Dubin are out.' (Harry Warren and Al Dubin are, in fact, the songs' composers, as they were for *42nd Street* and *Gold Diggers of 1935,* for which they wrote their classic, 'Lullaby of Broadway', that was to win them an Oscar.) Some of the comedy is quite risqué. When one of the showgirls Fay (Ginger Rogers) starts to say, 'If Barney could see me in clothes … ', another inter-rupts sharply, 'He wouldn't recognize you.' There is a nice visual joke when the girls manage to hook in their neighbour's milk for them-selves by using a pair of tongs, but its deeper significance is not lost: the extremes to which they must go in order to survive, and also how their survival might depend on their success in hooking what they need – like, for example, Brad's brother and the family lawyer, who succumb to the attractions of Carol and Trixie and then find they have been lured into embarrassing, even compromising, situations that could leave them open to blackmail. As a line from the showgirls' opening song says, 'We've got a lot of what it takes to get along'; and it seems to mean more than simply musical talent. Even the posters for the film focused heavily on the erotic appeal of the dancers' legs.

For the director of the film, Mervyn LeRoy, *Gold Diggers of 1933* represented something of a change of pace. Prior to that film, he had been mainly associated with hard-hitting dramas such as *Little Caesar* (1930) – the first major gangster film of the sound era – and *I am a Fugitive from a Chain Gang* (1932), a savage indictment of the penal system; and later in the decade he was to make *They Won't Forget* (1937), a powerful criticism of lynch-law justice. His subsequent career was less remarkable, though he did direct much-loved and popular films such as *Random Harvest* (1942) and *Quo Vadis?* (1951). LeRoy was one of those unobtrusive craftsmen of the studio era who could be relied on to do a competent job but who has never been considered as an *auteur*: that is, the kind of director who puts his personal stamp and style on a project. One might say that, in the case of a genre like the musical, it would be particularly difficult to do this, because it is a genre where the director is dependent on so many specialist talents of more or less equal importance. Nevertheless, if *Gold Diggers of 1933* is still remembered and considered as a film musical milestone, the reason has to do with the contribution of one man, Busby Berkeley, perhaps the most celebrated and controversial choreographer in the history of Hollywood.

Having rapidly gained a reputation as an exceptional dance director on Broadway in the 1920s, Berkeley had been brought to Hollywood by producer Samuel Goldwyn to choreograph the musical numbers for the comedies of Eddie Cantor, which were extremely popular at the time. However, it was his work on the Warner Brothers' musicals of the 1930s that brought him most acclaim, particularly through the way his production numbers transcended the boundaries of theatre, taking the camera to places where no theatre director (or audience) could go. He invented a monorail to facilitate the fluidity of his camera movement, and even bored holes in the ceiling of Warner Brothers' sound stages to achieve the aerial shots of choreographic patterns that became his trademark. Such strategies were not without attendant dangers; and when a minor earthquake struck Los Angeles during the rehearsal of one of the numbers, some of the girls fell off the ramp and were injured, though not seriously. Berkeley's numbers were not really dance-routines in the manner of Fred Astaire's 'Top Hat' performance, say, for they were collective more than individual displays and celebrated choreographic formation rather than the dancers' brilliance. For example, in 'The Shadow Waltz', the dancing girls hold neon-lit violins: the pleasure generated comes not from their individual skills but from the way Berkeley orchestrates their movements on camera, so that, for example, from above, they form themselves into the shape of a violin being bowed.

This picks up one aspect of his style that has been subject to criticism: namely, the demeaning use of women as objects and spectacle, serving his purpose towards the creation of his erotic and aesthetic geometry. This hostility has sometimes been taken a step further and Berkeley's method likened to that notorious propagandist on film of Nazi ideology, Leni Riefenstahl who, in a film like *Triumph of the Will* (1936), constructed a style where a multitude of young people were shown to be moulded into a single entity by the will of a charismatic leader, Adolph Hitler. In his famous 'Springtime for Hitler' number in *The Producers* (1967), director Mel Brooks alluded to this connection when he cut mischievously to a Berkeley-like aerial shot of the chorus-line as they spin around and we see that, from above, they are in the formation of a swastika. Nonetheless, it seems a bit harsh to suggest Berkeley as a musical Riefenstahl when the contexts and intentions are so different. Indeed, one could argue that the ideological implication of the method is the reverse of Riefenstahl's: namely, this is not obeisance to a charismatic leader, but an emphasis – at the time of the Depression and President Roosevelt's promise of a 'New Deal' – on the importance of everyone's pulling together in harmony if the enterprise is to be successful.

The specific social context of the film makes a dramatic reappearance at the finale, which has also attracted adverse comment. As Carol, Joan Blondell sings 'Remember My Forgotten Man' as a tribute to the work-force currently suffering the effects of America's economic crisis. A chorus representing the mass unemployed joins her and silhouetted behind them are representations of the men they were in the First World War, fighting for a country that has now consigned them to the scrapheap. The difference between this and an earlier number like, say, the deliriously romantic 'Petting in the Park' could hardly be greater and, in the July 1933 issue of the magazine *New Outlook,* Cy Caldwell expressed a common view when he condemned the sequence as offensive, in bad taste and incongruous in a musical comedy. Utopian joy, fantasy and energy are supposed to be at the heart of the movie musicals, not misery and unemployment. But then, genre conventions were made to be subverted, and it was a mark of this film – and Warner Brothers' musicals of this time – that it was not afraid to inject a bit of contemporary bleakness into the brashness even while maintaining an energy and imagination that in themselves exude optimism and a belief in a better future. 'My Forgotten Man' is also the definitive repudiation of those who see nothing in Berkeley's routines but geometric glitz and voyeuristic vulgarity. In this number he showed he could put across a social message with sensitivity as well as spectacle; it is the most poignant musical and choreographic evocation of Depression Era America.

Further reading

Rick Altman, *Genre: The Musical,* London, Routledge, 1981.
Jane Feuer, *The Hollywood Musical,* 2nd edn, London, Macmillan, 1993.
Martin Rubin, *Showstoppers: Busby Berkeley and the Tradition of Spectacle*, New York, Columbia University Press, 1993.

NEIL SINYARD

IT HAPPENED ONE NIGHT (1934)

[Production Company: Columbia Pictures. Director: Frank Capra. Screenwriter: Robert Riskin. Cinematographer: Joseph Walker. Music: Howard Jackson and Louis Silvers. Editor: Gene Havlick.

Cast: Clark Gable (Peter Warne), Claudette Colbert (Ellie Andrews), Walter Connolly (Alexander Andrews), Jameson Thomas (King Westley), Roscoe Karns (Oscar Shapeley), Alan Hale (Danker).]

It Happened One Night was a runaway hit about a runaway heiress. Opening modestly in New York to respectful rather· than rave reviews, it began to gather word-of-mouth recommendation among audiences in second-run theatres in the United States and by the end of the year had become one of 1934's most successful films. It then proceeded to win all the major awards at the Hollywood Oscars in 1935 – best film, best actor, best actress, best director, best screenplay – a feat that was not to be equalled until *One Flew Over the Cuckoo's Nest* (1975) 40 years later.

The popularity of the film had taken Hollywood by surprise. It was a modest subject without lavish production values, and was produced by Columbia Pictures which at that time was a minor studio without previous Oscar success. (It was essentially this film that put Columbia 'on the map'.) The original material, a short story called 'Night Bus' by Samuel Hopkins Adams, had been bought for little money and there was comparatively little enthusiasm for the project when it looked like proving difficult to sell as a movie. Two 'bus movies' – MGM's *Fugitive Lovers* (1933) and Universal's *Cross Country Cruise* (1933) – had failed with the public the previous year and there was little expectation that this new vehicle would fare any differently.

Casting also proved a major headache. In his autobiography, *The Name Above the Title* (1971), director Frank Capra recalled that several actresses (including Miriam Hopkins, Myrna Loy, Margaret Sullavan and Constance Bennett) turned it down before Claudette Colbert accepted it, although only on condition it would be finished in five weeks so that she could go on holiday and that she would receive twice her usual salary. She still seemed unconvinced the film was anything exceptional, even when it proved popular and garnered Oscar nominations; she had booked a journey to New York on the night of the awards and had to be driven hastily to the ceremony with a motorcycle escort. On loan from MGM, Clark Gable was only cast for the leading role when Robert Montgomery turned it down (on the grounds that he did not want to do another bus movie). With the possible exception of *Casablanca* (1942), it is hard to think of another classic film that had such an unpromising preparation and launch.

Capra was later to claim that a key turning-point came with the intervention of the studio's story-editor, Myles Connolly, who identified the weaknesses of the original script. Make the heroine not just an heiress but a reluctant heiress, Connolly argued: this will make her more sympathetic to a general audience. Also, if you change the hero from an artist to a working man – a journalist, say – he too becomes a character with whom a popular audience can more readily identify. The plot – a familiar standby about a couple whose initial antagonism on meeting turns to love as they share various adventures – was essentially a modern variation on *The Taming of the Shrew* and that has invariably proved a winning formula. Capra's regular screenwriter at this time, Robert Riskin, got to work on this new concept with his customary intelligence and imagination and the material suddenly seemed to gel.

The spark that ignited all these ingredients was Capra himself, who was just entering the most creative phase of his career and about to become arguably the major Hollywood director of the decade: he was to follow this film with best directing Oscars for *Mr Deeds Goes to Town* (1936) and *You Can't Take It With You* (1938) as well as making classics like *Lost Horizon* (1937) and *Mr Smith Goes to Washington* (1939). Comedy had always been Capra's particular forte. He had begun his film career in the silent era as a gag-man for the legendary Mack Sennett and then written and directed the early hit comedies of Harry Langdon, *Tramp, Tramp, Tramp* (1926), *The Strong Man* (1926) and *Long Pants* (1927), which had briefly put Langdon on a par in terms of popularity with Charlie Chaplin, Buster Keaton and Harold Lloyd. Always ferociously ambitious in reaction against his impoverished childhood, Capra had moved to Columbia Pictures and had rapidly become their star director. He had made a bold and stylish film about racial prejudice and misunderstanding, *The Bitter Tea of General Yen* (1933); and then been nominated for an Oscar for *Lady for a Day* (1933), being left to squirm with embarrassment when, responding to the call of the presenter Will Rogers, 'Come and get it, Frank!', he realized halfway to the podium that Rogers was actually summoning another nominee, Frank Lloyd, to collect the award for *Cavalcade* (1933). This only made Capra more determined to win, and although *It Happened One Night* might not have seemed immediately to be the kind of property that would bring this about, it did have all the components that played to Capra's comic strengths: pace, situations that were funny but also believable, and, above all, a strong and sympathetic sense of humanity across a broad social spectrum. Capra's best films were always to be optimistic fanfares to the common man.

In his book about Hollywood screenwriters, *Talking Pictures* (1975), the critic Richard Corliss suggested you could summarize the plot of this film in a single headline couched in the style of its reporter-hero:

'Star Reporter Trails and Nails Heiress – for Life.' On the run from her wealthy father (Walter Connolly) who disapproves of her marrying a playboy aviator, King Westley (Jameson Thomas), Ellen Andrews (Claudette Colbert) has hopped on a bus to New York to be united with King, but, in so doing, she inadvertently occupies the seat of a brash reporter, Peter Warne (Clark Gable), who has just been fired from his job. Warne quickly sizes up her situation, but promises to help her if he can report her story exclusively and win himself back into his editor's favours. As the journey proceeds, they fall in love.

If the plot is slight, the film, thanks to the inventiveness of Capra and Riskin, teems with memorable bits of comic business. The antagonistic interplay between Gable and Colbert is incessant, ranging from the best way to dunk a doughnut, in which he mocks her refined habits, to the best way to hitch a lift, where she undercuts his arrogance by demonstrating that the display of a shapely leg is more effective than the waving of a thumb. Most famous of all perhaps is the blanket Gable drapes across the middle of their shared motel room – the so-called 'Wall of Jericho' – that decorously separates their living space and which might be Capra's and Riskin's joke at the expense of the new Production Code which was tightening up on Hollywood's depiction of sexual morality. When Gable's character reveals during this section that he wears nothing under his shirt, movie legend has it that the revelation led to a 40 per cent reduction in the sale of men's vests: evidence of Hollywood's influence on the fashions of the time!

Like Dickens, Capra also always gave as much life to his minor characters as his major ones, knowing that they too had a story to tell, a history and a mystery about them. Roscoe Karnes has an excellent cameo as a salesman on the bus who tries to ingratiate himself with Ellen and then uncovers her identity, only to be frightened off by Peter who pretends to be an armed gangster and that Ellen is part of his kidnapping plot. (It was daring of Capra and Riskin to make a joke about kidnapping so soon after the notorious kidnapping of the child of Charles Lindbergh and its tragic outcome.) Alan Hale storms into the picture when he offers the couple a ride, cannot stop singing in the car, but is revealed to be a small-time thief when he attempts to run off with their things. (Peter somehow manages to overtake his speeding car on foot: by this time, the film is obeying its own comic logic.) There is an especially happy sequence that seems spontaneous and semi-improvised when the passengers on the bus take turns in singing a verse of 'That Daring Young Man on the Flying Trapeze' and where even the driver, hitherto a peripheral and rather gloomy figure, is so caught up in the joyful spirits that he joins in. It is a scene with the kind of vigour and generosity of spirit that is quintessential Capra. Hitchcock used to say that if you have four good scenes, you have got a picture; *It Happened One Night* was taking no chances – it has close on a dozen that live in the memory.

The film has been seen as a trailblazer in being the first successful example of a new genre – the so-called 'screwball comedy'. The term 'screwball' derived from baseball, describing a pitch with a wicked and unexpected curve on it, and also tied in with the English expression of 'having a screw loose' to suggest someone behaving in a lunatic manner. Generally speaking, screwball comedy was noted for its verbal witticism, frantic pace and slapstick craziness, with a particular emphasis on an evenly balanced battle of the sexes and also often a class conflict with a significant wealth divide between the two antagonists that love reconciles. Both *Twentieth Century* and *The Thin Man* had opened in the same year as *It Happened One Night* with some of these characteristics, but the former lacked the sympathetic characterisation of the Capra and the latter allied (and diluted) the sizzling verbal wit exchanged between husband and wife, Nick and Nora Charles (William Powell and Myrna Loy) with a murder mystery plot. Screwball comedy was to achieve its most complete expression in classics such as Leo McCarey's *The Awful Truth* (1937), Howard Hawks's *Bringing up Baby* (1938) and Preston Sturges's *Palm Beach Story* (1942).

Much has been written about *It Happened One Night* in the context of the screwball genre: how characteristic it is and whether it can truly be claimed to be the originator. How far is the film a sophisticated striking back at the Production Code, appearing to adhere to its rules (even down to its 'Wall of Jericho') while actually circumventing them? No one could miss the sexual elements in the film even though no intimacy is shown. The film's sexual politics has also generated a lot of discussion over the years. Beneath the wit and the supposed equality of the characterization, is the film still reinforcing the values of patriarchy, as a rebellious young woman is brought to heel by a man who can control her; or is it alternatively showing a new kind of heroine prepared to sacrifice wealth and position for the freedom to make her own moral, material and marital choices? Whatever one concludes, there is no doubt that *It Happened One Night* was one of those rare screen comedies, like *The Graduate* (1967) in the 1960s, like *Annie Hall* (1977) in the 1970s, that caught the mood of the time, answering an audience's need for romantic escapism and its hope for a harmony between wealth and worth. Capra himself had the simplest explanation for the film's popularity and it

In his massive 1998 book *'You Ain't Heard Nothin' Yet': The American Talking Film, History and Memory, 1927–1949*, Andrew Sarris includes essays about a number of directors of silents, including Chaplin. The Chaplin essay begins, 'Charles Chaplin is arguably the single most important artist produced by the cinema, certainly its most extraordinary performer and probably still its most universal icon' (Sarris 1998: 139). David Robinson, a Chaplin biographer, whose recorded introductions are included in the Chaplin DVD releases, describes the Tramp as 'the most universally recognized representation of a human being in the history of mankind' (Robinson 1985: xiii).

While silent films may seem remote in ways that even early sound films may not, Chaplin films have lost neither their charm nor their power to invoke laughter. Because silent film depended not on dialogue but on pantomime, the silents crossed language barriers in ways that sound film never will. Chaplin was one of the first international film stars, and remained the most international of film stars through the end of his career as a director and star of silent films. The Little Tramp was most recognizable film character in the world from the mid-teens until his final screen appearance in *Modern Times*.

Chaplin was the most rigorous of perfectionists: he rehearsed, shot, and re-shot until he was thoroughly satisfied. His unmatched popularity, feverish work ethic, and shrewd business sense made him one of the most independent filmmakers in the history of Hollywood. One can graph the astonishing rise in his popularity, the expanding market for film entertainment (and Chaplin's aggressive negotiating tactics) through his contracts. Chaplin had grown up in London slums and had appeared on stage since he was a child. His first film contract, with Keystone studios, signed in December 1913, guaranteed Chaplin $150 a week, good money in 1913. Signing this contract meant retiring from his career in a touring musical comedy company and joining the troupe, supervised by Mack Sennett, that produced three comic pictures per week, each 10–30 minutes long. After a year in which he appeared in 33 Keystone films, several of which he also directed, Chaplin signed a contract with Essanay in November of 1914. The new contract guaranteed $1250 per week, with a $10,000 signing bonus. Chaplin directed and appeared in 11 Essanay films, then signed with Mutual in February 1916. The legendary Mutual contract guaranteed Chaplin $10,000 per week, with a signing bonus of $150,000. After directing and starring in several of his most acclaimed short films, Chaplin moved to First National in 1917, where he signed a contract with an annual salary of $1,075,000. By January of 1918, he was working in the studio he had built. In 1919,

Chaplin joined with the period's other big stars, Douglas Fairbanks and Mary Pickford, and director D. W. Griffith to form United Artists. He had just turned 30.

Two months after the 1927 premiere of *The Jazz Singer* – the mostly silent film which marked the beginning of the end of silent cinema as a viable commercial enterprise – Chaplin began work on *City Lights*. *City Lights* took more than four years to complete, premiering in high style in February 1931. By this time the transition to sound film, the most wrenching artistic and economic storm to hit Hollywood, exacerbated by the onset of the Great Depression, was more or less complete. The careers of some of the most famous silent film stars and directors were over. New actors and comedians had already begun to take their places. *City Lights* included a few sound effects, and a score composed by Chaplin, but no dialogue. It is recognizably a silent film. And yet it was one of the year's most successful films, critically and commercially (Doherty 1999: 370–1).

The most astonishing fact about *Modern Times* is its release date – 1936 – almost nine years after the release of *The Jazz Singer*. To put this date in perspective, it's worth considering how far into the sound era Hollywood had traveled by 1936. After a careful build-up, silent film star Greta Garbo had spoken in *Anna Christie* (1930). In an attempt to maintain Garbo's international appeal, this film was released in English, German, and Swedish versions. German cabaret performer and film star Marlene Dietrich had made nine English language films, including an English-language version of *The Blue Angel* made simultaneously with the German version. The Marx Brothers had made their most memorable films. Fred Astaire and Ginger Rogers had danced together in four films.

Glancing through films represented in this volume, we see that, by the time *Modern Times* was released, Howard Hawks had killed Scarface in an audible hail of bullets. Busby Berkeley had directed the dance and musical numbers in *Gold Diggers of 1933*, Frank Capra had directed *It Happened One Night* (1934), one of the first and finest of screwball comedies, a genre that depends – more than almost any other – on dialogue.

Technically, *Modern Times* is not a silent film. It has a recorded soundtrack, but the soundtrack contains only sound effects, a musical score (composed by Chaplin), and some recorded speech, none of it dialogue. Most of the speech is mediated by technology. Speech is transmitted through a PA system, a video-screen, a record, or a radio. *Modern Times* does contain the first and only film sequence in which The Tramp opens his mouth and words come out. In the film's final minutes, while working as a singing waiter, he is compelled to perform a song. He writes the lyrics on his (detachable) shirt cuff but, during his opening dance, he flings off his cuffs and is forced to improvise. The words that come out of his mouth sound vaguely Italian, perhaps with some French inflection, but they are entirely gibberish. Most of the conversation between characters is communicated either through pantomime or via a handful of intertitles, which had otherwise vanished from the screen. The Tramp still communicates through Chaplin's extraordinary control of his body and extraordinarily expressive face.

Chaplin was generally seen as left leaning, with his films as evidence, and was considered politically suspect enough to be a subject of FBI interest from 1922 until his death in 1977. Certainly his films provide plenty of evidence that Chaplin sympathized with the poor. Chaplin spent 18 months traveling after the release of *City Lights*. During this time he developed an economic theory intended to lessen the consequences of the Depression. This interest emerged in part from visiting European countries that were suffering the economic consequences of depression, consequences that were already having a political impact. *Modern Times* in particular is legible as a critique of the dehumanizing power of technology and, by extension, of industrial capitalism.

The opening factory scenes in *Modern Times* owe a great deal to Fritz Lang's *Metropolis* (1927). *Metropolis* makes melodrama out of the achingly repetitive work of assembly line workers and of the dangerous gulf separating the capitalists from the labourers on whose work they depend. In *Modern Times*, the critique of the assembly line is played for comedy. Chaplin's film spends much less screen time on the capitalists. This time is efficiently damning, however: the factory owner monitors his workers through video screens, and pushes them to work harder and faster. Apart from doing surveillance, he sits at his desk doing jigsaw puzzles. The critique of technology is also legible as a critique of sound cinema. The harsh recorded voices contrast with the lyrical elegance of Chaplin's dancing comedy. The amazingly funny sequence in which the Tramp tests out the eating machine, casts suspicion on the idea that technology can improve any experience: technology is just as likely to destroy the pleasure of a sensual experience.

When the film leaves the factory, the focus on technology disappears. The concern for the poor does not. The Tramp was always an economically marginal figure and usually an urban one. Chaplin films routinely make comedy out of the Tramp's pretense to respectability despite his poverty. *Modern Times* was the first Chaplin movie conceived during the Great Depression. *Modern Times* is concerned with widespread poverty, not just with the marginality of a particular poor character or a particular region of a city.

At the same time, *Modern Times* contains Chaplin's most astute, and funniest comment on how his fame makes his politics visible and suspicious. This anticipates his banishment from the US, two decades later. In the second of the film's four acts, Chaplin sees a flag fall off the back of a truck (even in black and white, we know the flag is red). Chaplin picks up the flag and chases after the truck, waving the flag as he does so. A march of unhappy workers appears behind him. Waving the red flag, Chaplin accidentally finds himself leader of a movement.

Modern Times is read as one of Chaplin's most overtly political films, along with *The Great Dictator* (1940), the distinctly weird parody of Adolf Hitler, which trades on the striking resemblance between two of the most famous men in the world, born four days apart in 1889. Chaplin plays both Adenoid Hynkel, Dictator of Tomania, and a Jewish barber, one of the persecuted residents of Tomania's ghetto. The barber resembles the Tramp, but he speaks. The character plays on the widespread suspicion that Chaplin was a Jew, something he refused to deny, although he was not. He was happy to be considered Jewish, especially during the Nazi period, when he saw it as an expression of solidarity with European Jews (Robinson 1985: 154–5). It almost goes without saying that neither *Modern Times* nor *The Great Dictator* were released in Germany. West German audiences had to wait until 1956 to see the Little Tramp as factory worker, until 1958 to see Chaplin as Hynkel; East Germans had to wait until re-unification.

During the McCarthy era, Chaplin was a prime target for anti-communist witch hunters. Puritanical ideas about sex were as apt to cause suspicion as were leftist politics. Chaplin's marital history – four marriages, all to much younger women, plus a paternity suit which found him guilty of fathering a child out of wedlock, despite a blood test which proved he could not have been the child's father – did not help his cause. Despite his decades of work in the US, he never took US citizenship. In 1952, Chaplin set sail for Europe and his re-entry visa was revoked. He spent the rest of his long life living in Switzerland, and did not return to the US until 1972, when he received a series of honors, including a special Academy Award.

In recent years, cineastes have been apt to compare Chaplin to Buster Keaton, another one-time Keystone comedian who struck out on his own as director and star in the 1920s. Keaton never had the control over his productions that Chaplin had, and his character did not survive the earthquake of sound, although he continued to appear in movies and on television until his death in 1966. Keaton now looks like a more innovative filmmaker, more apt to experiment with film technology and movie magic. But discussion as to who one should rate more highly seems a little silly. As viewers, we are lucky that these two men made brilliantly funny silent films, and that so much of their work has survived.

Further reading

James Agee, 'Comedy's Greatest Era', in *Agee on Film: Criticism and Comment on the Movies*, New York, Random House, 2000, pp. 391–412.

Thomas Doherty, *Pre-Code Hollywood: Sex, Immorality, and Insurrection in American Cinema, 1930–1934*, New York, Columbia University Press, 1999.

Charles J. Maland, *Chaplin and American Culture: The Evolution of a Star Image*, Princeton, NJ, Princeton University Press, 1989.

David Robinson, *Chaplin: His Life and Art*, New York, McGraw-Hill, 1985.

Andrew Sarris, *'You Ain't Heard Nothin' Yet': The American Talking Film, History and Memory, 1927–1949*, New York, Oxford University Press, 1998.

ELLIOT SHAPIRO

GONE WITH THE WIND (1939)

[Production Company: MGM. Producer: David Selznick. Directors: Victor Fleming, George Cukor and Sam Wood. Screenwriters: Sidney Howard, Oliver Garrett, Ben Hecht and Jo Swerling. Cinematographer: Ernest Haller. Music: Max Steiner. Cast: Clark Gable (Rhett Butler), Vivien Leigh (Scarlett O'Hara), Leslie Howard (Ashley Wilkes), Olivia de Haviland (Melanie Hamilton), Hattie McDaniel (Mammy).]

If one were to put a date on the moment that indelibly marked the highpoint of Hollywood in its heyday, one might suggest 15 December 1939. This was the date of the premiere of *Gone with the Wind* in Atlanta, Georgia, an event attended by over 50 film stars and nearly two thousand dignitaries and regarded as so special that the Governor had declared a state holiday. Nothing was more remarkable about the film than the fact that it lived up to its own publicity. It was to win ten Oscars and to be a colossal box-office success, being seen at that time by more people than any other motion picture in history (a record, many say, that still holds). It was a fittingly spectacular end to the year of 1939, which has since often been looked on as a golden year for Hollywood film production; and indeed in some ways it is the culmination of Hollywood's dominance of the 1930s as the Mecca of mass entertainment and appeal.

The driving force behind all this was the producer, David Selznick, son-in-law of the head of MGM, Louis B. Mayer, but a fiercely independent spirit who was determined with this project to top all his previous successes. The story behind the film (and no film has inspired so many books about its making) was to be as dramatic as the film itself. On acquiring the rights to Margaret Mitchell's novel, Selznick rapidly became aware that he was not just adapting a text but a literary phenomenon with a fanatical following. Within six months of its publication, the publishers had been obliged to publish nearly half a million copies to keep pace with demand; and with that came a loyal readership holding strong views about what the film should be like and who should play the leading roles, demands that Selznick would have to satisfy.

No effort or expense was spared in the endeavour to bring to the screen a cinematic realisation that did justice to the novel. The bulk of the screenplay was written by Sidney Howard, a respected dramatist and adaptor of others' material, particularly admired for his play and then screenplay based on Sinclair Lewis's novel, *Dodsworth* (filmed by William Wyler in 1936): sadly, Howard was to die before the film opened. Nevertheless, no fewer than 16 other writers worked on it at different stages, including such eminent figures as Scott Fitzgerald and Ben Hecht. Although in the end the direction was credited solely to Victor Fleming (who had come onto the film after directing most of another enduring classic of that year, *The Wizard of Oz*), the first director on the film was George Cukor, who had done a year's preparation on it but who, after three weeks of filming and to the distress of his leading actresses, was fired because of what were called 'creative differences' with the producer. Director Sam Wood was also called in to help out towards the end of the picture when Fleming had a nervous collapse after yet another blazing row with his leading actress, which had left him, he was to say later, with the urge to drive off the nearest cliff. Meanwhile Selznick's indefatigable chief publicist, Russell Birdwell, was devising ever more ingenious strategies to keep the film in the public eye, even to the extent of sending the press foreign-made typewriters with the initials of the film highlighted by coloured keys.

The main publicity inevitably centred on the casting of the two central roles, the tempestuous lovers at the heart of the drama, Rhett Butler and Scarlett O'Hara. The public had already made up its mind about who must play Rhett: the leading heart-throb of the day, Clark Gable. Selznick had to pay a high price to persuade his father-in-law to release Gable from his MGM contact for the film; and indeed, by providing half the film's financing in return for world distribution rights and half the profits, MGM did very well out of the deal. But the real teaser, which Selznick exploited to the full for publicity purposes, centred on the question of who was to play Scarlett O'Hara. Thirty-two actresses were tested and a decision had still not been made when the film began shooting with the famous burning of Atlanta sequence, which had to be shot first to make room for the other sets. Legend has it (and it has never been contradicted by anything as mundane as the truth) that Selznick's younger brother, Myron, a top Hollywood agent, was visiting the set at that time in the company of Laurence Olivier and Vivien Leigh, who were lovers and shortly to be married. 'Hey, genius', Myron called out to his brother, 'meet your Scarlett O'Hara!' David turned round, took one look at Vivien Leigh against the background of the flames, and realized his search for Scarlett was at an end.

The phrase 'gone with the wind' comes from a love poem 'Cynara' by the nineteenth-century poet, Ernest Dowson, and its famous refrain 'I have been faithful to thee, Cynara! in my fashion' might have suggested to Margaret Mitchell something of the tempestuous on–off romance of her two strong-willed leading characters. In the context of the film, however, as an opening title penned by Ben Hecht reveals, 'gone with the wind' refers to the world and values of the American South blown away by the forces of war and change. The film is a saga of destruction and reconstruction during and after the American Civil War. Against this background of an aristocratic society collapsing then struggling to adjust to harsh new commercial and social realities, the love affair between Rhett and Scarlett flickers, then flames into passion, but then burns out, leaving only ashes. Rhett consigns Scarlett to damnation at the very moment she recognizes that her long infatuation with Ashley Wilkes (Leslie Howard), who has encouraged her feelings while having no intention of leaving his devoted wife Melanie (Olivia de Haviland), has been a false romantic illusion. When Melanie dies and Ashley cocoons himself in egoistic self-pity, she realizes her mistake, but it is too late. 'What's to become of me?' she cries, to which Rhett delivers the immortal reply: 'Frankly, my dear, I don't give a damn.' It was an expensive reply, too. Such profanity was forbidden under the Production Code and Selznick had to pay $5,000 to the Motion Picture Producers and Distributors of America for permission to use that line, the shock effect being slightly diluted by Gable's delivery, where he shrewdly places emphasis on the word 'give' rather than 'damn'.

As Butler, a pragmatic realist who sees the writing on the wall before his Southern friends and adjusts his life and expectations accordingly, Gable's performance cannot be faulted: it has all the romantic charisma the part requires, but he seasons it with a wicked wit, never more so than in his dealings with Scarlett, whose selfish deceptions attract as much as appal him because he recognizes something of a kindred spirit. 'We're alike', he tells her at one stage, 'selfish and shrewd, but able to look things in the eye and call them by their right name.' As Scarlett, Vivien Leigh seems at first all feminine caprice, which must later turn to ruthless self-preservation, but she also always conveys underneath the frivolous surface the character's sharp intelligence that is to captivate Rhett. She is a character with dynamism in a society that does not value or encourage such qualities in a woman, so that much of her energy and potential, one feels, becomes warped by the delusion that love should be the consuming goal of her life. In this respect, it is a performance that anticipates her definitive portrayal of another Southern belle of later vintage, also clinging to her romantic illusions as her body and her property are threatened by violation, Blanche du Bois in *A Streetcar Named Desire* (1951), which, like *Gone with the Wind*, also won her an Academy Award.

The film is an awesome spectacle that even today would be hard to match: perhaps a reason that thus far it has never been re-made. The burning of Atlanta remains an exciting set-piece. Some of the individual shots are breathtaking, none more so than the moment when the camera cranes away from Scarlett as she searches for a doctor at the Atlanta depot to reveal hundreds of wounded soldiers lying in the street awaiting treatment: a masterful visual exposition of an individual's plight being subsumed and overwhelmed by national tragedy. At moments like this, one is reminded that, for all Selznick's desire to please the public, he was not afraid to take risks. There are no battle scenes to add spurious excitement; there are moments of striking brutality (an amputation suggested by shadow, Scarlett's shooting of a Yankee deserter at point-blank range in the face); and, of course, an open rather than happy ending.

It is inevitable that the film would have dated in some respects, though even that is interesting in the sense that it tells you something about the tastes and values of the time. Historically, it has little to say about the causes of the War. The black characters now look either patronized or caricatured, though Hattie McDaniel succeeds in creating a strong and admirable character out of Scarlett's maid, Mammy, and also created history by being the first black performer to win an Oscar. The sexual politics look dubious now, and a feminist writer, Angela Carter, has expressed outrage at the notorious and, for its time, daring 'marital rape' scene, when a drunken Rhett carries Scarlett to bed; particularly when it is implied that Scarlett appears to have enjoyed the experience. On the other hand, it must be pointed out that other audiences have seen Scarlett as a precursor of feminism in her bravery, business acumen, determination and resilience. Certainly, one of the great moments of the film occurs when, half-starving amidst the fields of her beloved home Tara that has been ravaged by war, she rails at the heavens. 'If I have to lie, steal, cheat, kill', she cries, 'as God is my witness, I'll never be hungry again!'

Gone with the Wind remains a monument of Hollywood craftsmanship and the ultimate Hollywood film of the 1930s in terms of style and conception. It is big, brash and romantic, all this heavily underlined by the soaring music of Hollywood's top composer of the age, Max Steiner. It is star-studded and confident of its appeal, which is more emotional than intellectual, directed more at the heart than at the mind. It has colossal narrative authority and, even allowing for Selznick's over-arching control, it is essentially a triumph of corporate more than personal filmmaking. Dozens upon dozens of supreme professionals combined their talents on a project which, as de Haviland suggested at the time, they seemed to sense was not only something special but even promised immortality. The theme of a society suffering and then surviving a terrible war undoubtedly struck a chord at the end of that difficult and tormented decade. More than that, though, in its lament for a vanishing world, it contained its own implicit forecast and comment on the film capital itself. After *Gone with the Wind*, Hollywood was never to look quite so self-confident again.

Further reading

Sidney Howard, '*Gone with the Wind*' *Screenplay*, edited and with an introduction by Richard Harwell, London, Lorrimer, 1981, republished Faber, 1990.

Ted Sennett, *Hollywood's Golden Year 1939*, New York, St Martin's Press, 1989.

Helen Taylor, *Scarlett's Women: 'Gone With the Wind' and its Female Fans*, London, Virago, 1989.

David Thomson, *Showman: The Life of David Selznick*, New York, Knopf, 1992.

NEIL SINYARD

STAGECOACH (1939)

[Production Company: Walter Wanger Productions. Director: John Ford. Screenwriters: Dudley Nicholas and Ben Hecht. Cinematographer: Bert Glennon. Music: Gerard Carbonara. Art Director: Alexander Toluboff. Cast: John Wayne (The Ringo Kid), Claire Trevor (Dallas), Thomas Mitchell ('Doc' Boone), Andy Devine (Buck), John Carradine (Hatfield), Louise Platt (Lucy Mallory), George Bancroft (Marshal Curly Wilcox), Donald Meek (Samuel Peacock), Berton Churchill (Henry Gatewood).]

Stagecoach is a very attractive film for those of us who study or teach about cinema – especially the cinema of 'classic' Hollywood. It was released during the highpoint of that cinema in 1939 and invites consideration as a key film of the western genre. Like many of the major films of that period, its strength is derived from a clear narrative and I will follow that narrative in my writing to explore other issues. For example, its director John Ford was a key figure in the development of *auteur* theory and in John Wayne we see an emerging star of the Hollywood system supported by a typical Hollywood ensemble of character actors.

In fact, there are four 'stars' in *Stagecoach* although one – the director – is invisible. Two of the others, Monument Valley between Utah and Arizona and the eponymous stagecoach appear with the opening credits. Then, after an opening sequence which alerts us to the danger posed by Geronimo and his Apaches, we are introduced to the characters occupying the stage to Lordsburg. They include the crooked, opinionated banker, Gatewood; the stagecoach driver, Buck; and the town's marshal, Curly, who volunteers to ride shotgun. We see the drunken but eloquent Josiah Boone MD and the warm-hearted 'whore', Dallas, both run out of town by what Boone calls a 'foul disease called social prejudice' administered by the ladies of the Law and Order League. As he departs town, the doctor is enthralled to make the acquaintance of the nervous Mr Peacock, a whiskey salesman, and there is also the mysterious, stylish gambler, Hatfield, who offers his protection to the 'angel' and 'great lady', Mrs

Mallory – who is apparently sickly, but actually pregnant and is travelling to join her husband, an army officer.

As the stagecoach drives towards the great towers of the valley, Ford uses typical orchestral arrangements of American folksongs to provide a romantic, often exuberant, commentary on the unfolding narrative. He makes extensive and effective use of music throughout the film, supporting, anticipating and translating the action and emotional moods of the film.

Curly, the marshal, is pursuing the film's central character, the 'Ringo Kid' who has broken out of jail and is on his way to Lordsburg to take revenge on the Plummer brothers who have murdered his father and brother. Curly considers Ringo to be a 'fine boy' and believes 'the only safe place for Ringo is in the pen' away from a confrontation with the dangerous Luke Plummer. Curly is essentially pragmatic. When Buck accuses him of pursuing the reward, Curly responds reproachfully, 'Why the Kid's old man and me was friends', but adds pensively, 'besides I can use that five hundred in gold.'

Seventeen minutes into the film we see the eponymous stagecoach and accompanying soldiers ford a shallow river, whereupon the film cuts to a youthful, statuesque, dusty cowboy, brandishing a shotgun and halting the stage. The camera here 'zooms' into the face of the 'Ringo Kid', played by the legendary John Wayne in his first major role. Wayne is the fourth star of *Stagecoach*.

From here, *Stagecoach* unfolds in a rhythm of episodes around three key locations – the interior of the coach with its group of different yet complementary characters, the threatening open spaces of Monument Valley and the further spaces offered by occasional staging posts along the way. In the latter, two key issues emerge. In terms of the narrative, we find continual tensions and narrative shifts, as the soldiers' orders are altered in response to the actions and apparent intentions of Geronimo. Mrs Mallory's husband and his troop seem always one step ahead and the danger and threat of death to the passengers are ever present. At the same time individual characters and motivations develop through the intimate exchanges in the two interior locations. Nick Browne carried out a marvellous visual analysis of the meal scene at the first staging post, demonstrating how Ford's use of shots and angles supported the depiction of the growing social tensions between the 'respectable' group that surrounds Mrs Mallory, and the social rejects – especially Ringo and Dallas. Ford separates the two groups pictorially, depicts the snobbish rejection of Dallas by Mrs Mallory yet also hints at possible romance in a close-up of the two outsiders sharing supper to the orchestral strains of the popular melody 'I Dream of Jeannie.'

There follows a safe but bitterly cold journey through the mountains to the next staging post, run by the Hispanic, Chris, whose wife is an Apache, or as the usually timid Peacock, who will elsewhere request 'a little Christian charity' exclaims, 'a savage!' Chris meanwhile reveals that yet again, 'there ain't no soldiers – soldiers have gone', taking the badly wounded Captain Mallory to Lordsburg. Inside the post, Mrs Mallory collapses, apparently from the shock but in fact from her advanced if barely visible pregnancy. Despite her earlier rejection, the warm-hearted Dallas and Hatfield assist her while 'Doc' Boone sobers up sufficiently to help the birth and we see the happy consequences, as Dallas emerges holding the newborn girl. The men gather around now as one coherent group and Ford's use of shot–reverse shot which previously stressed the tensions between the two women is now used to signal the growing attraction between Dallas and Ringo – confirmed in the following outdoor night-time sequence. Unlike the pronounced visual and social separation of the previous meal scene Ringo and Dallas are becoming more integrated into the group. Ringo tells Dallas about his 'real nice' cabin adding 'a man could live there – and a woman'. The invitation is clear but Dallas hesitates, troubled by her own sense of self and of right-and-wrong. During these and other sequences, Ford examines a range of personal, moral dilemmas while also commenting further on broader economic and political issues through his depiction of the crooked banker Gatewood and Hatfield – a man out of time and place, embodying the contradictions between genteel social conventions and opportunism in this 'new' country.

Throughout *Stagecoach*, Ford presents a group of differently motivated individuals confronted by complex decisions of a practical or moral nature. As Dallas says, 'That's it – things happen' and each of these 'things' is a test for the participants in the drama. Ringo and Dallas demonstrate a flexibility and strong inner core as they wrestle with personal circumstances and social responsibility and similarly 'Doc' Boone is required to overcome his craving for the mental oblivion of alcohol in order to care for his patient. On the other hand, Ford is less sympathetic to the more 'civilized' characters, showing repeatedly the inflexibility of the 'polite' and 'proper' – whether Mrs Mallory, the Law and Order League, Gatewood or Hatfield. Whereas they reject Dallas for her reputation and what she appears to be, Ringo tells Dallas 'I know all I want' in offering her a life with him.

The next brief, frantic passage through an apparently hostile environment takes them to the third staging post which has been demolished by the Apaches who, unknown to the occupants, are still following the stagecoach. The passengers, erroneously believing they are approaching safety are allowed a brief moment of reconciliation before an arrow hits Peacock and the chase is on. Once again, Ford explores the responses of the various characters with Gatewood still motivated entirely by selfish greed, Hatfield by the urge to protect Mrs Mallory and Dallas to protect the baby, while Ringo responds with sheer physical heroism. The chase is archetypal, with magnificent stunts, travelling camera shots and the threatening Apaches enclosing the once open spaces. The soundtrack draws us into the drama of Hatfield saving his last bullet for Mrs Mallory as the music segues effortlessly into the diegetic sound of the bugle charge. Just in time, the cavalry arrive and the passengers are saved – except for Hatfield, killed at the moment of rescue.

It is night-time as the stage pulls into Lordsburg where the narrative and its key relationships are resolved. Dallas and Mrs Mallory (whose husband is safe) part with kindness, Peacock is taken away on a stretcher, Gatewood is arrested and the news is taken to the Plummers that 'the Ringo Kid's in town'. The unshaven Luke Plummer abandons a winning hand and downs one last whiskey as the piano rings out. Ringo arranges for Curly to take Dallas to his ranch and the noise and bustle of the town crowd fades as Curly allows Ringo to walk with Dallas before the final confrontation. As they do, we see the stagecoach for the last time behind Curly, Buck and 'Doc', the three men who care about Ringo, watching him walk away with his girl. The couple walk along main street past the gaudy sights and sounds of what Dallas believes to be her past and future home and workplace but Ringo, of course, is constant ('I asked you to marry me, didn't I?') and tells her to wait for him.

Once again, the action moves from indoors – the Plummers in the saloon – to outdoors where Ringo is waiting. In his second moment of redemption, 'Doc' Boone prevents Plummer from leaving the saloon with a shotgun and, once again, Ford shifts us from the primitive scenario of revenge and lawlessness to the modern world of media representations as the newspaper office prepares the story. The gunfight is shot in pronounced chiaroscuro but Ford cuts away at the vital moment to Dallas's anguish at the gunshots and then back to the saloon as Plummer re-enters. For a moment we believe Ringo must be dead but Plummer collapses and as we see Dallas and hear Ringo's footsteps we realize he is safe. Finally, the 'Doc' observes that Ringo and Dallas can be 'saved from the blessings of civilization' as he and Curly engineer the couple's escape to their little cabin and a life together.

I have described the narrative in some detail, for two main reasons. The first is to stress that the film 'works' principally because it is a great cinematic story, adapted from a short magazine story 'Stage to Lordsburg'. It is a story of exciting, separate episodes with two constant threads: the conflict between white and native Americans, and Ringo's pursuit of justice (or is it revenge?). The second reason is to point out that while it seems to us now as archetypal in its tale of the old West, of physical danger, heroism, romance, class snobbery and constant moral challenges, it is not clichéd because it played a major part in establishing the norms rather than following them.

Stagecoach is a product of the high point of Classical Hollywood Cinema, and because it is a product of its time we can applaud the magnificence of the storytelling through the fine command of sound and image while asking other questions. These are broadly to do with the contradictions inherent in the growth of modern civilization in a recently 'primitive' largely unspoiled country and also more specifically with representations of 'ordinary' people, and – of course – specifically women and native Americans. The latter are a constantly implied threat but almost faceless and allowed no opportunity to state their case in a context where they were often treated shamefully. The women – particularly Dallas and Mrs Mallory – are presented more clearly and in a more thorough way. But they still conform precisely to the twin stereotypes of mother and whore in a way which might be barely acceptable today. We are now more liberal, sophisticated and conscientious in our representations; whether we make better films is far less certain.

Further reading

Nick Browne, 'The Rhetoric of the Specular Text with Reference to *Stagecoach*', in John Caughie (ed.), *Theories of Authorship*, London, Routledge, 1981.
Edward Buscombe, *Stagecoach*, London, BFI, 1992.

DAVE ALLEN

HIS GIRL FRIDAY (1940)

[Production Company: Columbia Pictures Corporation. Director: Howard Hawks. Screenplay: Charles Lederer, based on the play 'The Front Page', by Ben Hecht and Charles MacArthur. Cinematography:

Joseph Walker. Editor: Gene Havlick. Cast: Cary Grant (Walter Burns), Rosalind Russell (Hildy Johnson), Ralph Bellamy (Bruce Baldwin), Gene Lockhart (Sheriff Peter Hartwell), Frank Orth (Duffy), John Qualen (Earl Williams), Helen Mack (Mollie Malone), Billy Gilbert (Joe Pettibone), Edwin Maxwell (Dr Max J. Eggelhoffer).]

A popular joke about Hollywood in the 1930s has it that, once the movies learned to talk, they wouldn't shut up. Hollywood produced hundreds of movies in the 1930s that are not fast-talking comedies. But the fast-talking comedies from the 1930s and early 1940s – from the reality-bending productions of the Marx Brothers, to the hetero-normative screwball romances that brought together skilled actors including William Powell and Myrna Loy, Clark Gable and Claudette Colbert, and Cary Grant and a string of leading ladies – are among the most satisfying products of an extremely satisfying decade in American cinema. At decade's end, *His Girl Friday* (1940) stands out as one of the fastest – and funniest – films of all time.

Films from the 1930s are unmatched not just for the speed of the dialogue but for their wit, thanks to the journalists, playwrights, short story writers, satirists, and novelists hired by the studios after sound film became the central product of the Hollywood system. Viewed in retrospect, it is striking, and anomalous, that in these films the women got lines as good as the men's. The most prominent comedians of the silent film era were men: Charlie Chaplin, Buster Keaton, Harold Lloyd. So were most of the comedians who made the transition from Broadway, vaudeville, or silent film to the talkies: the Marx Brothers, Laurel and Hardy, W. C. Fields, Bob Hope. Mae West, performer and playwright, was a notable exception. But the enforcement of the Production Code beginning in 1934 more or less put West out of business. From the 1970s through the first decade of the twenty-first century, when US comedies have been vehicles for male comedians who made their names in stand-up comedy or on *Saturday Night Live*, women have existed mostly to look pretty. In the early twenty-first century, David Denby has identified a genre of comedies that he terms 'slacker-striver romance[s]' (2007). Of the typical heroine in these pictures, Denby writes, 'She doesn't have an idea in her head, and she's not the one who makes the jokes.'

Comedies of the 1930s and 1940s feature actresses like Loy, Colbert, Carole Lombard, Irene Dunne, Katherine Hepburn, and *His Girl Friday's* Rosalind Russell – actresses who get terrific dialogue and the opportunity to demonstrate that they are terrific comic actresses. Even when they are enmeshed in plots that fail to imagine roles for women much beyond the roles available to Jane Austen heroines, their verbal acuity gives them a kind of presence that is rare in Hollywood pictures of any era. As in Austen's novels, even when the plot moves women inexorably towards marriage, a sense of possibility accompanies the sheer pleasure of seeing (or reading about) women who are as smart as men and are not afraid to show it.

Even in this group, *His Girl Friday* is unusual. The film's female lead is not a society girl choosing between two potential husbands, as in *It Happened One Night* (Frank Capra, 1934) or *The Philadelphia Story* (George Cukor, 1940), or a charming sparring partner for her detective husband, as in the *Thin Man* movies. Hildy Johnson is a working woman, an ace reporter, the best writer on the criminal justice beat in some big city. The script for *His Girl Friday* is based on *The Front Page*, a stage play written by Ben Hecht and Charles MacArthur. (The play was adapted for the screen under its own name in 1931 and again in 1974.) While audiences who saw *The Front Page* on stage in New York or London missed most of the local references, they knew the play took place in Chicago. When the play moved to the screen, the local references disappeared – the script is careful to indicate that the film does not take place in Chicago, New York, Baltimore, or any recognizable city. The Production Code, enforced most rigorously between 1934–41, included the following clauses, 'the presentation must not throw sympathy with the criminal as against the law … The *courts* of the land should not be presented as *unjust*' (Doherty 1999: 351). If Joseph Breen, the man in charge of administering the Production Code, saw the film as an indictment of contemporary politicians, he could have halted production. *His Girl Friday* takes place in a generic city and features generic yellow journalists. In case we miss the point, the opening disclaimer announces, 'you will see in this picture no resemblance to the men and women of the press today'.

This 1940 adaptation of *The Front Page* is built around one radical decision: in the play, Hildy Johnson – protégé of Walter Burns, reporter for the *Chicago Herald and Examiner* – is a man. He has chosen to leave the newspaper business, marry Peggy Grant, move to New York, and work in an advertising firm owned by his fiancée's uncle. In *His Girl Friday*, Hildy is a woman and Burns's ex-wife. Peggy Grant becomes Bruce Baldwin, an insurance salesman from Albany, who apparently resembles movie actor Ralph Bellamy. Burns is less a mephistophelean, thoroughly unscrupulous manipulator than a charming rogue. Choosing between Burns and Baldwin, Hildy is given the same choice, and the same stacked deck, given to Irene

Dunne's character in *The Awful Truth* (Leo McCarey, 1937). Who would choose Ralph Bellamy over Cary Grant?

A good deal of mythology surrounds the decision to turn Hildy into a woman. Howard Hawks tells a story in which he reads the play out loud with a female employee reading the reporter's part. When he heard the lines read by a woman, he decided it sounded better that way (Breivold 2006: 26, 142). Whether this story is true, it says a great deal about Hawks's control over the production process during his long and productive career. He began as a screenwriter during the silent era, directed his first film in 1926, his first sound film in 1930, and his 45th and final picture in 1970. From 1932 on, he produced his own films. Never tied to a particular studio, Hawks produced and directed films for all eight of Hollywood's major studios. He is recognized as a director who managed to produce outstanding films across a range of genres. He directed films still considered among Hollywood's finest examples of the gangster film, the adventure film, film noir, western, and comedy.

Hawks's early adventure films are stunningly male-oriented (and strikingly homosocial). By the late 1930s, Hawks proved himself exceptionally good at romantic comedies. In some of his most successful movies, notably *To Have and Have Not* (1944), he combined genres, bringing adventure and flirtation together in a single confection. Despite this extraordinary range, Hawks films have recognizable characteristics. But it took the French film critics of *Cahiers du Cinema*, inventors of the idea of the *auteur,* and auteurist critics such as Robin Wood and Peter Bogdanovich, to articulate the signatures of a Hawks film. The time span represented in the diegesis tends to be limited to a few days or even hours. The action is linear, presented without flashbacks, parallel action, or technical wizardry. The pace is snappy. The mastery of continuity and invisible editing is unmatched. The camera is positioned at eye-level. Camera position and shot duration tend to show multiple characters in space, allowing the actors to move around and interact with each other. Less frequently noted is the fact that the films almost always feature musical performance, although they are rarely musicals (*His Girl Friday* is an exception). Most of all, the films are fun to watch, no matter what the genre.

The scene in Walter Burns's office, at the beginning of *His Girl Friday*, illustrates these qualities as well as any Hawks-directed scene. The scene lasts more than 10 minutes and takes place entirely in a small office. For more than nine of those minutes, the only characters in the room are Hildy and Walter, except for a brief cut to the

Morning Post's city editor, and a foiled attempt by the same editor to enter the office. Hildy and Walter spend those nine minutes talking to each other. Stage business is limited to answering a phone, standing up and sitting down, taking a glove off and putting it back on, lighting a cigarette, putting a carnation into a lapel. But nothing about this scene feels confining. There are a few brief close-ups, and a few brief shot/reverse shot sequences, but most of the time both characters are in the shot, usually in medium shots that show head, shoulders and torso.

These characteristics carry through to the rest of the film. While the play takes place entirely in the press room in the criminal courts building, the film adds almost 25 minutes in other settings to the beginning of the film. Once Hildy arrives at the press room, we are there for most of the rest of the film. This confinement doesn't feel stagey. Nor does the speed of the dialogue wear on viewers. For this, it's hard not to give Hawks credit. Hawks is a master of pace, using silence as effectively as dialogue. Mollie Malloy's speech to the newsmen shames them into silence. Her exit is followed by almost 20 seconds in which no one speaks, and then only to answer a phone. Twenty seconds of silence is deafening in a film that talks as fast as this one.

As a film about a career woman, *His Girl Friday* anticipates the movement of women into the workforce during the 1940s in numbers that would not be matched for 30 years. During World War II, male military conscription, and the expanding wartime economy, made women's employment an economic necessity and a patriotic duty. World War II movies feature women who work. After the war, when an ideology of domesticity pushed women back into the home, domestic melodramas feature women who must choose between career and family. Women who try to have both, such as the title character in *Mildred Pierce* (Michael Curtiz, 1945), are punished. Hildy Johnson has the remarkable opportunity to choose both marriage and career.

Two of the films cited in Laura Mulvey's landmark essay in feminist film criticism 'Visual Pleasure and Narrative Cinema' (1988) are Howard Hawks films: *Only Angels Have Wings* (1939) and *To Have and Have Not* (1944). Both screenplays are credited in whole or part to Jules Furthman, one of Hawks's frequent collaborators. Furthman also wrote *Morocco* (Josef von Sternberg, 1930), Marlene Dietrich's Hollywood debut, and another film discussed in Mulvey's essay. All three films feature women who work at the morally questionable profession of stage performer. All three films dramatize the sacrifices women must make to demonstrate the devotion that will make them worthy of the leading man's attention. While Johnson gets to choose husband *and* career (thus avoiding the sacrificial trap in which the heroines of melodramas are routinely placed), the movie dramatizes a shift in the balance of power between Hildy and Walter. At the movie's outset, she has left him for a life of respectability. He spends the film in pursuit. By the end, she is prepared to return to her earlier life, apparently on terms identical to those she rejected before.

Robin Wood describes Hawks films as products of and celebrations of collaboration (2006: xvii). He gives Hawks credit for exerting exceptional control over his productions. We must give Hawks similarly paradoxical credit for creating female characters like Hildy Johnson − smart, confident, self-assured − and then for placing them in movies in which they must learn to submit to their men.

Further reading

Scott Breivold (ed.), *Howard Hawks Interviews*, Jackson, University of Mississippi Press, 2006.

David Denby, 'A Fine Romance', *The New Yorker*, 23 July 2007, pp. 58–65.

Thomas Doherty, *Pre-Code Hollywood: Sex, Immorality, and Insurrection in American Cinema, 1930–1934*, New York, Columbia University Press, 1999.

Ben Hecht and Charles MacArthur, *The Front Page: From Theater to Reality,* edited by George W. Hilton, Hanover, Smith and Kraus, 2002.

Gerald Mast, 'From Howard Hawks, Storyteller', in Gerald Mast and Marshall Cohen (eds), *Film Theory and Criticism*, 3rd edn, New York, Oxford University Press, 1985, pp. 563–71.

Laura Mulvey, 'Visual Pleasure and Narrative Cinema', in Constance Penley (ed.), *Feminism and Film Theory*, New York, Routledge, 1988, pp. 57–68.

Peter Wollen, 'The Auteur Theory', in *Signs and Meaning in the Cinema* (1969), Bloomington, IN, Indiana University Press, 1972, pp. 74–115.

Robin Wood, *Howard Hawks* (1968), Detroit, Wayne State University Press, 2006.

ELLIOT SHAPIRO

CITIZEN KANE (1941)

[Production Company: RKO Radio Productions. Director: Orson Welles. Screenwriters: Herman J. Mankiewicz and Orson Welles. Cinematographer: Gregg Toland. Music: Bernard Herrmann. Editor: Robert Wise. Cast: Orson Welles (Charles Foster Kane), Joseph

Cotton (Jedediah Leland), Everett Sloane (Bernstein), Dorothy
Comingore (Susan Alexander Kane), Ray Collins (James W. Gettys),
Agnes Moorehead (Mary Kane), Ruth Warrick (Emily Norton
Kane), George Coulouris (Walter Parks Thatcher), Paul Stewart
(Raymond).]

Few films have enjoyed, or been encumbered with, a reputation
quite as high as that of *Citizen Kane*. In 1952, the British film periodical *Sight and Sound* asked leading film critics from around the
world to choose their ten best films. *Citizen Kane* didn't feature in
that first 'top ten' list but when the survey was repeated ten years later
in 1962, it appeared at number one. It has continued to top the poll
at each ten-year interval since then (the most recent being in 2002).
In 1992, *Sight and Sound* introduced a second poll based on the views
of an international panel of film directors and again *Citizen Kane* was
placed first on both occasions that this survey has been undertaken.[1]
Similarly, the American Film Institute's 'Top 100 Movies of All
Time' recently confirmed the status of *Citizen Kane* by placing it at
number one.[2] Such consistent acclaim also creates its own hazards in
that the film has almost become beyond criticism. Its elevated position can be daunting to any student approaching the film for the first
time. Can any film avoid arousing feelings of disappointment when it
trails such unrivalled levels of expectation behind it?

A further obstacle to examining the film dispassionately has been
the problem of disentangling *Citizen Kane* from the wider legend of
its principal creator, Orson Welles. The opening of David Thomson's
biography of Welles conveys something of the mythology when he
writes: 'He had moved people, men and women, with anecdotes,
laughter, heady company, genius, beauty, the brightest heaven of
invention. He had been loved, admired, revered' (Thomson 1997: 3).
Another biographer, John Russell Taylor, alerts us to Welles' own
tendencies towards self-mythologizing, noting that 'his favourite
image for the artist in general and himself in particular was that of a
stage magician, an illusionist' (Taylor 1999: vi). The legend tells us
how the 'boy genius' bluffed his way into a job as an actor at Dublin's
prestigious Gate Theatre when he was just 16, and how the 23-year-
old Welles had convinced America that Martians were landing with
his infamous radio production of *War of the Worlds*. *Citizen Kane*
remains a lynchpin of the myth, the masterwork of a 26-year-old
first-time director, destined to be the greatest film ever made. The
myth also encompasses Welles' later decline into obesity and chat-
show celebrity, a development seemingly paralleled by the 'rise and
fall' plot of *Citizen Kane*. This part of the legend also includes the

erroneous assumption that he was never to achieve the heights of *Citizen Kane* again; an idea belied by the vitality and artistry of subsequent films such as *The Magnificent Ambersons* (1942) and *Touch of Evil* (1958).

One straightforward way to approach *Citizen Kane* is by way of the *auteur* theory, seeing the film as the first cinematic expression of Welles' characteristic themes and stylistic traits. Regarding the former, Welles has often been seen as a director fascinated by the figure of the Shakespearian hero. Obvious evidence is provided for this in the form of his three film adaptations of Shakespeare – *Macbeth* (1948), *Othello* (1952) and *Chimes at Midnight* (1966) – as well as by the characters he portrays in *Mr Arkadin* (1955) and *Touch of Evil*. The narrative arc of these films presents the rise and fall of charismatic, romantic but flawed figures, brought down through their own weaknesses and by fatal over-reaching. This is certainly part of the fascination of *Citizen Kane* as we follow Charles Foster Kane from the dynamism and high-minded principles of his youth, when he turns the failing newspaper the *Inquirer* into a populist, campaigning 'voice of the people', to his final isolation and despair, imprisoned in the fantasy palace he has created at Xanadu, lonely and embittered. A much celebrated sequence which conveys this with characteristic cinematic bravura shows Kane and his first wife in a series of breakfast table encounters over the course of their marriage. A montage of shot–reverse shot combinations depicts the gradual change from intimacy to coldness as Kane's priorities shift to his political career. The final sections of the film, with the elderly Kane lumbering round the vast, empty interiors of Xanadu, contrast strikingly with the exuberance of early scenes at the *Inquirer* where an ever-smiling Kane fires up his team of young reporters with energy and idealism.

Auteurist examinations of the film have thrown up a number of other interpretations of Welles' intentions. For James Naremore, *Citizen Kane* is a fundamentally political film, offering a critique of the corruption endemic in American capitalism (2005: 341–58). This is most apparent in the close correlation between Kane's story and that of the American media magnate William Randolph Hearst who is generally assumed to have provided the real-life model for Kane. In contrast, Laura Mulvey has read the film as both a political allegory (in which Kane's final desperate loneliness is a metaphor for America's own isolationist stance to the war in Europe) and a text that invites psychoanalytical interpretation; the latter leading her to a meticulous reading of the film's complex rendering of the inner life of its central character, as well as providing a meditation on the power of memory. Mulvey neatly summarizes the rich possibilities which the film offers to those attempting auteurist textual evaluations when she argues that 'its elusiveness is one of the qualities that makes it infinitely re-viewable, re-debatable' (1992: 9).

Even attempting an *auteur* reading of the film is not without its complications. The original publication in 1971 of *The Citizen Kane Book* with its extended introductory essay, 'Raising Kane', by Pauline Kael is indicative of this (Kael *et al.* 1974: 1–71). One of Kael's central intentions was to highlight the contribution made by the film's co-writer, Herman J. Mankiewicz, even to the extent of implying that much of the credit for the film's startling visual panache and thematic content was derived from ideas developed by Mankiewicz at the scripting stage. Welles' later apparent decline might, therefore, be at least partially attributed to the fact that Welles never worked again with the unjustly overlooked Mankiewicz. As David Thomson points out, Kael's argument was based on insecure, highly selective research (1997: 396–8) and subsequent film historians have confirmed Welles' significant role in developing the screenplay and extending its conception in the actual filming. Kael herself subsequently publicly conceded the weaknesses of her own argument.

Another approach to the film has been to focus on it purely as a cinematic text. This has led to a good deal of work which considers the various technical innovations and manipulations of cinematic form which distinguish *Citizen Kane*. In the most reductive instances, the film has almost been seen as a training manual for would-be directors, providing a catalogue of the differing effects of tone and atmosphere which cinema can achieve. In Richard Barsam's *Looking at Movies*, it is the use of sound which comes under scrutiny, particularly in the party sequence at the offices of the *Inquirer* (2007: 306–11). For Robert Kolker, it is the highly distinctive deployment of deep focus photography in the arrangement of shot compositions, which calls for close examination (2006: 70–4). Bordwell and Thompson's now classic *Film Art: An Introduction* instead turns its attention to the narrative construction of *Citizen Kane*, systematically breaking this down into 'segments' to illustrate the complexities of its construction and the sophisticated handling of time transitions (2004: 91–102).

It is certainly understandable that the film has been read as a technical tour-de-force. From the use of ceilinged sets and fly-away scenery, through the overlapping dialogue (which Welles had previously used as a director and actor with his Mercury Players theatre company), to the barrage of acute camera angles, swooping crane shots and startling lighting effects, the film offers a shot-by-shot repertoire of dazzling cinematic devices. This may account also for the oft repeated claim that the film's principal weakness lies in the emotional coldness which arises as a consequence of Welles' fascination with surface effects. In contrast, it is precisely these qualities which account for the film's continuing fascination, according to Peter Wollen. For Wollen, all other interpretations are ultimately flawed and it is only for 'its virtuosity, its variety of formal devices and technical innovations and inventions' that it can be considered a film landmark. Wollen sees it almost as a work of cinematic abstraction, whose importance lies in its 'elaboration of a formal poetic ... a text which is a play with meaning rather than a vehicle for it' (1998: 29). Wollen is dismissive of evaluations which seek to place *Citizen Kane* in any wider social or cultural context. In retrospect, his essay is symptomatic of dominant theoretical trends in film studies during the 1970s and few would be likely to support his position today. It seems eminently sensible to suggest that the film might be seen as a product of the Hollywood studio system in the classical period. Even the technical qualities which Wollen celebrates are in part a consequence of the resources which RKO put at Welles' disposal. Welles acknowledged this by giving his cinematographer, Gregg Toland, equal billing with himself on the film's end credits.

Other film historians, including Kael, have chosen to examine Welles' use of William Randolph Hearst as a source for the film's content, or considered the attempts made by Hearst to suppress the film and have Welles ostracized by Hollywood. Such approaches acknowledge the complex relationship between Welles and the studio system which both furnished him with the opportunity to create *Citizen Kane* and then set about making sure that he would never be given such a free hand again.

What this short appraisal has hopefully made abundantly clear is the extraordinary breadth of theoretical approaches which have been applied to *Citizen Kane*. In addition to those already listed, there is barely space to acknowledge André Bazin's immensely influential analysis of the film which held it up as an example of 'total cinema', its use of deep focus and sequence construction combining to produce what Bazin saw as a form of heightened realism.[3] Perhaps what all of these viewpoints indicate is that the real reason for the continuing fascination of *Citizen Kane* is that, rather like the Charles Foster Kane himself, the film is all things to all people; its riches lie its ambiguities and contradictions.

Notes

1 See *Sight and Sound*, Vol. 12, No. 9, September 2002, for full details of all the polls published to date.
2 See www.afi.com for the full list.
3 See André Bazin, *Orson Welles: A Critical View*, New York, Harper and Row, 1979.

Further reading

James Barsam, *Looking at Movies: An Introduction to Film*, New York, W.W. Norton, 2007.

David Bordwell and Kristin Thompson, *Film Art: An Introduction*, New York, McGraw-Hill, 2004.

Pauline Kael, Herman J. Mankiewicz and Orson Welles, *The Citizen Kane Book*, St Alban, Paladin, 1974.

Robert Kolker, *Film, Form, and Culture*, New York, McGraw-Hill, 2006.

Laura Mulvey, *Citizen Kane*, London, BFI, 1992.

James Naremore, 'The Magician and the Mass Media', in Jeffrey Geiger and R. L. Rutsky (eds), *Film Analysis: A Norton Reader*, New York, W.W. Norton, 2005.

John Russell Taylor, *Orson Welles*, London, Pavilion, 1999.

David Thomson, *Rosebud: The Story of Orson Welles*, London, Abacus, 1997.

Peter Wollen, 'Introduction to *Citizen Kane*', in John Hill and Pamela Church Gibson (eds), *The Oxford Guide to Film Studies*, Oxford, Oxford University Press, 1998. Originally published in *Film Reader*, No. 1, 1975, pp. 9–15.

ROBERT SHAIL

CAT PEOPLE (1942)

[Production Company: RKO Radio Pictures. Producer: Val Lewton. Director: Jacques Tourneur. Screenwriter: DeWitt Bodeen. Cinematographer: Nicholas Musuraca. Music: Roy Webb. Editor: Mark Robson. Cast: Simone Simon (Irena Dubrovna), Kent Smith (Oliver Reed), Jane Randolph (Alice Moore), Tom Conway (Dr Louis Judd).]

Released a few months after *Citizen Kane*, and produced by the same studio, RKO, *Cat People* was intended as a low-budget competitor to Universal's successful stream of horror films. Opening to an indifferent critical response, it went on to gross eight times more than *Citizen Kane*, save RKO from bankruptcy and become the box-office phenomenon of the year.

In the early 1930s, Universal's 'Monster Movies' had dominated horror with their adaptations of Mary Shelley's *Frankenstein* (James Whale, 1931), Bram Stoker's *Dracula* (Tod Browning, 1931) and H. G. Wells' *The Invisible Man* (James Whale, 1933). But by the 1940s, they were struggling to sustain an audience for their increasingly derivative monster-fare. Titles like *Son of Frankenstein* (Rowland W. Lee, 1939) and *The Invisible Woman* (A. Edward Sutherland, 1940) showed a studio struggling for inspiration. Audiences were ready for something new.

Cat People elevated its genre beyond mere shock tactics to a subtler disturbing exploration of the modern psyche. It set the template for the urban contemporary horror we have today, blending romance, melodrama, noir and horror. Proving a major hit with the public, critics returned for an unheard of second viewing, re-evaluating the film they had initially dismissed as simply another routine scare-machine. What they had missed the first time around now became more apparent. *Cat People* was no simple monster movie. Instead, quite remarkably, it used the tropes of this much maligned genre to show ordinary people dealing with ordinary problems; jealousy, marital infidelity, sexual desire, etc. This was a film which dealt with universal situations rarely addressed in popular cinema. How this came about is largely down to the film's producer, Val Lewton. Having been assigned the less than promising title by RKO, Lewton chose to turn his back on the formulas of the day.

Cat People introduces us to Irena Dubrovna, a young attractive Serbian artist haunted by the peculiar fear that should she become aroused or angered, she will turn into a vicious panther. Irena believes she is from a long line of Serbian 'cat people' cursed by feline trans-formation and forever thwarted from finding happiness in love. Enter clean-cut American architect Oliver Reed, who sees only Irena's beauty and has little time for her neurotic superstitions. After a brief romance the pair marry but Irena can't bring herself to consummate their relationship. The couple's marriage deteriorates rapidly and Oliver, losing patience with Irena, falls for his colleague Alice. Through jealousy and isolation, Irena's worst fear metamorphoses from psychological affliction into physical threat, endangering the lives of her husband, her psychiatrist and, most especially, her rival, Alice.

Cat People's financial success initially sparked a raft of cheap copies but its reputation soon transcended both genre and budget. Notably, it made a strong impression on Alfred Hitchcock, directly inspiring elements from *The Birds* (1963) as well as his seminal Freudian study of schizophrenia and sexual anxiety, *Psycho* (1960). A clear line can be drawn from Hitchcock through Roman Polanski's *Rosemary's Baby* (1968) to virtually the entire output of Canadian auteur David Cronenberg. In 1982, *Cat People* was loosely remade by Paul Schrader, the American laureate of urban alienation. Although Schrader wrote modern American classics such as *Taxi Driver* (1976) and *Raging Bull* (1980), his *Cat People* never managed to capture the public's imagination in the way the original did. Many critics blamed the remake's lack of success on its literal and explicit depiction of its heroine's dilemma: the emotional core is all but lost in a welter of animatronics. The original *Cat People* is remarkably subtle, and for this reason more believable and terrifying than its 1982 shadow. Irena's transformation in the original is not simply from woman into panther. The physical transformation is largely inferred and unseen. It is merely a metaphor for her transformation from loyal, loving and frustrated wife to a betrayed victim falling back on violence as a last resort.

Cat People was initially conceived as a period piece set in old Europe, as many of the Universal monster movies had been. But Lewton decided to use a contemporary setting, a decision RKO would have approved of; it's always cheaper to set a film in the present, saving on the cost of specialist set-dressing and props. Lewton believed his audience would identify more with characters placed in a familiar environment rather than somewhere safely distanced through history. This led to the groundbreaking use within the genre of *Cat People*'s recognizable city setting. Its power draws heavily on its unsettling placing of horrific events in banal locations – a world of offices, diners and apartments, frequently peculiarly deserted – expressing a palpable paranoia through the urban nightfall. The film was shot in something approaching the chiaroscuro noir lighting of the hard-boiled detective genre. The city itself seemed to project a sense of foreboding fear and threat.

The most famous scene, affectionately known today by editors and directors as 'The Bus', depicts Alice appearing to be stalked initially by Irena in human form, and then in feline. Alice is simultaneously saved and scared by the sudden arrival from off-screen of a bus. The entire sequence takes place on a deserted, dark, city street illuminated by pools of streetlight. This is followed by the subsequent attack on Alice in the basement swimming pool of her apartment block. Again this uses the notion of home invasion and extreme vulnerability to emphasize the terror. What could be worse than being trapped alone at night, almost naked and in the water of a deserted underground swimming pool? The final major set-piece before the climax is located in a late-night office. While the scene with Oliver and Alice initially holds the forbidden promise of an extra-marital affair, the audience is really being prepared for the familiar workspace to be used as a location for entrapment and eventual punishment for the moral transgression of infidelity. All three of these sequences have several things in common. They use isolation and vulnerability to generate fear. They emphasize the alienation, anonymity and loneliness of modern urban life. They use the dark as a source of the unknown, a blank canvas of the imagination onto which the audience is compelled to project their own fears. In all three sequences, the night is used to transform banal, safe, social places of the day into parallel expressions of urban loneliness and emptiness. Lewton famously remarked, 'If you make the screen dark enough the mind's eye will read anything into it you want.'[1]

Lewton and director Tourneur presented, for the time, a daringly topical exploration of Freudian sexuality to create a world of psychological terror. They were also well informed about Freud's writing on the Uncanny and how it 'derives its terror not from something externally alien or unknown but – on the contrary – from something strangely familiar which defeats our efforts to separate ourselves from it'.[2] This reflects perfectly Irena's seemingly irrational fear of transformation, evoking a response in the audience by straddling the line between reality and unreality. Until perhaps the very end of the film, which is still somewhat ambiguous, we barely see the panther and are never quite sure how much of Irena's fear is grounded in reality or neurosis.

Cat People's use of Freudian notions of sexual anxiety and lesbianism to unnerve its audience showed an unprecedented sophistication. Irena's metamorphosis into a murderous panther can clearly be read as a metaphor for sexual and emotional repression. Her inability to consummate her marriage seems rooted in a heady cocktail of inadequacy, shame and guilt creating an overpowering sense of isolation.

Irena's difference from Oliver, Alice and others is emphasized by the appearance at her wedding celebration of an exotic foreign woman who speaks hauntingly to Irena in Serbian. This woman addresses Irena as 'sister', reinforcing her outsider status simultaneously through language, gender, race and possibly sexual orientation. This scene explicitly illustrates one of the main tensions in Irena's life. She fears her own sexuality as something destructive. She wants to be a traditional American wife for her traditional American husband. She wants to fit in – but is singularly unable to. The scene links this feeling of estrangement from Irena's marriage and social position in

America to her being foreign.[3] Like Irena's sexuality, this further reinforces a subtext of cultural difference as a source of conflict and pathos in the film. *Cat People* collapses both monster and victim into one, using Irena as a prism through which to identify with her 'otherness' and to set audiences' sympathies in conflict with the other characters' apparent normality. Irena's situation accentuates an unexamined rootlessness typifying the Americans around her.

Made during World War II, *Cat People*'s sombre atmosphere seemed a valid response to the darkness hanging over America and the world. Cynicism and horror at the on-going war was spilling into American public consciousness and cinema found itself articulating the trauma its audience was experiencing. *Cat People*, perhaps unwittingly, uses America's nascent cultural identity – its lack of history – to critique a kind of optimism and naivety. This is particularly evident in the arrogant, selfish and slightly dim-witted 'hero' Oliver and is in stark contrast to Irena's complex, troubled and ancient European identity used to suggest unease and trouble. J.P Telotte notes Irena's 'deep cultural roots not only suggest a mysterious depth but also underscore a significant absence in the Americans here who seem quite divorced from history' (1985: 24). This Old Europe versus New America reading posits the film as a critique of America's role as a new world power. This is personified by all-American Oliver's domination of faltering European Irena. However, all is not quite as simple as it seems. If Oliver is the embodiment of American optimism and straightforwardness, then the flip-side to his apparently simplistic morality can be found in the modernity, cynicism and streetwise image of marriage-busting Alice.

So Irena's, and therefore *Cat People*'s, story is a tragedy of displacement. The film's high standing in American film culture is assured because it expresses a nightmare at the very heart of America's self-image and is just as relevant now as it was in 1942. America may be conceived of as a country fashioned from global migration and fuelled by a mix of egalitarian ideals, escapism and reinvention. Yet the nightmare is to find oneself once more in a place wracked with conflicts which threaten to consume society. Assimilation, whether sexual, racial or political, is the goal and true horror lies in being forever condemned to the status of outsider.

The outsider is a key theme for the American horror film. In addition to Schrader's aforementioned 1982 *Cat People*, it's fascinating to note how often horror films dealing with this theme have been remade to take into account contemporary social upheavals: *Invasion of the Body Snatchers* (Don Siegel, 1956) was remade in 1978 by Philip

Kaufman, in 1993 by Abel Ferrara as *Body Snatchers*, and again in 2007 as *The Invasion* by Oliver Hirschbiegel. Similarly, *The Fly* (Kurt Neumann, 1958) was remade in 1986 by David Cronenberg, and *The Thing From Another World* (Nyby, 1951) was remade by John Carpenter in 1982.

Poor Irena may rank as the least monstrous, most human, of all movie monsters. Irena's neuroses are not so different from those of any of us. She simply wants to belong.

Notes

1 *Life Magazine*, 25 February 1946.
2 *Standard Edition of the Complete Psychological Works of Sigmund Freud*, London, Hogarth Press, 1953–74, vol. 17, p. 217.
3 Both Lewton and Tourneur were European immigrants themselves and no strangers to cultural estrangement as they navigated Hollywood.

Further reading

Edmund G. Bansak, *Fearing the Dark: The Val Lewton Career*, Jefferson, NC, McFarland, 1995.
Chris Fujiwara, *Jacques Tourneur: The Cinema of Nightfall*, Jefferson, NC, McFarland, 1998.
J.P. Telotte, *Dreams of Darkness: Fantasy and the Films of Val Lewton,* Urbana, IL, University of Illinois Press, 1985.

SIMON WARD

CASABLANCA (1942)

[Production Company: Warner Brothers. Director: Michael Curtiz. Producer: Hal Wallis. Screenwriters: Julius Epstein, Philip Epstein and Howard Koch. Cinematographer: Arthur Edeson. Music: Max Steiner. Editor: Owen Marks. Cast: Humphrey Bogart (Rick Blaine), Ingrid Bergman (Ilsa Laszlo), Paul Henreid (Victor Laszlo), Claude Rains (Louis Renault), Conrad Veidt (Major Strasser), Sydney Greenstreet (Señor Ferrari), Dooley Wilson (Sam), Peter Lorre (Ugarte).]

Casablanca is seen as a Hollywood 'classic' but how has it attained this status? Does it arise from the combination of a melodramatic love story set within a threatening world, a strong star presence enhanced by seductive cinematography, a satisfying cause-and-effect narrative that moves to an intense moment of resolution, a rhapsodic use of music reinforcing the melodrama,[1] an ironic script that counterpoints the melodrama, an exotic location enabling an escape from the everyday world, and noir lighting that reminds the spectator of the darker aspects of life that continue to exist around the fringes of this imagined space of gratification? Or is a 'classic' created as much by marketing as through thematic content and film style? *Casablanca* was rushed through production by Warner Brothers so its release would coincide with a major Allied conference in Morocco; it was further publicized by receiving eight Oscar nominations and winning three; it became a cult film in the 1960s; and with the advent of video and DVD, assorted anniversary box sets have maintained its profile.

As a product of the Hollywood studio system, *Casablanca* could be explored as an example of the way in which inputs of studio, cast and crew come together during this period in a collaborative production process. There is a distinctive industrial-creative process at work. Ultimate corporate control is exerted by the studio, Warner Brothers, but there are also creative inputs from producer, director, stars and other members of the cast and crew.[2] The screenplay alone involves several contributors: Howard Koch,[3] Julius and Philip Epstein,[4] and Casey Robinson.[5] The music includes recurring melodies by Steiner but also the distinctive delivery of songs ('As Time Goes By' in particular) by Wilson. In performance terms, there is the star presence of Bogart and Bergman but also the character-acting of Rains, Greenstreet and Lorre. Curtiz was an experienced operator having directed over 100 films (and this was Bogart's 45th Hollywood movie).[6] Overarching the whole process there is the presence of the studio dictating not only the overall 'look' of the product but also the political outlook.

The narrative shows how in wartime films Hollywood's dominant ideological concerns are altered to bring them into line with the demands of a war situation. 'Getting the girl' is not what matters in the end (such considerations are put off 'for the duration'). In the light of issues felt to be of such magnitude that they dwarfed personal relationships, Hollywood emphasizes self-sacrifice and duty. The final shot is of male bonding between Rick and Renault (America and Free France).

Our engagement with the melodrama can obscure the centrality of ideology to this film. Those involved were driven by a desire to address the political and (at the time) pressingly contemporary issue of German fascism. This was a fundamental concern for Warner Brothers' executives but also for liberals like Bogart, cast members like Veidt[7] and Lorre[8] who had fled Nazi Germany and Curtiz who had earlier come to Hollywood from Europe. This was a 'wake-up call' for America; as Rick Blaine (Bogart) says, 'I bet they're asleep in New York. I bet they're asleep all over America.' Blaine has confronted the Italians by supplying guns to Ethiopia in 1935 and fought in Spain against the fascists in 1936; and contemporary hardships of refugees in Europe are presented in a documentary style that conflates this fictional narrative with newsreels of the period. Significantly, the film is set in December 1941, the month of Pearl Harbor. The script deals with the brutality not only of Germany but also of Marshal Pétain's Vichy France administration in collaborating with the Germans against the Free French resistance. The dark presence of concentration camps in occupied Europe is behind everything we see. Often, even Rick's one-line asides carry serious bite ('What do you want for Sam?' produces 'I don't buy or sell human beings.'). At the same time, despite (or because of) these intense underpinning issues, the Germans and Italians are also often presented in stereotypical comic-book fashion, and there are comic interludes as with the pickpocket and the bumbling stereotypical English couple.

The 'What do you want for Sam?' line from Greenstreet's Ferrari carries weight, beyond what Warners is likely to have intended, since Sam is African American. There are stories of audiences in all-black cinemas in America demanding the projectionist rewind Sam's parts and replay them as it was so unusual to see a black actor with anything approaching a substantial role in a Hollywood movie.[9] And yet, how we should read the presence (or present absence) of Sam within the film is a contentious issue. In theory, as Rick says, he is within the narrative free to make his own decisions but, in reality, Sam maintains the dutiful sense of subordinate loyalty expected in a master–servant relationship. The very notion of including a designated 'free' black man in the film within the context of an American society (and Hollywood films) founded upon segregation should not be underestimated. But, do we in fact have conservative racial politics within a film that purports to expound liberal views? At the very least, it would seem a major suppression within the text to have America exalted as the bastion of democratic freedoms and cosmopolitanism (see the nationalities represented within Rick's Café Americana) while Sam is forced to passively represent millions socially and economically designated as second-class citizens in that country.[10] Just as tellingly, Moroccans are almost totally absent from the film. There is one named supposed 'Moroccan', Abdul, the doorman (Dan

Seymour), and Casablanca itself as presented bears no relation to the actual place.[11]

If we are to place the film within the context the script demands, we need to know about the Italian colonial enterprise in Ethiopia, the Spanish Civil War, the American debate over whether or not to become involved in World War II, the Vichy administration of France, the social and economic realities of racial segregation in America, and the nature of the way in which North African countries and peoples were looked upon by America and other European powers. We need to be aware of the seriousness of life and death in Occupied Europe as well as some light-hearted clichéd cultural perspectives held in 1940s America.

Above all, we should note how America is represented as the Promised Land for refugees, a place of safety and a guardian of freedom and democracy. This is from one perspective a factual truth of American history. Religious and political refugees (as well as economic refugees) had been among those crossing the Atlantic from Europe. In the 80 years or so before World War II, Europeans flooded in beneath the shadow of the Statue of Liberty. They formed a large percentage of both the national population and the Hollywood film-making population; as a result, there was always likely to be support for the dispossessed and oppressed of Europe. However, at the same time, the United States had during the inter-war years followed a strongly isolationist foreign policy, determinedly keeping out of overseas conflicts. There was, therefore, a heated debate during the late 1930s and early 1940s about whether to enter the war or not. Warner Brothers was in favour of America joining the war and *Casablanca* was part of its on-going film-based contribution to the debate, or, if you like, propaganda for its point of view. Franklin Roosevelt had moved the country steadily nearer to war, repealing the Neutrality Act, for instance, in order to supply Britain and pushing through an act to lend or lease supplies when Britain could no longer afford to pay. But, it was not until after the Japanese bombing of Pearl Harbor on 7 December 1941 that the debate was finally clinched in favour of intervention.

If *Casablanca* is to be understood as more than a romantic wartime drama, it has to be seen within a historical and political context. There is pleasure to be gained from the romance, and the suspense (as the film also operates as a thriller), but there is an additional depth of understanding that goes with grasping the contexts within which the film was made and originally shown. Imagining this being shown in the United States or Britain as the war was going on (the turning globe and narrator's voice-over at the beginning clearly suggesting this war is inescapably affecting the whole world) enables us to understand the film in a fuller, more complete way. It may also alert us to ways in which this film could be read in relation to the postwar emergence of the United States as a global imperial power.

Finally, returning to the ideological complexities of the film, if we were to consider the lead female role we might be struck by the passivity of Ilsa. She is the dutiful wife and the woman who asks her man to think for her. The film may advocate liberal values in the face of fascism but it also suppresses important issues with regard to both race and gender.

Notes

1 See Martin Marks 'The Sound of Music', in Geoffrey Nowell-Smith (ed.), *The Oxford History of World Cinema*, Oxford, Oxford University Press, 1997, p. 253.

2 This was the first project for Wallis as a unit producer at Warners. In *Round Up the Usual Suspects: The Making of Casablanca*, Aljean Harmetz sees him as the key creative force, overseeing production down to details of lighting and costume.

3 Howard Koch wrote plays for Broadway in the 1920s and adapted H.G. Wells' *War of the Worlds* for Orson Welles' famous radio broadcast in 1938. He was blacklisted as a Communist sympathizer in 1951 and moved to Europe.

4 Julius and Philip Epstein worked as a writing partnership at Warners in the 1940s. Julius was investigated by the House Un-American Activities Committee, and when asked if he had belonged to any subversive organizations reportedly replied, 'Yes, Warner Brothers.'

5 Robinson is not mentioned in the credits.

6 Michael Curtiz was born in Hungary in 1886. He worked in the Hungarian film industry before making films in Austria and Germany. In 1926 Warner Brothers brought him to Hollywood. Whether the visual style of his films is attributable to him or the cinematographers and art directors he worked with has been much debated.

7 Conrad Veidt was a high profile German actor during the 1920s and 1930s, establishing his reputation as Cesare in *The Cabinet of Dr Caligari* (1919). He was a critic of Hitler in the early 1930s and eventually had to flee the country.

8 Peter Lorre had acted in plays by Bertolt Brecht in the 1920s and became famous as the child-killer in Fritz Lang's *M* (1931). He was born to a German-speaking Jewish family in Hungary and fled Germany in 1933.

9 Dooley Wilson toured Europe with his band as a singer/drummer during the 1920s and worked as an actor in the 1930s before getting a contract with Paramount who also loaned him to other studios. He was an influential member of the Negro Actors' Guild of America.

10 We might also consider that Sam is (reassuringly?) desexualized.
11 See Brian T. Edwards, 'Preposterous Encounters: Interrupting American Studies with the (Post)Colonial, or *Casablanca* in the American Century', *Comparative Studies of South Asia, Africa and the Middle East*, Vol. 23, Nos 1 and 2, p. 70.

Further reading

Aljean Harmetz, *Round up the Usual Suspects: The Making of Casablanca – Bogart, Bergman and World War II*, New York, Hyperion, 1992.
Clayton R. Koppes and Gregory D. Black, *Hollywood Goes to War: Patriotism, Movies and the Second World War from 'Ninotchka' to 'Mrs Miniver'*, London, I.B. Tauris, 2000.
Harlan Lebo, *Casablanca: Behind the Scenes*, New York, Simon & Schuster, 1992.
Richard Maltby, *Harmless Entertainment: Hollywood and the Ideology of Consensus*, Metuchen, NJ, Scarecrow Press, 1993.
James C. Robertson, *Casablanca Man: The Cinema of Michael Curtiz*, London, Routledge, 1993.
Thomas Schatz, *Boom and Bust: American Cinema in the 1940s*, Berkeley, CA, University of California Press, 1999.

JOHN WHITE

DOUBLE INDEMNITY (1944)

[Production Company: Paramount Pictures. Director: Billy Wilder. Producer: Joseph Sistrom. Screenplay: Billy Wilder and Raymond Chandler, based on the novella by James M. Cain. Cinematography: John F. Seitz. Editor: Doane Harrison. Music: Miklos Rozsa. Cast: Fred MacMurray (Walter Neff); Barbara Stanwyck (Phyllis Dietrichson); Edward G. Robinson (Barton Keyes); Porter Hall (Mr. Jackson); Jean Heather (Lola Dietrichson); Tom Powers (Mr. Dietrichson); Byron Barr (Nino Zachetti); Richard Gaines (Mr. Norton).]

Increasingly critics and scholars have ranked *Double Indemnity* as one of the greatest films noir, describing it as 'the gold standard of 40s noir', or 'archetypical noir'.[1] But what is film noir? One answer to this question points to specific aspects of the film, such as Barbara Stanwyck's performance as a femme fatale, the film's fatalism, its first-person approach that emphasizes psychological interiority, John Seitz's low-key cinematography, etc. A more general definition might say that *Double Indemnity* is a film noir because it inverts certain Hollywood conventions, such as a happy ending where the protagonist triumphs over the forces that oppose him. Instead, this film tells a story that is a dark reflection of the conventional Hollywood narrative; we can sum it up in an oft-quoted bit of Walter's dialogue, 'I didn't get the money and I didn't get the woman. Pretty, isn't it?'

Defining noir is tricky, however; it has been called 'one of the most amorphous categories in film history' (Naremore 1998: 11). So while it is impossible today not to celebrate *Double Indemnity* as a quintessential film noir, this designation should only be a first step in approaching the film and not a destination. After all, none of the people who worked on *Double Indemnity* would have had any idea what film noir meant. Bosley Crowther in his review for the *New York Times*, for instance, called the film a 'tough melodrama'. Unlike 'western' or 'historical drama', noir was not a term that filmmakers of the 1940s would have used; rather, it emerged retroactively from the vocabulary of critics.[2] So while some writing on *Double Indemnity* concentrates on identifying how the film fits into a predetermined category of noir, this article will present readings that enrich that concept by complicating and expanding our understanding of it.

One prominent method of approaching the film uses the insights of feminist psychoanalysis. Claire Johnston emphasizes how a male point of view tends to dominate the film, making the woman into an object of the masculine gaze. The way that Walter's voice-over narration structures the story, providing his perspective on the events, is a good example of this tendency. The repeated close-ups from Walter's point-of-view of Phyllis's ankle as she descends the stairs in her house are another way the film emphasizes the male position. In both instances, there is a marked disparity in power – it is the man who speaks/looks, and the woman who is the object of the story/look.

Johnston's point is not simply that the film is sexist, however. Instead, she argues that the film 'traces the precariousness of the patriarchal order and its internal contradictions' (1978: 103). By 'contradictions' she refers to the notion that the woman occupies a peculiar position in a patriarchal (i.e., male-dominated) society. In such a system, the woman signifies lack; she is without the phallus, without power, which makes her both fascinating and terrifying.

According to the psychoanalytic view, *Double Indemnity* enacts the fundamental scenario of Oedipal struggle. Walter wants to beat the system, which is another way of saying that he wants to test the authority of the Law, as symbolized by Keyes. Phyllis represents a way to achieve that desire; she embodies a kind of desire that exists outside of the sanctioned order, outside of the bounds of the family and the patriarchal law that designates woman as (sexual) property. The film attempts to contain the dangerous desire and to restore the status quo, both by introducing another, 'good' woman (Lola) and by (somewhat implausibly) dispatching the 'bad' woman (Phyllis). The question remains open, however, whether this attempted containment actually eradicates the interesting possibilities raised by the dangerous woman.

Another insight offered by a psychoanalytic approach to the film concerns the relationship between Walter and Keyes. Johnston raises the point, which other writers have pursued as well, that although Keyes may represent the Law of patriarchy, he also harbours a maternal side ('a heart as big as a house'). The upshot of this observation is to prompt us to think about the relationship between Walter and Keyes as harbouring the possibility of an alternative affective bond, which finds expression in the ritualized exchange of matches and the film's final line, 'I love you, too.' Whether this bond between Walter and Keyes can be characterized as homosexual in a contemporary sense is debatable. Some people insist that the relationship is a paternal one, but we can ask whether such an emphasis rules out the possibility of an erotic dimension.[3]

Psychoanalytic readings tend to construe films as closed systems, resulting in readings that rarely pursue questions related to the film's cultural contexts. Many readings, however, do consider how the world outside of the film has shaped what appears on the screen. The examples of a contextual approach that we will consider here focus on the film's relation to its source materials.

There are two accounts of the inspiration for the James M. Cain novella on which the film was based that can serve as entry points for contextual readings. When asked about the genesis of the story for *Double Indemnity*, Cain mentioned an anecdote he heard from H. L. Mencken about a newspaper typesetter who, after years of faithful service, purposely let a dirty typo in a headline slip through. The outline of this situation, where a faithful employee runs amok, is present in the film in a somewhat modified form when in Walter's voice-over narration he talks about 'the guy behind the roulette-wheel'. Regardless of the specific form this common thread takes, the basic germ of the story concerns someone trying to beat a system.

James Naremore picks up on this aspect of the film, arguing that a modernist critique of mass culture undergirds the film. He points out that a significant similarity in temperament that unites the three major creative contributors – Cain, Chandler, and Wilder – is an outsider's mentality (Cain came from the East Coast and Wilder from Austria and Berlin, Chandler grew up in England). This outsider's mentality manifests itself in a critique of life in an age of industrial capitalism that is encapsulated in the phrase 'straight down the line'. This phrase first occurs during Walter's initial sales patter, then gets picked up by Walter and Phyllis, who use it as a way to refer to their commitment to one another, and finally gets used by Keyes, who turns it into an image of a trolley ride whose final stop is the cemetery.

This metaphor signals a critique of what Naremore calls, referencing a Weimar intellectual tradition, 'Fordist Amerika', a view of American society that sees an assembly-line logic having permeated all aspects of material and mental life, turning people into alienated, robotic slaves, *à la Metropolis*. This line of argument leads to Naremore's provocative claim that the ending that Wilder originally envisioned for the film – a long, predominately silent sequence in which Walter is executed in the San Quentin gas chamber with Keyes as a witness – represents a better version of the film. This argument reverses the conventional wisdom about the gas chamber ending, which critics, following Wilder's own statements, have discounted as excessive and unnecessary. For Naremore, the gas chamber ending is the necessarily grim culmination of the film's engagement with the logic of 'straight down the line'.

Another contextual reading relies on the more frequently identified source for *Double Indemnity*, the trial of Ruth Snyder and Judd Gray. Snyder, a Long Island housewife, and Gray, a corset salesman who became Snyder's lover, murdered Snyder's husband. The trial was a major media event from March 1927 to January 1928. James M. Cain, whom critic Edmund Wilson called one of the 'poets of the tabloid murder', was working for *The New York World* during the trial and certainly would have been immersed in the coverage.

Penelope Pelizzon and Nancy West connect the coverage of the case in prominent New York City tabloids to its echoes first in the Cain novella and then in the film. This context allows Pelizzon and West to propose different readings of such textual features as the 'straight down the line' metaphor. They read this motif as Cain's adaptation of an insight in H. L. Mencken's review of Judd Gray's confession/ book, where Mencken analyzes Gray's thinking as an example of the notion of Presbyterian predetermination, which stipulates that some people are predestined to be sinners. This reading provides an interesting colouring to observations about this film's 'fatalism'.

A detail of the film's *mise-en-scène* that the Snyder–Gray context also illuminates is Barbara Stanwyck's blonde wig. This costume choice often has been seen as anomalous or dissident; it was famously singled out for ridicule at the time of production when Paramount production head Buddy De Sylva reportedly commented, 'We hire

Barbara Stanwyck, and here we get George Washington.' Wilder claimed that he realized the wig was a mistake after it was too late to make a change, but he also justified his choice by saying that he wanted Phyllis to have a 'sleazy' look. This adjective suggests how the wig can be connected to the Snyder–Gray trial; the tabloids frequently commented on Ruth Snyder's hairstyle, dubbing her 'the burning blonde' or 'the synthetic blonde murderess'.

The tabloid context also places the gas chamber ending in a different light. One of the most famous moments in the Snyder–Gray media coverage occurred during the executions when Thomas Howard, an enterprising photojournalist for the *New York Daily News*, strapped a miniature camera to his ankle and took a photograph at the moment the executioner threw the switch on Ruth Snyder. This sensational photograph took up the entire front page underneath the gigantic headline 'DEAD!' Pelizzon and West suggest that the cut ending, for which Wilder had an exact replica of the San Quentin gas chamber built, registers the power of the execution snapshot, 'those familiar with the photo might be tempted to see it as a palimpsest beneath Wilder's death chamber, as if the latter image were superimposed onto the earlier one' (2005: 212).

The connotations of tabloid journalism provide an important context for the film's initial reception as well. When *Double Indemnity* premiered, it was seen as 'provocative', which is to say sordid and trashy. Wilder's usual screenwriting partner, the urbane Charles Brackett, refused to participate in the project, which he considered in bad taste. Wilder, who consistently pushed the boundaries of censorship, tested the Hays code with *Double Indemnity* by taking on a literary property that was supposedly unfilmable; at the time of its making he described *Double Indemnity* as a film 'to set Hollywood back on its heels'.[4]

When Walter drives away from the Dietrichson household, he muses in voice-over, 'How could I have known that murder can sometimes smell like honeysuckle?' This striking juxtaposition of the foul and the sweet is not a bad emblem for noir more generally. Even though, noir is difficult to define precisely, we could do worse than to call it a beautiful mode of filmmaking about ugliness, an aesthetic approach to darkness, violence, and corruption, of which *Double Indemnity* is an extraordinary example.

Notes

1 [JWin], capsule review of *Double Indemnity* in *Time Out London*, issue 1838, 9–16 November 2005; consulted 19 June 2008 at http://www.

timeout.com/film/reviews/65700/double_indemnity.html; and Philip Kemp, 'Billy Wilder', in Sara Pendergast and Tom Pendergast (eds), *The International Dictionary of Films and Filmmakers*, Vol. 2, 'Directors', 4th edn, Detroit, St. James Press, 2001, p. 1079; accessed via the Gale Virtual Reference Library.

2 For an excellent genealogy of the concept of film noir, see James Naremore, 'The History of an Idea' (1998: 9–39).

3 For a theorization of how homosocial desire operates at the expense of women, see Eve Sedgwick, *Between Men: English Literature and Homosocial Desire*, New York, Columbia University Press, 1985.

4 Wilder in the *L. A. Times*, quoted in Sikov (1998: 194). For a perceptive chapter on *Double Indemnity* that, among other things, builds on Naremore's insights and pursues Wilder's connections to the field of journalism, see Gerd Gemünden, 'The Insurance Man Always Rings Twice: *Double Indemnity*', Chapter 2 in *A Foreign Affair: Billy Wilder's American Films*.

Further reading

James M. Cain, *Double Indemnity* (1936), New York, Knopf/Everyman's Library, 2003.

Gerd Gemünden, *A Foreign Affair: Billy Wilder's American Films*, New York, Berghahn Books, 2008.

Claire Johnston, '*Double Indemnity*', in E. Ann Kaplan (ed.), *Women in Film Noir*, London, BFI, 1978, pp. 100–11.

James Naremore, *More than Night: Film Noir in Its Contexts,* Los Angeles, University of California Press, 1998.

V.Penelope Pelizzon and Nancy M. West, 'Multiple Indemnity: Film Noir, James M. Cain, and Adaptations of a Tabloid Case', *Narrative*, Vol. 13, No. 3, October 2005, pp. 211–37.

Ed Sikov, *On Sunset Boulevard: The Life and Times of Billy Wilder*, New York, Hyperion, 1998.

Neil Sinyard and Adrian Turner, *Journey down Sunset Boulevard: The Films of Billy Wilder*, Ryde, Isle of Wight, BCW Publishing, 1979.

Billy Wilder and Raymond Chandler, *Double Indemnity* (1944), Berkeley, University of California Press, 2000.

Billy Wilder, with Cameron Crowe, *Conversations with Wilder*, New York, Random House, 1999.

OLIVER GAYCKEN

MILDRED PIERCE (1945)

[Production Company: Warner Brothers Pictures. Director: Michael Curtiz. Screenwriter: Ranald MacDougall. Cinematographer: Ernest

Haller. Music: Max Steiner. Editor: David Weisbart. Art Director: Anton Grot. Cast: Joan Crawford (Mildred Pierce), Jack Carson (Wally Fay), Zachary Scott (Monte Beragon), Eve Arden (Ida Corwin), Ann Blyth (Veda), Bruce Bennett (Bert), Jo Ann Marlowe (Kay), Butterfly McQueen (Lottie).]

Mildred Pierce was a huge hit when it was first released in 1945 and remains a favourite to this day. As the first film she made with Warner Brothers after her contract with MGM came to an end, it was responsible for revitalizing the flagging career of classical Hollywood icon Joan Crawford.[1] It was nominated for six Academy Awards in 1946, with Crawford winning Best Actress Oscar for her performance as the self-sacrificing heroine.[2] Based on a novel by James M. Cain, known for hard-boiled noir fictions, the screenplay reworks his plot, cutting characters and reorganizing the structure, but retains the sharp edge of the original.

Taking a hybrid approach that was relatively unusual for its time, the film embraces many key generic features of both noir *and* melodrama, setting itself up as a site of struggle and uncertainty in structural terms that is reflected by the emotional conflict between its main characters. Thus, the moody low-key lighting and disruptive shadows of noir are set against the cluttered sets and emotive score that are more familiar to viewers of melodrama. Themes of love, betrayal and revenge, suffering and torment, mother/father–daughter relationships, female solidarity and the burden of family duty are among those articulated in this complex tale.

Historically, the context of *Mildred Pierce* is the austere yet uncertain 1940s post-war era of social and economic transition. While this is not strictly a period piece in that it does not explicitly deal with a specific moment of history, the film nevertheless responds to key concerns of the time. As Corrigan and White have argued, *Mildred Pierce* 'visibly embraces a crisis in the public narrative of America' (2004: 252) with its heart-rending portrayal of the collapse of the nuclear family at a time when many women resisted attempts to force them back into the home. As a fictional story of intimate, personal experiences, it nevertheless resonated so intensely in large part because many women of the day could identify with Mildred's plight.

In contrast to the novel on which it is based, the film is structured as a fragmented flashback which gradually unravels the story of a murder. The deliberate omission of a standard reverse shot that would have clarified the situation, tricks the viewer into thinking there is no ambiguity regarding the identity of the murderer, but questions are raised and complexities gradually woven into the story as it progresses. Throughout, Mildred maintains her devotion to her daughters, especially the spiteful, hard-nosed Veda. When her neglected husband turns to another woman for attention and solace, Mildred asks him to leave and decides to fend for herself financially. Much to Veda's disgust, she finds work as a waitress; later, she summons all her powers of persuasion to buy a restaurant which she develops into a successful business. Still her daughter is resentful and her selfishness gets dangerously out of control, until eventually both mother and daughter must confront tragic consequences.

An intermittent voice-over narration delivered by Mildred confirms this as a story that privileges her point of view; it also acts as the principal device to establish identification between the spectator and the protagonist, thereby securing initial support for her position. This approach to storytelling, with its apparent focus on the female perspective, was very much at odds with the anti-feminist slant of most noir films. However, any tension provoked by this ambiguity is eventually relieved when Mildred's version of events is called into question by the detective who has spent all night listening to her only to reveal that he knows full well she is hiding the truth. The binding structure of sympathy that had been developed is abruptly ruptured, and an alternative view of Mildred as social menace is offered. She is finally punished for threatening patriarchy by causing the downfall of the three men in her life, and the representative of the Law is able finally to restore order and stability.

Partly because of its ambivalent relation to the genre system, *Mildred Pierce* is complex in terms of its articulation of gender issues, and attempts to interpret these have drawn on Marxist and psychoanalytic approaches to film theory. As part-melodrama, it is bound to give greater attention to its female characters than most other classic genres, while melodrama is also 'one of the few generic areas in Hollywood in which masculinity in general, and "virile" masculinity in particular, has been constantly qualified, questioned, impaired or castrated' (Neale 2000: 186). Indeed, in *Mildred*, the protagonist's own husband has his masculinity called into question by her supposed neglect of his emotional and sexual needs and his lack of employment. Meanwhile, suitor Wally Fay constantly sees his advances rejected and second husband Monte, who comes to rely financially on his wife, is punished for his deception and betrayal of her with the loss of his life.

In film noir, as E. Ann Kaplan points out, 'women are central to the intrigue' (1980: 2). Nevertheless, given that this is noir, the strong women portrayed must never be allowed to rise far above their station, and patriarchy must triumph in the end. Independent women such as Mildred who abandon the home, seek solace in female friendship and reject male comfort are regarded as a social menace, a threat to the order which upholds those capitalist values upon which western society rests. Mildred is a particularly complex character as she assumes both archetypal female roles of noir: the nurturing figure *and* the 'spider woman' described by Janey Place as the 'evil seductress who tempts man and brings about his destruction' (Kaplan 1980: 35). She becomes a 'tycoon' restaurateur, owning a chain of quite glamorous establishments; she lures Wally Fay into a trap that threatens his freedom by framing him as a murderer; yet she also remains a self-sacrificing mother, risking everything she owns for the sake of her daughters. Even more dangerously for patriarchy, she takes on the conventional father's role of providing for her daughters when Bert is no longer able to do so, denying him a social role (and effectively erasing him from most of the rest of the narrative).

Noir films often also include corrupt, duplicitous children, especially daughters, who have to be punished just as their mothers are. Here the excessive Veda, only around 14 at the start of the story, gradually steals the role of treacherous *femme fatale* from her more sexually uncertain mother. Since Veda is the source of most of the marital tension between her parents, she and Mildred have to be separated in order that husband and wife might resume their 'normal' relationship.[3] Even more shocking perhaps, as Pam Cook explains, is the way in which Monte and Veda's relationship verges on 'transgression of the ultimate taboo: that against father incest' (Kaplan 1980: 75).

As Corrigan and White point out, *Mildred Pierce* is so compelling partly because its narrative structure oscillates tantalizingly 'between the classical and alternative narrative traditions' (2004: 252), both deploying and deliberately tampering with the conventions of cinema storytelling. The extended flashback (lasting four years) proceeds in a linear fashion, pausing only a few times to return to the 'present' of her so-called confession before the detectives (lasting one night). This 'present' is where most of the noir conventions of the film are to be found and where, ultimately, its ideological force resides. However, this interpretation is complicated by a re-telling of the past from Mildred's point of view which more clearly draws on the features of melodrama, during which the increasingly elaborate costumes and sets reflect, at a glance, Mildred's changing social status and developing sexual allure. The multi-layered approach is reinforced by the use of noir lighting conventions that draw attention to shadows that suggest that all may not be revealed while by contrast, the more even, high-key lighting used in the sections recalled by Mildred gives the impression of plenitude and truth. That the latter eventually gives way to the former indicates that Mildred's account of events might be dubious, even before the detective confirms this suspicion.

In the end, despite all its complexities and transgressions, *Mildred Pierce* offers a 'reassuringly' conservative and conformist resolution. Mildred is forced to recognize the error of her independent ways, and returns to her ex-husband. Her 'confession', a strategy for maintaining control, is finally rebuffed. In effect, 'the temporal and linear progressions in Mildred's material life are ... ironically offset by her loss ... of emotional and spiritual life' (Corrigan 2004: 252) throughout the film. Her 'dangerous' sexuality has already been punished, for example, with the sudden death of her younger daughter, Kay, after her one night of illicit passion with Monte. While it is clear from the outset that Mildred wants to be found guilty of an actual crime of murder, according to the conventions of noir, she is *also* considered guilty of an offence against patriarchy: for having abandoned her marital vows and her domestic duties, albeit for the sake of her children.

In the film's final shot, the reunited couple leave the police station together and walk away from the institution that represents national law and order. As they become engulfed by the modern building's enormous structures and exit through the perfectly framed archway, the silhouette of the Empire State Building, absolute symbol of western capitalism, is clearly visible in the background. Meanwhile in the foreground, two women can be seen scrubbing the steps, on their knees, as a reminder of the inextricable link between domesticated repression and patriarchy.

After all, part of the project of *Mildred Pierce* was to highlight the need to restore clear gender-based boundaries, and to encourage 'acceptance of the repression which the establishment of such an order entails' (Cook, in Kaplan 1980: 63). Thus, finally, after the struggle, torment, loss and self-sacrifice, Mildred reluctantly acknowledges that it is her social duty to return to the family home and support her (ex-)husband. Her adventures as an independent career woman are over. Moreover, the ambiguity and blurred boundaries of generic hybridity are also finally resolved as the rational logic and cool intellect of noir overcome the emotional excess of melodrama.

Notes

1 Crawford later claimed she 'found' the part of Mildred which had already been turned down by arch rivals Bette Davis and Rosalind Russell. Jack Warner was sceptical about casting Crawford in this more mature role, but was rewarded with a hit that marked a change of direction in the star's career.

2 Nominations for Best Actress in a Supporting Role also went to Ann Blyth as Veda and Eve Arden as feisty restaurant manager, Ida. According to her daughter, Crawford desperately wanted to win the Oscar but was so nervous about attending the ceremony that she took to her bed with 'pneumonia', from which she miraculously recovered in time for the celebratory press photographs. See *Joan Crawford: The Ultimate Movie Star* (DVD Special Feature, 2002).

3 In feminist discourse, this enforced separation is described as a form of 'castration' in that the beloved child, in Freudian terms, is considered to be the extension of the female body, the phallus she refuses to let go.

Further reading

John Belton, *American Cinema, American Culture*, New York, McGraw-Hill, 2005.

Pam Cook, 'Duplicity in *Mildred Pierce*', in E. Ann Kaplan (ed.), *Women in Film Noir*, London, BFI, 1980, pp. 68–82.

Timothy Corrigan and Patricia White, 'Narrative Value in *Mildred Pierce* (1945) and *Daughters of the Dust* (1991)', in *The Film Experience*, Boston, Bedford/St Martins, 2004, pp. 252–4.

Steve Neale, *Genre and Hollywood*, London, Routledge, 2000.

Janey Place, 'Women in *Film Noir*', in E. Ann Kaplan (ed.), *Women in Film Noir*, London, BFI, 1980, pp. 35–54.

SARAH BARROW

GUN CRAZY (1949)

[Production Company: King Brothers Productions. Director: Joseph H. Lewis. Producers: Maurice King and Frank King. Screenwriters: Mackinlay Kantor and Dalton Trumbo. Cinematographer: Russell Harlan. Music: Victor Young. Editor: Harry Gerstad. Cast: Peggy Cummins (Annie Laurie Starr), John Dall (Bart Tare), Annabel Shaw (Ruby Tare), Barry Kroeger (Packett), Morris Carnovsky (Judge Willoughby), Harry Lewis (Sheriff Clyde Boston), Nedrick Young (Dave Allister).]

In the attention-grabbing style beloved of post-war B-movies, the title of this film announces its subject matter with all the seedy enthusiasm of a tabloid newspaper headline. Original posters followed the same line adding the more explicit sub-headings of 'Thrill Crazy' and 'Kill Crazy' while introducing a split-skirt, high-heeled image of the character, Annie Laurie Starr, full of the sexual promise found on the covers of pulp fiction novellas. The film does not disappoint; it focuses on the danger of young people becoming obsessed with guns in a way that echoes the type of gunplay moral panic frequently fostered by newspapers and the central female performance develops the suggestiveness of the poster into an expression of raw sexuality.

In line with the Hollywood moral imperative, the resolution naturally presents not only the defeat of the woman who expresses her sexuality too freely but also a clear depiction of the psychotic nature of such a woman. The transgression of social norms is shown to have led the central male character not only out of and away from the community into a position of social exclusion but also into a moral quagmire from which there is no escape. *Gun Crazy* is, thus, able to show wayward young people on the screen under the guise of a moral homily and display the spectacle of the female sex-drive while at the same time appearing to condemn it. The young couple succeed in escaping from restrictive, boring, claustrophobic small-town America into an expansive wider world of excitement but they must pay the price.

The final structure of the narrative may symbolically eradicate the social aberrant Bonnie-and-Clyde style couple[1] but their dominant presence within the film, standing out as fully rounded characters against a drab community backdrop peopled by dull time-serving flat representations of conformity, undermines the ending. Cummins and Dall's performances are played and directed with an enthusiasm that creates the energetic heart of the film. The exuberance of the cinematography (in using a long take and a hand-held camera in the car chase sequence, for example) both echoes and endorses the couple's desire for freedom. Working on the edge of Hollywood, producing low-budget B-movies, Joseph Lewis has, like the couple at the heart of his film, carved out some small measure of freedom for himself. He has found a space within which to gain performances from actors the like of which they would not attain again and he has been able to free the camera, taking it out of the studio and using it on location in an expressive fashion.[2]

It would, however, also be possible to suggest this film offers a more consistent condemnation of anti-social behaviour and female sexuality. Authority figures abound in the film, particularly in the opening scenes showing Bart's childhood. The opening credit sequence ends with the young Bart sprawling on a dark, rain-washed Main Street at the feet of a towering, black-clad figure of law enforcement. The court scene concludes with the didactic pronouncement of Judge Willoughby.[3] Bart's childhood friends, Dave and Clyde, settle down to be solid, upstanding members of the community.

Women in the film are represented as either sexually attractive and dangerous (Annie Laurie), or caring and homely (Ruby).[4] Ruby is commonly shown in her apron in the domestic space of the kitchen. She has had a difficult early life, coming from a poor area and having to bring up her younger brother, but as a woman she has worked to create a happy family atmosphere. By contrast, Annie is first seen in tight, hip-hugging trousers and a shirt that expresses the contours of her breasts. She is shot from a low angle that immediately emphasizes her dominance and the look she gives Bart is full of provocative self-assurance.

Annie emerges into the film fully formed as the femme fatale. We learn little about her past apart from the fact that she is from London, England, and therefore presumably able to be displayed as something other than the all-American girl of the American Dream. With Bart though, we are given privileged insights into his childhood and teenage years so that he becomes a much more rounded character with whom we identify. The early incident in which the young Bart kills a chick with his BB gun and internalizes the sorrow of death sets the tone for our whole understanding of the character. The cinematic device of the close-up on a clenching child's fist means we have a visual signifier that can be re-used at climactic moments of stress for the character in order to remind us that Bart cannot kill and remains essentially an innocent.

In common with other Hollywood movies, one of the things under investigation in this film is the way in which kids from the same community who have played together as youngsters can end up on opposite sides of the law.[5] Dave becomes a journalist in his home town, Clyde becomes the town's sheriff, but their childhood friend, Bart, ends up differently, hunted through mist-swirling swamplands. Why? Is the problem his obsession with guns, as Judge Willoughby suggests in his moral monologue when sentencing the young Bart?[6] Or is it his attraction to the femme fatale charms of Annie? The film can be seen to allow both the dangerous female sex-drive and worrying male fascination with guns to be exposed, outlawed beyond the boundaries of society and finally extinguished in a resolution that deals with what are perceived as threatening social problems. There also appears to be some expression of concern about the emerging post-war materialist society in which young people want or are moulded to want consumer goods.

In the end, however, don't we identify with Bart as he sprawls at the feet of authority and as he is brow-beaten by Judge Willoughby? The court scene might end with the judge's final verdict but his response is essentially lifeless, an expression of society's absolute inability to find adequate answers to address the half-formed yearnings of its younger generation. Dave and Clyde might become pillars of the community but essentially they conform and settle down to the humdrum routine existence required of them by the dull, low-horizon expectations of the American Dream. Bart has always been marked out as different from them. Significantly he is more sensitive: when they urge him to kill the mountain lion that they only see as a creature to be hunted, it is he who responds to the life and beauty of the animal.

The film was originally to be called 'Deadly is the Female' suggesting it is the woman who is being expected to carry the burden of responsibility for social ills; and the overt sexuality of the relationship between Annie and Bart is certainly suggested as being a driving, motivating force for their actions. The essential innocence of Bart is strongly established by the lengthy opening scenes; and at the end Clyde calls out, 'We know *you're* not a killer Bart', with the clear implication that Annie is. And in the final sequence Bart is seen as strong and Annie as weak (if not demonic), but is this the overall feeling an audience would take away? Because she arrives fully formed as the evil seductress fascinated by the phallic gun and the power it bestows, she is never given a chance to be redeemed by the script as Bart is. Unlike Bart, we never see her childhood and as a result never gain any sense of why she might have become what she has. And yet, she is also a powerful female figure with a determination to enjoy life and not to be constrained by socially imposed notions of the female.

It remains true that in line with noir films of the period there is a dark pessimism attaching to the trajectory of the central character; from the start there is a doom-laden atmosphere hanging over Bart. He is not the hero since he never seems capable of making any decisions; instead there is a fatalistic inevitability about everything that happens to him. He is the 'fall guy' commonly found in these films caught in a nightmare experience, and often trapped by a seductively alluring woman.

Is this the continuation of war-time trauma in a domestic situation?[7] When young men go off to war, to fight for democracy, it feels like an exciting adventure but the reality turns out to be a nightmare. Was there some sense of the world as a doomed place during this period? Is this anything to do with the Cold War fear of Communism? Does this reflect in some way the nightmare of film-makers caught up in the McCarthyite era? Is this an expression of male fear of the emerging 'new woman'? Is this more simply an economically driven transposing of popular pulp fiction to the screen? Or does this film succeed in containing within its structure some element of all of these contemporary social tensions?

Notes

1 This film creates the same essential trajectory as the better-known *Bonnie and Clyde* (Arthur Penn, 1967).
2 This was one of those films from Hollywood admired by directors involved in the French New Wave. It had a direct influence on their work demonstrating the possibilities made available by the use of a mobile camera.
3 'We're not trying you here today because you like to shoot, Bart. We're trying you because the thing you like so well has turned into a dangerous mania with you. You're here today because you committed grand larceny, burglary, breaking and entering. We all want things, Bart, but our possession of them has to be regulated by law. And you've broken the law. You've committed a very serious crime.'
4 The old dichotomy to be found in male representations of women: the whore and the virgin – in Biblical terms, Eve, responsible for the original fall of man, and Mary, the original template for the loving mother.
5 *Angels with Dirty Faces* (Michael Curtiz, 1938), for example, places its entire focus on this issue with Jerry (Pat O'Brien) growing up to become a priest while his childhood friend, Rocky (James Cagney), becomes a gangster.
6 The problem of an emerging youth culture expressing the rebelliousness of disaffected youth was certainly something that was dealt with by later films such as *The Wild One* (László Benedek, 1953) and *Rebel Without a Cause* (Nicholas Ray, 1955).
7 Within the context of the period, Bart is like thousands of others who have just returned from the war in the late 1940s. He is a young man who has had experience with guns, indeed, his sharp-shooting skills have been prized in the army, but now he is trying to fit into civilian life.

Further reading

Nicholas Christopher, *Somewhere In the Night: Film Noir and the American City*, New York, Free Press, 1997.
Andrew Dickos, *Street with No Name: A History of the Classic American Film Noir*, Lexington, KY, University Press of Kentucky, 2002.
E. Ann Kaplan (ed.), *Women in Film Noir*, London, BFI, 1998.

Jim Kitses, *Gun Crazy*, London, BFI, 1996.

James Naremore, *More Than Night: Film Noir in Its Contexts*, Berkeley, CA, University of California Press, 1998.

Robert Porfirio, Alain Silver and James Ursini (eds), *Film Noir Reader 3: Interviews with Filmmakers of the Classic Noir Period*, New York, Limelight Editions, 2002.

Alain Silver, James Ursini and Paul Duncan, *Film Noir*, Los Angeles, Taschen, 2004.

JOHN WHITE

SINGIN' IN THE RAIN (1952)

[Production Company: Metro-Goldwyn-Mayer. Directors: Stanley Donen, Gene Kelly. Producer: Arthur Freed. Cinematography: Harold Rosson. Editor: Adrienne Fazan. Art Direction: Randall Duell, Cedric Gibbons. Set Decoration: Jacques Mapes, Edwin B. Willis. Costume Design: Walter Plunkett. Cast: Gene Kelly (Don Lockwood), Donald O'Connor (Cosmo Brown), Debbie Reynolds (Kathy Selden), Jean Hagen (Lina Lamont).]

Singin' in the Rain holds a privileged place in the canon of American movies, comparable to the places held in the rock and roll canon by Elvis Presley and the Beatles. Among the various top ten, top twenty-five, top one hundred lists on which this 1952 nostalgia fest has appeared, the most emblematic (and most frequently cited) may be *Sight & Sound*'s 1982 poll of critics for the ten best movies of all time: *Singin'* came in fourth; no other musicals made the list. Indeed, while musicals were among the most popular forms of Hollywood entertainment during the 1930s, 1940s, and 1950s, and the genre remains beloved among devoted cinephiles, musicals tend to be marginal in film surveys. Among this collection's 50 'key' films, only four are musicals (*Applause* [1929], *Gold Diggers of 1933* [1933] and *West Side Story* [1961] are the others). Dramas, melodramas, and comedies dominate this and most comparable lists, along with representative thrillers and westerns and the occasional science fiction or horror film. Musicals are often cloying; their plots challenge even the most devoted viewer's capacity to suspend disbelief; the music doesn't always age well. What makes *Singin' in the Rain* different?

To address this question, it's worth asking another question: what is a musical? A few 'key' American films offer points of comparison. *Casablanca* (1942), many people's favourite movie, includes a good deal of diegetic music; five different songs are performed in their entirety within the imaginary world of the film. 'As Time Goes By' and '*La Marseillaise*' provide crucial thematic structure. But most people would not call *Casablanca* a musical.

One cannot define musicals as movies in which characters sing and/or dance without any plot motivation. The question of the relationship between musical numbers and the surrounding plot (if there is any) is often complex. In 'integrated' musicals, songs advance plot or develop a character in various degrees, while revues hardly have a plot. But distinctions are often not that clear. Backstage musicals, such as *Gold Diggers of 1933*, deal with the problem of characters spontaneously breaking into song or dance by locating their plot in the entertainment world. Nor can we limit the definition to movies, like *West Side Story*, which feature original music (original, in this case, to the stage show on which the film is based). Of the 12 songs performed in *Singin' in the Rain*, nine had appeared in earlier MGM musicals. Only two – 'Moses Supposes' and 'Make 'em Laugh' – were written for *Singin'*. (Even this is a stretch. 'Make 'em Laugh' has virtually the same musical structure as Cole Porter's 'Be a Clown', the finale of *The Pirate* [Vincente Minnelli, 1948].)

Singin' is the last, and best, of a post-World War II sequence of what are now called jukebox musicals. Warner Brothers started the trend with *Night and Day* (1946), a sanitized and fictionalized version of the life of Cole Porter. *An American in Paris* (1951) and *Singin' in the Rain,* both produced by the Arthur Freed unit, both starring Gene Kelly, represent the most successful examples of the MGM jukebox musical. *American* is built around a catalogue of songs composed by George Gershwin with lyrics by Ira Gershwin. *Singin'* is built around songs composed by Herb Nacio Brown, with lyrics by Arthur Freed. While neither is a biopic of the *Night and Day* genre, *Singin'* glorifies producer Freed – who began his MGM career as a lyricist – and Kelly – whose name appears in the credits three times: as above-the-credits star, as choreographer (with Stanley Donen), and as co-director (also with Donen).

Of course, this movie does more than glorify its creative team. *Singin' in the Rain* is about movie magic. Set in the historical moment when sound film threatened the supremacy of silent film, this movie mythologizes the development of the movie musical, and presents movie magic as evidence of film's superiority to the cinema's new, terrifying, and never mentioned competitor: television.

Singin' in the Rain's intertextual relationship to *Babes in Arms* (1939), the first musical produced by Freed, is particularly noteworthy. *Babes* is the prototypical 'let's put on a show in the barn' movie. Mickey Rooney and Judy Garland play children of vaudeville performers whose livelihood disappeared when sound film killed vaudeville. In *Babes*, the vaudevillians' children put on a musical show to forestall their parents' insolvency.

In *Singin'*, three characters hatch a plan to put on a musical movie and save a studio. The film dramatizes the transition from vaudeville to the movies twice: in the opening sequence, when Don Lockwood moves from vaudevillian to stunt man to star, and again in the 'Broadway Ballet' sequence, which dramatizes the ascent of a Lockwood-like character from no-name to Broadway star. Although this number glorifies 'The Great White Way', everything about it reinforces its cinematic qualities. The number demonstrates that the movies can encompass all other performing arts – song, music, dance – and offer them all up in a glossy package.

As a film, *Singin'* is structured by musical spectacle, nostalgia, and creative anachronism. Musical spectacle dominates the diegesis from the film's opening moments to its closing. The credits feature a very wet performance of the film's title song by the film's three stars: Kelly, Donald O'Connor, and Debbie Reynolds. The film's closing moments feature a duet of Kelly and Reynolds singing 'You are my lucky star', a number finished by an invisible choir as Kelly/Don Lockwood and Reynolds/Kathy Selden are transformed into bill-board images advertising a film called *Singin' in the Rain*. While this film qualifies as a backstage (or backlot) musical, and the plot motivates the performance of some musical numbers as entertainment or as components of a film within the film, other numbers, which express character moods, exist mostly as spectacle.

After the opening credits, the film locates us firmly in a nostalgia inflected past. A billboard at the center of the frame advertises the premiere of 'The Biggest Picture of 1927' at Grauman's Chinese Theatre in Hollywood. We settle in for the pleasures of a nostalgia film: we'll appreciate the retro costumes and antique cars, and smirk at the characters' inability to foresee a future that is already past. Viewers with any knowledge of film history will immediately note the significance of 1927, the year the *The Jazz Singer* was released, which along with other films signaled the beginning of the end of the silent film era. When studio chief R. F. Simpson (Millard Mitchell) shows a talking picture at the post-premiere party, his guests pronounce it: 'a toy', 'a scream' and 'vulgar'. A director intones, 'It'll never amount to a thing.' Cosmo Brown (Donald O'Connor) appears to be the only one with any foresight when he says, 'That's what they said about the horseless carriage.'

In the next scene, on the front lot at fictional studio Monumental Pictures, Cosmo reads a headline from *Variety* about *The Jazz Singer*'s smashing success in its first week. An extra looks up from his coffee to opine that it will be flop in the second. This kind of dramatic irony is frequently used by Hollywood to offer viewers a position of superior knowledge: in films made about the 1920s, characters fail to antici-pate the stock market crash. In films set in 1941, characters don't know Pearl Harbor is about to be attacked. In fact, experiments with sychronized sound go back virtually as far as experiments with film technology. Sound shorts were far from unknown before the release of *The Jazz Singer*. However, Warner Brothers was willing to bet the studio on a film starring Al Jolson, the most popular performing celebrity of the day, and were able to convince enough theatre owners to re-wire their houses for sound. A successful earlier short featuring Jolson convinced the Warners to build their gamble around him. Nonetheless, the transition to sound film did not happen over-night. It took three years for sound film to fully replace silents as the dominant product of the Hollywood system.

Some of the pleasures of *Singin'* come from the film's willingness to both grant us positions of superior knowledge and give us backlot passes. We see silent film production, and then see the new technol-ogies of sound film on display. We are granted the illusion that we are seeing how movies are really made. Just as we are privy to the artifice through which movies are created, we are privy to the artifice through which stars are created. As Kelly/Lockwood narrates the publicity department version of his career, we see images of the 'real' history: the education of a third-rate vaudevillian who started his movie career as an on-set musician and got a break as a stuntman. Of course, the 'real' story is as staged as anything else in the movie. Since we know we are watching a fictional film, we are in on the joke. The interplay between artifice and 'reality' continues throughout the film, from the invented romance between Don Lockwood and Lina Lamont through the dubbing which substitutes Kathy's voice for Lina's in the musical version of *The Dancing Cavalier*.

As with any film, artifice made visible to the audience masks other kinds of artifice. In *Singin'* the most mind-boggling joke played on us concerns vocal dubbing. While Reynolds sings for herself in 'All I do is dream of you' and 'Good mornin'', other voices are dubbed over Reynolds' when Reynolds/Kathy is shown dubbing in her voice for Lina Lamont's. Betty Noyes actually sings the song recorded for *The Dancing Cavalier,* while Jean Hagen, the actress who plays Lina, speaks the dubbed dialogue attributed to Selden.

The film creates a similar illusion about film history, compressing years of history into weeks or minutes. Even as we swallow the fictionalized version of film history, we are struck by a raft of anachronisms, many apparent even to casual moviegoers. The most significant anachronism is the use of dubbing technology to dub Kathy's voice over Lina's. Even if casual viewers were not aware that this technology was not available to the filmmakers of 1927, when synchronized sound was a technology in progress, they might notice the discrepancy between the 'Beautiful Girls' number and the later love scene from the *Dueling Cavalier*. When filming the *Dueling Cavalier*, the camera is placed inside a soundproof booth (an actual booth used in early sound pictures). The Monumental Pictures crew goes to great lengths to ensure that Lockwood and Lamont's voices get recorded without extraneous noise such as a thrown cane or the beating of Lina's heart.

Showing this rocky transition to sound, the film represents some real bumps on the road to sound film. However, when filming 'Beautiful Girls', not only is the camera freed from its booth, while sound is recorded through an overhead microphone, but R. F. Simpson manages to carry on a conversation with the director without interfering with the filming. The number concludes with an overhead camera shot of dancers forming kaleidoscopic patterns, a technique of choreographing and filming dance numbers pioneered by Busby Berkeley in the early 1930s, years after *Singin'* takes place. In the earliest film musicals, the camera films head-on while simultaneously recording the sound. The sound quality was often poor and the camera was mostly immobile.

More than most (or perhaps any) musicals from the period, *Singin' in the Rain* never feels wholly dated. The pace, the production values, and the quality of the performances are crucial. The interplay between artifice and greater artifice flatters viewers. The film can acknowledge the artifice of movie magic and still use movie magic to seduce its audience, which is fine with us – we would not be watching if we did not want to be seduced. Steven Cohan makes this point succinctly in his argument about *Singin' in the Rain*'s status as 'the first camp picture'. He writes: '*Singin' in the Rain* stands out as "the ultimate MGM musical" because it can simultaneously be appreciated as one of the best films every made *and* as feel-good escapism from a bygone era that still works its movie magic' (2005: 202–3).

Produced when Hollywood was panicked about a new competitor – television – this glorification of movie magic, and of the all-encompassing capacity of the musical, reminds viewers to remember the silver screen. That tiny black and white TV set might help you keep up on old movies, but nothing can match the glorious feeling you get from the big screen, technicolor, star-studded, MGM musical.

Further reading

Rick Altman, *The American Film Musical*, Bloomington, IN, Indiana University Press, 1989.

Steven Cohan, *Incongruous Entertainment: Camp, Cultural Value, and the MGM Musical*, Durham, NC, Duke University Press, 2005.

Scoto Eyman, *The Speed of Sound: Hollywood and the Talking Revolution*, New York, Simon & Schuster, 1997.

Jane Feuer, *The Hollywood Musical*, 2nd edn, Bloomington, IN, Indiana University Press, 1993.

ELLIOT SHAPIRO

ON THE WATERFRONT (1954)

[Production Company: Columbia Pictures and Horizon Pictures. Director: Elia Kazan. Producer: Sam Spiegel. Screenwriter: Budd Schulberg. Cinematographer: Boris Kaufman. Music: Leonard Bernstein. Cast: Marlon Brando (Terry Malloy), Lee J. Cobb (Johnny Friendly), Rod Steiger (Charley), Eva Marie Saint (Edie Doyle), Karl Malden (Father Barry), Pat Henning ('Kayo' Dougan).]˙

This film has always been mired in controversy because of its intimate connections to the post-war Communist witch-hunt in the United States. Three of the key creative personnel, who had been in the Communist Party (Elia Kazan, Budd Schulberg and Lee J. Cobb), went before the House Un-American Activities Committee that was investigating Communism in Hollywood and named others they knew to be party members. (Cobb went before the Committee just the year before *On the Waterfront* was made.) Not only were they then able to continue working in the film industry while others were blacklisted as a result of their testimony but they then made a film about giving evidence to a crime commission in order to break a mob's grip on a community. Former Communist Party members who refused to 'name names' were, in the terms of this film, acting as if 'D and D' (deaf and dumb) in support of a corrupt organization. Marlon Brando, for one, was not keen to work with Kazan because he had testified and was even less enthusiastic about the project when he realized he also had to work with Schulberg and Cobb.

The film itself provides the audience with a classic Hollywood-style narrative in which a downtrodden community gains the self-confidence to fight back as a result of the actions of one heroic character. In effect, it is a western played out in the New York docklands, or as Kazan called it, an 'eastern'. Criticism of the upper echelons of society is paired down to the absolute minimum, effectively amounting to one cutaway shot to the home of a rich businessman within the courtroom scene as the central character, Terry Malloy (Brando), gives evidence against the union boss, Johnny Friendly (Cobb). The anonymous businessman's comments make his involvement in the corruption clear, and since he is essentially faceless, it is implied that he represents a whole group or class. However, the focus of the film is not on the privileged capitalist elite but on the union as a brutal organization that rules through terror. There is no real analysis of how extreme poverty and hardship have become a feature of the lives of those living in the docklands, although there is genuine sympathy for the community being portrayed as expressed through the documentary realism employed.

For many the most striking thing about *On the Waterfront* is the performance of Brando[1] as the docker who journeys towards an understanding of the corruption with which he is surrounded and an awareness of the need to stand against it, not only because it is morally right to do so but also in order to achieve some restored sense of self-worth. Kazan spoke of 'the contrast of the tough-guy front and the extreme delicacy and gentle cast of his behaviour' and of 'the depth of guilt as well as tenderness' he felt Brando managed to achieve in his performance (Bruccoli 1991: xxxi – xxxii). As far as Kazan was concerned, 'If there's a better performance by a man in the history of film in America, I don't know what it is.' The *New York Times* review from 1954 described Brando's presentation of Terry as 'a shatteringly poignant portrayal of an amoral, confused, illiterate citizen of the lower depths' (Rapf 2003: 153). A full investigation of Brando's performance would need to consider the body language (the walk and the gestures used, for example), the facial expressions (the movements of the eyes and direction of the gaze, for instance) and the delivery of lines (including crucially, pauses, mumblings and silences). When Edie confronts him with the simple notion of certain actions being right and others wrong because they either amount to treating others with decency or a lack of decency, Terry's verbal response is simply: 'You're such a fruitcake.' However, Brando's facial and bodily response totally contradicts the dismissive nature of these words, revealing the intense awkwardness he feels when in effect being confronted by his conscience. He shifts uneasily and looks down, anywhere but at Edie. He knows the harsh reality of world of the docks doesn't naturally provide a space for Edie's humanity but equally he has a side to his character, exemplified by the gentleness with which he cares for his pigeons, that recognizes what Edie says. Brando may not have got on with either of them but the performances of Cobb (Johnny Friendly) and Rod Steiger (Charley) match his own. Cobb's speech, 'My mother brought us up on a stinking watchman's pension ... ' jolts the viewer into a realization of the depth of these characters; it is not just the character of Terry that has been formed by his experience of life. Steiger's facial expression of the turmoil of emotions as he finally decides to sacrifice himself for his brother is at least as good as anything Brando does and seems to have been given in defiance of Brando who had left him to complete the scene on his own. Maybe it was the tensions between the actors and between Brando and the director that brought out these performances, the determination to show the others what you could do.

According to Schulberg(!), Kazan described this as one of the best three scripts he had ever received; the other two being Arthur Miller's *Death of a Salesman* and Tennessee Williams's *A Streetcar Named Desire*. What is clear is that Schulberg had real empathy for the community he was attempting to portray. He describes time spent researching the material in the waterfront districts of New York, drinking in local bars listening to the stories that were told and sitting in the kitchen of the man who was showing him around, writing down 'lines I could never make up' (Bruccoli 1991: xi). As a result, there is a documentary dimension that attaches to the writing; the script, to some extent at least, grows out of the everyday experiences and language use of longshoremen, their families and others living in the docklands community during the particular historical moment of the late 1940s and early 1950s.[2] Schulberg also points out that while they were in Hollywood attempting to get a studio to back the project, Kazan was heavily involved in re-writing parts of the script. But a further contribution to the script also apparently came from the producer, Sam Spiegel, who forced re-write after re-write. 'He thought it was over length and sometimes discursive. Lots of times he was right,' says Schulberg (Bruccoli 1991: xvii).[3] The re-writes meant Kazan and the cast had an already tight script with which to work, the only remaining perhaps overly didactic section being Father Barry's speech in the ship's hold after the death of 'Kayo' Dougan. In an article from 1954, Schulberg said after initially becoming involved in trying to write a script based on dockland corruption, it was 'four years and at least eight full scripts later' before the film reached the screen (Rapf 2003: 151).

Further reinforcing the social realist style embodied in the documentary aspects of Schulberg's approach to the script was Kazan's decision to shoot on location in Hoboken, New Jersey, during harsh, winter conditions of 1953–54. Although the famous 'I coulda been a contender' scene between Brando and Steiger playing Terry's brother Charley (the mob's lawyer) was a studio rig-up, little else seems to have been. Schulberg says the film was made 'without a single set being built' (in Rapf 2003: xvi) by using the piers, bars, rooftops and coldwater flats of Hoboken. The dialogue, derived from close observation of the community, and the location filming, work together to create a social realism somewhat at odds with Hollywood norms. If we consider any single location, however – outside of the church where the railings seem to pen Terry in and where the swing helps to connote the childlike aspect to his character, for example – it is clear that the selection of place has been a carefully considered aspect of film construction. Similarly with sound – if we move slightly beyond the environs of the church, we see Terry and Edie in a scene played out on wasteland at the edge of the water where a siren is realistically but also symbolically able to tear through their conversation. The symbolism is on occasion too obvious – the pigeons that are clearly indicative of a softer side to Terry's nature are contrasted with the hawks who prey upon them, and the coat is passed as the mantle of truth from Edie's brother to 'Kayo' Dougan and eventually to Terry – but also has an integral role to play in the construction of meaning.

At one level, the film is an investigation of human potential thwarted by social environment. Terry is consistently referred to as 'slow', but Edie recognizes his potential. Asked by Terry how she would have got a better response from him at school, Edie says through showing him kindness. And, of course, although the Golden Warriors gang strand of the narrative doesn't ring true in some places, the boys relate to Terry because he gives them time and attention. What Terry has (and we are constantly reminded of this) is a conscience. After Charley is killed, Terry to some extent becomes the traditional male hero, especially in leading the men back to work in the final scene; but unconventionally, he defeats Johnny Friendly through the courts and is actually physically beaten at the end (although morally triumphant). As we see Terry rejecting his old way of life, Edie's keynote lines become increasingly significant: 'Shouldn't everybody care about everybody else: isn't everybody a part of everybody else?'

Kazan had been a Communist for two years (1934–36) but testified before the Un-American Activities Committee in 1952. He continues to put forward socialist views in this film (although couched in strongly Christian terms) while attacking corruption among trade unions. Many scenes fleshing out the extent of that corruption were apparently cut as the script was honed to a tight, essentially Hollywood structure.

> In truth, I had started with a broader canvas, wanting to tell not only Terry Malloy's personal story, but the waterfront priest's, and to set it all in social perspective. I wanted to define the pecking order, right up to the Mayor and the 'Mr Big' who owned him.
>
> (Schulberg, in Rapf 2003: xvi)

When Father Barry is speaking in the hold of the ship after the murder of Dougan, if we take away the dog collar, we have a straight didactic speech on socialism. Even those who are corrupt are shown to have their corruption founded upon the hardship of their upbringing (*Johnny Friendly*: 'My mother brought up ten of us on a stinking watchman's pension.'). Terry needs the active agency of Edie (and to some extent Father Barry) to be 'saved' from his harsh experiences as a child and young man, but the film also shows honest, hard-working people like Edie's father defying all the odds to maintain their integrity.

Notes

1 Frank Sinatra was initially lined up for the part of Terry but was passed over when it became clear Brando could be brought on board (Schickel 1991: 88).
2 Schulberg based the idea for the screenplay on articles written by Malcolm Johnson for the New York *Sun*, in which he exposed the bribery, 'pay-offs' and extortion that went on in the docks.
3 'He did have an instinctive story sense; he knew it had to be unrelenting as it unfolded, and it should never let up tension and always aim for the end,' says Kazan (Bruccoli 1991: xxi).

Further reading

William Baer, *Elia Kazan: Interviews*, Jackson, University Press of Mississippi, 2000.
Leo Braudy, *On the Waterfront*, London, BFI, 2005.

Matthew J. Bruccoli (ed.), *On the Waterfront: Budd Schulberg*, London, Faber and Faber, 1991.

Elia Kazan, *Kazan on Kazan*, London, Faber and Faber, 2000.

Darwin Porter, *Brando Unzipped*, New York, Blood Moon Publications, 2005.

Joanna E. Rapf, *On the Waterfront*, Cambridge, Cambridge University Press, 2003.

Richard Schickel, *Brando: A Life in Our Times*, London, Pavilion Books, 1991.

JOHN WHITE

REBEL WITHOUT A CAUSE (1955)

[Production Company: Warner Bros. Pictures. Director: Nicholas Ray. Screenplay: Stewart Stern. Producer: David Weisbart. Music: Leonard Rosenman. Cinematography: Ernest Haller. Editor: William H. Ziegler. Cast: James Dean (Jim Stark), Natalie Wood (Judy), Sal Mineo (John 'Plato' Crawford), Corey Allen (Buzz Gunderson), Edward Platt (Ray Fremick), Jim Backus (Frank Stark), Ann Doran (Carol Stark), William Hopper (Judy's father), Rochelle Hudson (Judy's mother), Virginia Brissac (Jim's grandmother), Marietta Canty (Crawford's maid), Dennis Hopper (Goon), Jimmy Baird (Beau).]

Rebel without a Cause was symptomatic of the 1950s as a transitional era. A WarnerColor Cinemascope production starring James Dean and Natalie Wood, borrowing its title from a 1944 nonfiction book, the film was part of a larger shift in Hollywood towards addressing a teenage audience, at a time when teenagers started to be seen as a distinct subculture in marketing terms. The film tapped into some of the era's pertinent social issues: teenage angst and delinquency, family conflicts in white middle-class suburbia, social conformity, changing gender norms among both the parental generation and their children, the nuclear holocaust, and the violence all these tensions in social relations so easily engendered. In doing so, it anticipated the larger cultural revolution that was to rock society and Hollywood cinema in the 1960s.

Not least because it was seen as targeting a teenage audience, the Production Code Administration (PCA), which enforced the Production Code, a lengthy document outlining what could not be shown on screen, adopted by the film industry in the 1930s, voiced concerns about *Rebel without a Cause*. Juvenile delinquency especially was a hotly debated topic – *The Saturday Evening Post* had run a series on the subject under the title 'The Shame of America' (Simmons 1995: 58). Other films, such as *The Wild One* (László Benedek, 1953) and *Blackboard Jungle* (Richard Brooks, 1955) tackled similar themes, the former starring Marlon Brando as a biker, the latter Sidney Poitier as a teen in a racially troubled high school. Not least because the state of America's youth was a hot-button topic, and because opinion as to the causes of juvenile delinquency was divided, the PCA objected to any 'derisive gesture' toward police officers, to what they (erroneously) took be the smoking of marijuana, to the implications of incest, to teenage sexuality, and to violence (the film originally started with Buzz's gang senselessly assaulting and beating a young man at night). These concerns were partially voiced from the increasingly important foreign market. The British Board of Film Censors (BBFC), which had banned both *The Wild One* and *Blackboard Jungle*, ordered cuts in *Rebel without a Cause* and limited its exhibition to those over 15 years old (Simmons 1995).

The tensions and contradictions that caused censorship concern were made visible on the level of acting – specifically James Dean's Method acting – which exemplified 'a daily psychic tug of war between personal identity and social identity, or, … individualism and conformity, alienation and patriotism' (Braudy 1996: 193). Going back to the Group Theatre in New York City in the 1930s, and developed by Lee Strasberg at the Actor's Studio in the 1940s and 1950s, Method acting was an 'art based on the armature of the body', producing 'models of being' and 'models of social behaviour in post-war America' (Braudy 1996: 196, 195). In that sense, it was part of a larger discourse about the performance of the body, which can also be found, for instance, in the fiction of Jack Kerouac or the poetry of Allen Ginsberg (ibid.: 194). Such acting produced a 'layered self', depths of feeling in which the repressed became visible. Its ascendancy coincided with the rise of rebellious new male stars – Montgomery Clift, Marlon Brando, James Dean (ibid.: 191–204).

Jim's anxiety has everything to do with the troubled nature of the post-war, white, suburban family. The film gestures towards post-war affluence – 'Don't I buy you everything you want?' Jim's father asks, and Plato's dad's contact with his son consists of his generous alimony checks. But money and consumerism cannot sustain families. Moreover, Jim's family is torn by gender conflicts, many of which center on the father's emasculation. After having seen his father wearing a flowery apron over his gray-flannel suit, Jim becomes increasingly disillusioned about the possibility of getting help from his father, and assertively kicks in his mother's portrait when he storms out of the house after an argument in a later scene. *Rebel without a Cause* can thus easily be called a paternal melodrama – where what is at stake is the ability of fathers to become role models. And we might add that the context of and anxieties about the Cold War do not help stabilize paternal authority. 'It's just the age', Judy's mother says; 'the atomic age', Judy's little brother exclaims and shoots his toy rifle at the dinner table. Likewise, the otherwise so cockily performing teenagers look up in fascination and terror as they witness a cosmic explosion and the end of Earth at the Planetarium (the Griffith Park Observatory in Los Angeles): 'Man, existing alone, seems himself an episode of little consequence. That's all', the lecturer finishes. No wonder that the film perceives the authority of the father and the post-war patriarchal family structures as being besieged on all fronts. It mourns the loss of fatherly authority while simultaneously criticizing its continued existence, most notably in the case of Judy's stern father.

The film's concern about the contradictions within the nuclear family was part of a larger post-war discourse about the effects of suburbanization. In 1950, sociologist David Riesman published *The Lonely Crowd,* in which he suggested that that the suburbs changed people's psychic life: equipped with an internal 'radar', they constantly scan those around them and adjust their behavior accordingly, thus becoming 'other-directed'. Riesman's work was part of a larger interest in – and anxiety about – how the post-war suburban economy affected especially male psyches. In 1955, the same year *Rebel without a Cause* came out, *The Man in the Gray Flannel Suit* was published, Sloan Wilson's novel about a World War II veteran with domestic troubles working for an oppressive and conformist mental-health network. The following year, *The Man in the Gray Flannel Suit* was made into a film, and William Whyte's bestselling book, *The Organization Man*, was published, suggesting that corporate planning affected employees' inner lives, and ending with a chapter on suburbia – the 'organization man at home'. In these contexts, suburban men are successful, but other-directed businessmen who struggle with conformity, oppression, and emasculation. Above all, more valiant forms of masculinity, more likely to be found outdoors (or in Western films) than in the suburbs, no longer seemed possible. The suit under Jim's father's apron did not suggest a masculine alternative.

Rebel without a Cause's trouble, however, extends beyond the family and beyond the suburbs. Already the PCA was concerned with the implications of a homosexual relationship between Jim and Plato, though it remained unable to determine what part of the script contained that inference, so that they dropped the issue (Simmons 1995: 59). From the opening scene at the police station, Jim is drawn into two different directions: Judy and Plato. The latter keeps a picture of actor Alan Ladd in his school locker, and competes with Judy for Jim's love and attention. Not unimportantly, in line with Hollywood's homophobia, Plato is also marked as the most disturbed character; and his potential queerness is deflated by an effort to stage the scene at the abandoned mansion – quite possibly the most utopian moment in the film – as a possible alternative nuclear family, with Jim as father, Judy as mother, and Plato as son. 'If only you could have been my father', Plato says to Jim.

Nonetheless, the film's gender and sexual politics are ambiguous and contradictory enough to be read in multiple ways. Judy longs for Jim's 'different' and 'sincere' masculinity: 'a man who can be gentle and sweet, like you are', she tells Jim. Of course, this longing itself may speak to changing notions of masculinity in the post-war era. But critics have also read it differently, as suggesting, for instance, Jim's 'butch' identity. In this context, Rebel without a Cause becomes a film about ambiguous gender identity, a film that can be read in lesbian terms, with Jim in the role of the butch and Judy in the role of the femme. As Kelly Hankin as wittily observed, Jim 'suffers from bathroom trouble', walking towards the women's bathroom in his new high school (1998: 7). Ray had directed gender-troubled films before, maybe most famously Johnny Guitar (1954), a Western where the final shootout occurs between two women. Dean's ambivalent sexuality – he appears to have had relationships with both men and women – also facilitates such a reading through extratextual knowledge about the film's star. Of course, a queer reading of Rebel without a Cause has become easier in subsequent decades, not least because in 1955 homosexuality was illegal, classified as a mental disease, so that lesbians made up part of the incarcerated or institutionalized youth (Cartier 2003: 447).

Rebel without a Cause is remarkable for how it mobilizes cinematic style to emphasize and draw out the instability of gender and social conventions. Filmed in widescreen and brilliant colour, Rebel without a Cause was one of these films Hollywood thought could compete with television, which had emerged as a major force in entertainment, but which still remained constrained in terms of its aspect ratio and black and white image. In Rebel without a Cause, Ray uses the widescreen format effectively in terms of suggesting the tensions among the characters. In the early scene at the police station, for instance, he first films Jim, his father, mother, and grandmother in one frame, with the two women standing between the two men (literally and figuratively), and then follows up with a shot-reverse-shot pattern between Jim, on the one hand, and his father, mother, and grandmother, on the other. The three adults share the frame, with the grandmother intervening between the parents, in a way that suggests both their conflicts as well as their combined overpowering force. Another memorable scene occurs later in the film, when Ray films a conflict between Jim and his parents on the stairs in their suburban home, making use of the wide frame, the *mise-en-scène* (particularly the difference in height due to the stairs) as well as lighting. The film's conflicts, that is, are very much worked out and suggested on the stylistic level.

As a film that addressed both social problems and a teenage audience, *Rebel without a Cause* can be placed within a larger group of widely diverging films, ranging from George Lucas' *American Graffiti* (1973), to the teen comedies of John Hughes, and the more politically charged *Boys Don't Cry* (Kimberly Peirce, 1999), based on the actual murder of a transgender man in Nebraska. That *Rebel without a Cause* is connected to such widely different films suggests how it can be read in different ways, how in the guise of popular entertainment, it laid bare the contradictions within American social conventions.

Further reading

Leo Braudy, '"No Body's Perfect": Method Acting and 50s Culture', *Michigan Quarterly Review*, Vol. 35, No. 1, Winter 1996, pp. 191–215.

Marie Cartier, 'The Butch Woman Inside James Dean or "What Kind of Person Do You Think a Girl Wants?"', *Sexualities*, Vol. 6, 2003, pp. 443–58.

Thomas Doherty, *Teenagers and Teenpics: The Juvenilization of American Movies in the 1950s,* revised and expanded edn, Philadelphia, PA, Temple University Press, 2002.

Kelly Hankin, 'A Rebel without a Choice?: Femme Spectatorship in Hollywood Cinema', *The Velvet Light Trap*, Vol. 41, Spring 1998, pp. 3–18.

David Riesman, *The Lonely Crowd: A Study of the Changing American Character,* New Haven, CT, Yale University Press, 1950.

Jerold Simmons, 'The Censoring of *Rebel without a Cause*', *Journal of Popular Film & Television*, Vol. 32, No. 2, Summer 1995, pp. 56–63.

J. David Slocum (ed.), *Rebel without a Cause: Approaches to a Maverick Masterwork*, Albany, NY, State University of New York Press, 2005.

William H. Whyte, *The Organization Man,* New York, Simon & Schuster, 1956.

Sloan Wilson, *The Man in the Gray Flannel Suit,* New York, Simon & Schuster, 1955.

SABINE HAENNI

THE SEARCHERS (1956)

[Production Company: C.V. Whitney Pictures. Director: John Ford. Screenwriter: Frank Nugent. Cinematographer: Winton Hoch. Music: Max Steiner. Editor: Jack Murray. Cast: John Wayne (Ethan Edwards), Jeffrey Hunter (Martin Pawley), Natalie Wood (Debbie Edwards), Vera Miles (Laurie Jorgensen), Ward Bond (Reverend Captain Samuel Clayton), Henry Brandon (Scar), Hank Worden (Mose Harper).]

With 'Red Indians' set against homesteaders and John Wayne playing the strong, silent hero, the basic elements of the plot of *The Searchers* might suggest the film is likely to present simplistic interpretations of both the history of the American West and the nature of human psychology. What emerges, though, is something that is much more complex and resistant to easy analysis. The film moves towards a re-evaluation of Hollywood's version of 'Wild West' history within the changing post-war world.[1]

Initially the representation of Native Americans is as the threatening brutal savage set against the home-making, peace-loving white folk, in other words, as part of the classic, anticipated binary opposition of westerns. However, although Ethan Edwards (John Wayne) and the Comanche chief, Scar, are constructed as diametrically opposed foes, the strong similarity between them is at least as important to the dynamics of the film. The Native American has literally been scarred by his experience of the clash of civilizations that has occurred and in this he is clearly presented as a parallel to Ethan (and possibly his alter ego, a self that is able to play out the full extent of Ethan's restrained savagery). Together they represent a past that needs to be purged so that the future can be shaped by a new generation.

The way in which Martin and the homesteaders need Ethan as a protector has often been commented upon but it is the younger man who actually rescues his adopted sister and kills Scar, leaving Ethan with only the opportunity to re-emphasize his repressed brutality by scalping Scar. Martin displays the same tenacity in trying to find his sister as his uncle but with the difference that he is driven by the motivation to save life rather than to take life. Ford denies both us and Ethan (the old-style hero) the classic final 'shoot-out'. The emerging new liberal hero, Martin, kills not within the context of glorifying ritual spectacle but simply, off-screen and of forced necessity. He rejects the racism not only of Ethan but of his fiancée, Laurie, who demonstrates the deeply ingrained nature of prejudice; and he reacts with simple compassionate humanity both to the plight of white women driven insane by their experiences at the hands of 'Indians' and to the massacre of women and children by the 7th Cavalry.

By contrast, Ford steadily exposes the reality of the nature of Ethan, the old order hero. In blind hatred, for example, he shoots out the eyes of a dead Comanche in order that his soul should not enter the spirit world and slaughters bison in manic fashion in order that the tribes should not be able to feed themselves. The viewer, certainly in 1956 when Wayne was at the height of his popularity, is placed in the potentially uncomfortable position of having to reject the values embodied in the character played by the iconic star.

On the other hand, it is also true that Ethan's motivations are more complex than is often allowed. To see him simply as seeking revenge is to neglect the extent to which he is also driven by guilt. He is the Indian-hater who knows his adversary's ways better than others, and yet he allows himself to be drawn away from the home, allowing the massacre of his brother's family and the woman he loves.

Ethan is full of the contradictions that Ford seemed to see in the contemporary United States. He is the brutal man who scalps Scar and then lifts Debbie to the sky with such compassion. Wayne's character in many senses remains the traditional hero: he knows what to do in any situation, can deal with any foe, and is never scared, even in the face of his own death. Yet, he is also a frightening man with dark corners to his personality – in many ways an anti-hero. Frequently Ford uses careful direction and shot composition as well as dialogue and action to show us this complex man; but when Wayne, the jocular hero of so many westerns, shifts suddenly to the dark anti-hero, the dislocation is stark. The viewer is disorientated and faces the central flaw in the film – the way in which it uncomfortably straddles the divide between an older Hollywood version of 'how the West was won' and a new emerging perspective on history and nationhood.

If Ethan's similarities with Scar are at least as important as their opposition, the same is also true of his relationship with Martin. Old and young, avenger and saviour, traditional hero and new emerging hero, they might be but at the same time Martin is Ethan's natural heir and the one who is able to carry Ethan's inheritance into the future. Like Ethan, Martin's natural element is the outdoors; he arrives in the film bare-chested and riding bare-back suggesting his mixed blood but also the way in which he is at home in the landscape. He has Ethan's determination but is shaped by a new outlook. Their interaction throughout the film has all the tensions of a father–son relationship.

The Searchers is set in the past and yet in many ways mirrors the tensions and fears of late 1950s America. Reactionary forces are perceiving the uncertain loyalties of some as a threat while at the same time new understandings of old conflicts are attempting to shape a new world. The Civil Rights movement is underway and the strongly perceived external and internal threat posed by the Soviet Union and Communism hangs over every political decision. From our vantage point *The Searchers* can be seen as a politically flawed product of the 1950s, a strongly situated historical construct revealing the cultural perspectives of the period in which it was made. The issue of racism is at the heart of both the film and the central character. The Civil Rights movement has made the question of race unavoidable and this film reflects that contemporary reality. From the start, despite being part-Native American, Martin is welcomed into the family by Ethan's brother and his wife. Ethan, the racist, respects the domestic sphere but the performance clearly shows us he only grudgingly accepts Martin's presence at the dinner table. Both Martin and Debbie are orphaned by the violence of the past and are seen by Ethan as in different ways tainted by their contact with the formerly excluded Native American 'Other'; but both are welcomed back into the community.

The film is set in Texas in 1868. This is a crucial period in the history of the United States: massive westward expansion is underway and this brings with it the inevitability of clashes with the Indian nations. The Cheyenne-Arapaho wars (1861–64) and the Sioux wars (1862–67) have only just ended and more are to follow. In addition, the American Civil War (1861–65) has only just finished and slavery has only just been abolished (1866). The Jorgensens with their East European/Scandinavian background contribute towards showing the United States as an ethnic melting pot. Martin is one-eighth Cherokee, with the rest Welsh and English. The film, it seems, aims to include references to almost every aspect of conflict embodied in the American 'invasion' of the West.

Yet, despite all that has been said here regarding the seriousness of the issues at stake, humour is often used: do these scenes act effectively as comic relief, or do they flaw the whole concept? The episodes involving 'Look', who is later slaughtered by the cavalry, embody the most simplistic stereotyping imaginable of both women and the Native American 'Other'. On the other hand, it is also a woman, Mrs Jorgensen, who often puts the events of the film into some perspective, acting as a voice of reason. She fully recognizes that it is the harsh nature of the pioneering experience that lies at the heart of the hardship suffered ('It's this country killed my boy') and begs for something better for the next generation beyond that which she fears Ethan offers, 'Don't let the boys waste their lives in vengeance.'Ford's direction means as much is revealed through facial expression, physical stance and subtle gesture as through dialogue. Insights into characters are conveyed by body language and looks that carry implied meaning, for example, Wayne's unspoken love for Martha and Aaron's uncertainty about Ethan. The cinematography clearly contrasts the inner spaces of the homesteads with the vast open tracts of landscape outdoors but again how this should be interpreted is not so easy to decide. Martha and Aaron's home is solid, homely and warm but it is also overbearing and claustrophobic (see the low angle shots revealing the heavy, low ceiling). It is clearly designed and shot as a place of safety and refuge but proves to offer no security. Outside, the vast panoramas offer a sense of both beauty and freedom but it is a harsh beauty and the apparent emptiness of the space harbours the unseen threatening savagery.

Ultimately, the film is filled with contradictions. As both minister and soldier, the concept of the character of Clayton embodies the moral dilemmas of frontier life. Both Indians and whites are capable of alternating compassion and brutality. There are no easy answers, nothing as simple as good versus evil; unless that is we look for both good and evil within each character. The cavalry massacres men, women and children at the settlement and Scar has had two sons killed by white men.

It is the importance of the future that is consistently emphasized. Martin represents that future and Ethan recognizes this when he leaves him everything in his will. Debbie is perhaps symbolically even more a representation of the future than Martin and Laurie (see how many ethnic groups come together in their union). Debbie is that which is being searched for, she is hope, she is reconciliation, she has lived in both cultures and in that sense is the future.

Note

1 This is particularly the case when the film is read alongside its contrasting but in many ways companion volume from a few years later, *The Man Who Shot Liberty Valance* (Ford, 1962). In this film, Ranse Stoddard (James Stewart) embodies democratic values – education for all, a free press, law and order. The very ordinary people who come to the school he establishes are given a sense of ownership; it is pointedly 'our' country, and a republic, we are told, is a state in which the people are 'the bosses'. Pompey (significantly as the African American) recites from the

Declaration of Independence, 'We hold these truths self-evident that all men are created equal.' Yet, in the end, even Stoddard has to admit, 'When force threatens, talk's no good any more.' Ultimately, he needs Tom Doniphon (Wayne, again) to defeat the baddie, the ironically named Liberty Valance. This it seems is the ultimate belief upon which Ford's type of democracy is built, that in the end you sometimes have to defend democracy and the rights it brings.

Further reading

Lindsay Anderson, *About John Ford*, London, Plexus, 1981.

Ian Cameron and Douglas Pye, *The Movie Book of the Western*, London, Studio Vista, 1996.

Arthur M. Eckstein, 'Darkening Ethan: John Ford's *The Searchers* from Novel to Screenplay to Screen', *Cinema Journal*, Vol. 38, No. 1, 1998, pp. 3–24.

Arthur M. Eckstein and Peter Lehman, *The Searchers: Essays and Reflections on John Ford's Classic Western*, Detroit, Wayne State University Press, 2004.

Scott Eyman and Paul Duncan, *John Ford: The Complete Films*, London, Taschen, 2004.

Julia Leyda, 'Home on the Range: Space, Nation and Mobility in John Ford's *The Searchers*', *The Japanese Journal of American Studies*, No. 13, 2002.

Armando Jose Prats, *Invisible Natives: Myth and Identity in the American Western*, Ithaca, NY, Cornell University Press, 2002.

Gaylyn Studlar and Matthew Bernstein (eds), *John Ford Made Westerns: Filming the Legend in the Sound Era*, Bloomington, IN, Indiana University Press, 2001.

JOHN WHITE

INVASION OF THE BODY SNATCHERS (1956)

[Production Company: Walter Wanger Productions. Director: Don Siegel. Screenwriters: Jacky Finney, Daniel Mainwaring and Richard Collins. Cinematographer: Ellsworth Fredericks. Music: Carmen Dragon. Editor: Robert Eisen. Cast: Kevin McCarthy (Dr Miles J. Bennell), Dana Wynter (Becky Driscoll), Larry Gates (Dr Danny Kaufman), King Donovan (Jack Belicec), Carolyn Jones (Theodora 'Teddy' Belicec), Jean Willes (Nurse Sally Withers).]

As both a tale concerning invading alien pods and a stark critique of small-town America, *Invasion of the Body Snatchers* stands as a significant US film; whether it is considered merely a low-budget science fiction B-movie, a fantastic story that serves as an allegorical warning, or an accurate portrayal of suburban life in the 1950s, the film continues to challenge modern audiences.[1] This is a taut mixture of conspiracy narrative and contemporary fears; a film noir tale (Booker 2006: 59), as told by its main protagonist, Dr Miles Bennell, of the 'outsider' as threat to a supposedly tranquil American idyll. David Seed rightly places the film within its cultural contexts, stating that:

> A cluster of films from the mid-fifties demonstrates a consistent paradigm of such invasion-as-conspiracy where the battle for the nation's mind is played out in Smalltown USA.
>
> In *Invasion* and these other contemporary films, the instrumentality of threat comes from outside (creatures from Mars or Venus, pods from outer space) but the real power of these films is carried by their transformation of humans rather than the crude 'monstrous' devices, their fracturing of the nuclear family or local community.
>
> (Seed 1999: 132–3)

The last point is crucial, since the family and community were seen by many politicians, including those involved with the Communist witch-hunts of Senator Joseph McCarthy and the House Un-American Activities Committee (HUAC), as important weapons in the fight against Communism and the socialist threat to American capitalism. *Invasion*'s significance partly lies in its role as a social barometer for America in the 1950s but also in the fact that it dared to compare the imaginary invading 'other' with the then largely unrecognized danger posed by America's consumerist ideology.

Mark Jancovich (1996: 15) points out that most critics of the decade's invasion narratives see them as being inextricably linked to Cold War ideology. American films of the decade, this critical orthodoxy claims, demonized both the Soviet Union and any resistance to the status quo, ensuring that the institutions and authorities of the country were protected from the so-called 'red menace' that was seen as permeating the nation. Americans were given two choices: either support America or be seen as a Communist sympathizer – in *Invasion*, this distinction is clearly represented between Miles and the residents of Santa Mira as they try to persuade him to become a pod person. This distinction meant that there was a clear line between right and wrong, America and the alien 'other'. However, Jancovich contends American culture was itself going through a sort of identity crisis as men returned from war to face changes in the work and domestic spheres. The so-called 'suburban dream' was little more than a cover for a loss of individual identity, the threat posed by the Communist as 'alien' was not as pressing as the threat posed by the push to conform:

men having to go to work in the city dressed in grey flannel suits and return home to idealized, yet all too similar, modern suburban homes. The technological advancement of consumer culture that had promised so much was instead stifling Americans' own self-worth:

> It has often been pointed out that the qualities that identify the aliens with the Soviet Union are their lack of feelings and the absence of individual characteristics. It was certainly the case that during the 1950s many American critics claimed that in the Soviet Union people were all the same; that they were forced to deny personal feeling and characteristics, and to become functionaries of the social whole. It should also be noted, however, that … it was common in the 1950s for Americans to claim that the effects of scientific-technical rationality upon their own society was producing the same features within America itself.
>
> (Jancovich 1996: 26)

Despite the contradictory reasons for America's feeling of vulnerability in the 1950s, the fact remains that the alien, its desire to conquer Earth and technological pre-eminence, were common themes in films of that decade. Along with *Invasion of the Body Snatchers* films such as *The Day the Earth Stood Still* (1951), *War of the Worlds* (1953) and *Invaders from Mars* (1953) presented America and the world in the grip of emergencies – emergencies 'that jeopardized the future of the race; they were not national, nor even international, but planetary' (Biskind 2000: 102). *Invasion* took that external threat and made it a discernibly internal one by focusing on the invasion of the human body by an alien force (Hendershot 1998: 26). Yet, what makes this film stand out is its constant ability to contradict itself, to offer the audience competing definitions of what might be the most attractive lifestyle to have.

In Miles, the audience has an ideal role model, a successful professional man loved by the local community. His race to prevent the pods from spreading to the rest of the West coast and perhaps the entire country is a heroic representation of American masculinity. At that time, such masculinity was valorized as part of the nation's Communist containment strategy: 'the decade's focus on rigid gender roles, respect for authority, patriotism, and hygiene was part of a larger fear that [America] might unravel from within' (Caputi 2005: 142).

For Elaine Tyler May (1999), the Communist threat could be contained by a return to the family values of a pre-World War II America where men went to work and women stayed at home.

However, with the disruption that the war brought, husbands were displaced in both the home and at work by their wives; this led to a sense of masculinity in crisis as the traditional male bread-winner role became increasingly obsolete. Thus, like the male protagonists of popular books such as Sloan Wilson's *The Man in the Gray Flannel Suit* (1955) and William Whyte's *The Organization Man* (1956), Miles is a man caught in a suburban nightmare, unable to escape the encroaching conformity symbolized by the white picket fences and mundane daily routine of work and family responsibility. The kiss between Miles and Becky Driscoll towards the end of the film, and his revulsion as he realizes she has become a pod person, has been read as an indicator of emasculating femininity and symbolic of Miles' latent homosexuality – a common theme in science fiction films of this period (Benshoff 1997). Christine Cornea, for example, links the role of women in the film to the then contemporary theory that domineering mothers who smothered their teenage male off-spring posed a threat to the patriarchal status quo (2007: 43–4). However, what really appears to be at stake here is the notion that America's changing society is the threat to Miles; neither the pods as Communism nor Becky as the feminine are as critical as the choice he has to make between becoming a pod person or continually run-ning from the conformity that a pod society ultimately represents.

When Miles and Becky are confronted by the pod versions of Jack Belicec and Dan Kaufman, they are offered the choice to become pod people. The complicated emotions of modern life such as 'love, desire, ambition, faith' would be destroyed and life would be simpli-fied; and since the pod people have no need for these 'human' traits, their society would be one without conflict and pain – Miles and Becky would be 'reborn into an untroubled world'. This scene is an important signifier of the social contradictions at the heart of 1950s America, conformity to the status quo would offer a safe society in which to bring up the nuclear family – free from a Communist threat and wealthy enough to participate in a consumer lifestyle; yet con-formity also signals an end to the individualist ethos of American culture – the business ethos of the period was creating a society of 'clones' with no individual creativity. What is truly horrific and unnerving in this exchange and underlies the tensions beneath the film's narrative is that both choices are attractive:

> Amid all this critical activity, one might also note that there is a definite emotional appeal to the idea of being 'taken over' which goes beyond the inherent attractions presented by the

pod-psychiatrist in *Invasion of the Body Snatchers* ... That added emotional attraction is 'no more responsibility'. Being 'taken over' can be likened to being drafted, to having to follow orders. 'Taken over', we cannot be held accountable for our crimes – passionate or passionless.

(Sobchack 1998: 123)

It is the mundane appeal of conformity, the normality and familiarity of small-town life, which the film makes out to be threatening. The look and feel of the film underscore the contradictions in individual identity; the audience becomes vigilant in watching for anything that looks out of the ordinary. The low-budget *mise-en-scène*, black and white colour, and flat characterization contribute to painting a picture of domestic drudgery that was both desired and despised: 'What is visually fascinating and disturbing ... is the way in which the secure and familiar are twisted into something subtly dangerous and slyly perverted' (Sobchack 1998: 124). Humans in this film are dehumanized in such a way that we can neither tell them apart nor perhaps want to differ from them.

Note

1 Produced on a shoestring budget, *Invasion of the Body Snatchers* continues to stand the test of time both visually and in terms of narrative. Contesting accounts of the production budget put the film's price tag as low as $382,000 (LaValley 1989: 3), dead on $400,000 (Booker 2006: 64), and as high as $417,000 (Cornea 2007: 71). In an interview with Stuart Kaminsky (1976: 77), Don Siegel specifies $15,000 went on the special effects that produced the transforming pods and replica corpses. Although these figures appear insignificant compared to other more special-effects-orientated science fiction films of the decade, they do draw attention to the understated nature of the film's production and the important role this plays in the construction of a believable and, at first glance, normal small-town setting.

Further reading

Harry M. Benshoff, *Monsters in the Closet: Homosexuality and the Horror Film*, Manchester, Manchester University Press, 1997.

Peter Biskind, *Seeing is Believing: How Hollywood Taught Us to Stop Worrying and Love the Fifties*, London, Bloomsbury, 2000.

M. Keith Booker, *Alternate Americas: Science Fiction Film and American Culture*, Westport, CT, Praeger, 2006.

Mary Caputi, *A Kinder, Gentler America: Melancholia and the Mythical 1950s*, Minneapolis, University of Minnesota Press, 2005.

David Castronovo, *Beyond the Gray Flannel Suit: Books from the 1950s that Made American Culture*, New York, Continuum, 2004.

Christine Cornea, *Science Fiction Cinema: Between Fantasy and Reality*, Edinburgh, Edinburgh University Press, 2007.

Barry Keith Grant, 'Movies and the Crack of Doom', in Murray Pomerance (ed.), *American Cinema of the 1950s: Themes and Variations*, New Brunswick, NJ, Rutgers University Press, 2005, pp. 155–76.

Cyndy Hendershot, 'The Invaded Body: Paranoia and Radiation Anxiety in *Invaders from Mars*, *It Came from Outer Space*, and *Invasion of the Body Snatchers*', *Extrapolation*, Vol. 39, No. 1, 1998, pp. 26–39.

Mark Jancovich, *Rational Fears: American Horror in the 1950s*, Manchester, Manchester University Press, 1996.

Stuart M. Kaminsky, 'Don Siegel on the Pod Society', in Thomas R. Atkins (ed.), *Science Fiction Films*, New York, Monarch Press, 1976, pp. 73–83.

Al LaValley (ed.), *Invasion of the Body Snatchers: Don Siegel, Director*, New Brunswick, NJ, Rutgers University Press, 1989.

Elaine Tyler May, *Homeward Bound: American Families in the Cold War Era* (revised edn), New York, Basic Books, 1999.

David Riesman, *The Lonely Crowd*, New Haven, CT, Yale University Press, 1950.

David Seed, *American Science Fiction and the Cold War: Literature and Film*, Edinburgh, Edinburgh University Press, 1999.

Vivian Sobchack, *Screening Space: The American Science Fiction Film*, New Brunswick, NJ, Rutgers University Press, 1998.

J.P. Telotte, *Science Fiction Film*, Cambridge, Cambridge University Press, 2001.

LINCOLN GERAGHTY

PSYCHO (1960)

[Production Company: Shamley Productions. Director: Alfred Hitchcock. Screenwriter: Joseph Stefano (from a novel by Robert Bloch). Music: Bernard Hermann. Cinematography: John L. Russell. Editor: George Tomasini. Cast: Anthony Perkins (Norman Bates), Janet Leigh (Marion Crane), Vera Miles (Lila Crane), John Gavin (Sam Loomis), Martin Balsam (Arbogast).]

As with several Hitchcock films, *Psycho* has at the heart of its plot the violent abuse of a woman by a man and could be read as a misogynistic text. Through both the central character of Marion Crane and Norman Bates' mother, women are represented as deceptive, manipulative, controlling and, from a male perspective, unfailingly unpredictable. The key passage in the film that has become one of the most famous scenes in the history of cinema – the shower scene – focuses in intimate detail upon the brutal murder of a vulnerable woman. In a film often seen as the original 'slasher' movie, this is the central action towards which everything prior to this leads and from which everything after it follows. The scene is graphic for the period – only being passed for viewing after well-documented tactical exchanges with the censors (and retaining one frame in which the knife penetrates flesh) (Rebello 1998: 145–6). Marion is 'raped' via Norman's preceding voyeuristic act as well as through the use of the phallic dagger.

Adding to the disturbing nature of the attack is the fact that as a result of the preceding voyeuristic observation of the 'prey', the violence is clearly presented as sexually motivated. As an infant whom the domineering mother has not allowed to develop into adulthood, the discovery of a woman who rouses the sexual adult can lead it seems to only one outcome. Furthermore, from a 'male' perspective, as viewers, we could be said to be implicated in the voyeurism, not only by sharing Norman's view of Marion through the peephole in the previous scene but also as a result of any pleasure we may gain from viewing Janet Leigh as Marion in all her naked vulnerability in the shower prior to the attack.

On a first viewing the spectator would not be expected to see the attacker as Norman (although this would depend upon how much prior knowledge of the storyline has been gained from friends or background reading before coming to the film). On subsequent viewings the spectator's involvement in the scene will essentially shift from the shock or surprise created as a result of the original restricted perspective on events to a sense of expectation attaching to our now omniscient knowledge of the narrative. Our identification with Marion (and hence our sympathy for her) should never be in doubt since it has been her and the events that have happened to her that we have followed from the beginning of the film. In the parlour we have heard her announce her intention to return to Phoenix to seek redemption and in the shower we have seen her symbolically washing away her guilt (so that she goes to her death with a restored sense of innocence). But, still, we do spy on her from Norman's perspective, we do observe her in her nakedness beneath the shower, and we do experience the knife attack from the attacker's perspective. The positioning of the viewer, whether male or female, via film construction, and more importantly the way in which that position is accessed and activated by the viewer, become critical for the individual's reading of the shower scene moment.

If we move beyond the issue of whether or not this scene and this film might be said to be misogynistic, *Psycho* offers the possibility of an even more disturbing overall perspective. If the central image of woman is of someone at the mercy of voyeurism and physical abuse, the image of man in the form of Norman is of a creature at once vulnerable and weak while also being predatory and brutal. This is not presented as an unsympathetic portrait of a serial-killer; Norman is not seen simply and comfortingly as a monstrous aberration, on the contrary, in both his importance to the narrative and the achieved emotional impact upon the viewer, his presence completely over-powers the role of Sam as the conventional heroic Hollywood male. John Gavin (Sam) has a cardboard cut-out of a part that reflects not just Hitchcock's lack of interest in (and therefore, weak focus upon) this aspect of the narrative but more fundamentally the shift of atti-tudes within society away from confident idolization of the 'good guy' hero towards an almost mesmeric fascination with the darkness existing just beneath the veneer of civilization. This may be too sim-plistic in that films and filmmakers have always shown an interest in darker characters but to see *Psycho* within the context of a loss of faith in John Wayne-style heroes at least moves us towards considering this film within a wider social context rather than as a simple expression of the vision of Hitchcock the auteur.[1]

Furthermore, if the image of man that is presented could be said to be as bleak as that of the brutalized woman, the image of male–female relationships hardly reinforces the concept of the 'American Dream'. The opening scene makes the bitter failure of Sam's first marriage clear; and in the next scene the best Cassidy can do for his daughter, even with all of his money, is to buy off unhappiness. Moments of pleasure, like that of Sam and Marion in the hotel room, it seems, have necessarily to be obtained surreptitiously and against society's wishes. The social institutions of marriage and the family are placed under intense scrutiny. In the opening scene, despite the con-text of the illicit hotel rendezvous, Marion actually demonstrates her allegiance to an idealized notion of marriage that she aspires to attain seemingly at any cost. Ironically, the moment at which she realizes that the false allure of this socially constructed norm can lead you into a trap is the point at which because of her innocent openness towards another being her fate is sealed. The central theme of life as a process that constantly ensnares people into traps from which (it seems) they find it impossible to extricate themselves is made clear in this scene in the parlour between Norman and Marion. Norman's entrapment and its origin within a 'family' comprising an absent father and dom-ineering mother are given powerful visual representation in the final haunting superimposition of the mother's face over his.

Depending on your perspective, *Psycho* (as with Hitchcock's wider body of work) can be seen to be underpinned by either a murky, unforgiving view of life or an entirely realistic view of humanity. It seems as if everybody has guilty secrets; even Caroline (Pat Hitchcock) in the early office scene, hemmed in by a husband and a mother who continually check up on her (effectively at the mercy of family and marriage) has a secret supply of tranquilizers that help to make her life bearable. Each character is motivated by self-interest or uncontrollable desires, or a combination of the two. Civilized behaviour is no more than skin deep. The killer is in our midst but cannot be easily detected. In a parody of the supposed best aspects of a civilized society Norman offers hospitality and friendship but this it seems is a cover for the savagery that is just below the surface, a savagery nurtured within the most cherished institution of Western civilization. The psychiatrist may offer the conventional comforts of the Hollywood resolution that has an authoritative male-figure demonstrating a reassuringly controlled understanding of events, but we do not end on this note, we end with not only the image but the haunting words of the absent presence of Hitchcock's caricature of cherry-pie 'mom'.

From the beginning, the examination of contemporary US society has been clear. We open with Marion and Sam taking part in an extra-marital relationship in a cheap downtown hotel that rents rooms by the hour during the middle of the day. This might focus on individuals but it is about the condition of a whole society. Sam feels trapped by his life as Marion does by hers. The temptation to transgress social boundaries of acceptable behaviour is present for each character. And we are not left out of the equation; we have our position as voyeurs very clearly marked out for us from the outset by the elaborate opening camera movement that slips us in through the partially open hotel window to view a couple's intimate behaviour and listen in on the personal details of their lives. From scanning the city skyline, we are taken in beneath the surface of society to view just one example of the lives being played out everywhere.

When Norman leads Marion into his parlour behind the reception area of the Bates Motel, editing emphasizes the stuffed birds. There is the predatory owl in mid-swoop followed by the ominously sharp-beaked shadow of a crow, a harbinger of death (or perhaps a raven, even more strongly associated with the gallows in English folklore). Owls are clearly associated with hunting and the eating of flesh: crows (and even more so ravens) with being meat-eating scavengers but also as capable of dispatching defenceless, unsuspecting prey. The pheasant positioned behind Norman symbolizes a species bred purely for the purpose of being ritually slaughtered. Meanwhile Marion nibbles thoughtfully on bread and milk, a nurturing food associated with mothering and helping the young and otherwise weak. Nor should we miss the paintings of classical nudes on the walls: the female body displayed in all its naked vulnerability before the essentially male gaze. Norman wrings his hands, lurches between one position and another ('I say I don't mind, but I do.'), leans forward to seemingly take Marion into his confidence, leans back as she retreats from his position of confidentiality, and finally moves from nervous smile to aggressive confrontation. Marion perches on the edge of her chair, her body posture and arms in a tight defensive position as she weighs her words thoughtfully. What is said makes it clear that Norman's and Marion's positions are effectively metaphors for the general state of being experienced by us all.

Note

1 Writing about *Notorious*, Chopra-Gant suggests that when considering Hitchcock's work, it is important to consider the ways in which 'the films register contemporaneous discourses that articulate key social anxieties of their historical moment' (Chopra-Gant 2005: 361). His point in relation to *Notorious* is that moral decline is being linked to the absence of parental authority during the early post-war period and maternal domination, or 'momism', to the infantilization of men.

Further reading

Charlotte Chandler, *It's Only a Movie: Alfred Hitchcock, a Personal Biography*, London, Simon & Schuster, 2005.

Mike Chopra-Gant, 'Absent Fathers and "Moms", Delinquent Daughters and Mummy's Boys: Envisioning the Postwar American Family in Hitchcock's *Notorious*', *Comparative American Studies*, Vol. 3, 2005, pp. 361–75.

Raymond Durgnat, *A Long Hard Look at Psycho*, London, BFI, 2002.

Janet Leigh and Christopher Nickens, *Psycho: Behind the Scenes of the Classic Thriller*, New York, Wings, 2005.

Patrick McGilligan, *Alfred Hitchcock: A Life in Darkness and Light*, Chichester, Wiley, 2003.

Stephen Rebello, *Alfred Hitchcock and the Making of Psycho*, London and New York, Marion Boyars, 1998.

Donald Spoto, *The Dark Side of Genius: The Life of Alfred Hitchcock*, London, Plexus, 1983.

JOHN WHITE

THE MISFITS (1961)

[Production Company: United Artists/Seven Arts. Director: John Huston. Screenwriter: Arthur Miller. Cinematographer: Russell Metty. Music: Alex North. Editor: George Tomasini. Cast: Clark Gable (Gay Langland), Marilyn Monroe (Roslyn Taber), Montgomery Clift (Perce Howland), Thelma Ritter (Isabelle Steers), Eli Wallach (Guido), Kevin McCarthy (Raymond Taber).]

The Misfits may be the most compellingly flawed film discussed in this book. It fascinates as a symptomatic work; that is in the way some films seem to show more than they intend, gathering together their times and displaying them in ways that writer, director and actors could never have conceived. This film is also revealing about the nature of acting for cinema, just at the moment when the medium was falling from grace with its audience. *The Misfits* plays with its starring cast in a very knowing way, using the politics of charisma with remorseless cruelty. Of all the elements that contribute to a successful film, the work of the actors is rarely given enough attention in critical writing, and this film seems to show what acting for the screen truly is, even as it fails to convince as film fiction.

The Misfits in part represents the studio majors at a loss, increasingly unsure of their audience. It is a product of that moment when, no longer capable of staging great emotions through the conventions of the world's most successful mass-audience entertainment, 'American cinema shrank into seriousness ... History may show that the feature form was exhausted by 1960, waiting to be transformed by diversity and experiment' (Thomson 2003: 342, 743). As a decayed western, *The Misfits* is a cruel parody of the conventions of a major Hollywood genre that could no longer work on its old terms. Yet there is no nostalgia for 'the lost West', only unflinching realism about what life in that territory has become, when Nevada is the 'Leave It' state, a dumping ground for everything from former wives to atom bombs. There are scenes and shots suffused with a peculiarly American bleakness, which is portrayed on the cusp between two very different decades. The film seems to face in opposed directions: the ethos of the 1950s is acted and filmed in a way that anticipates the raw cinema of the 'Nouvelle Vague', John Huston directing with a casual, brutal truthfulness of the kind Jean Luc Godard so admired in American cinema. Godard's *Pierrot Le Fou* (1965) could be the French New Wave's remake of *The Misfits*.

Huston was the difficult, seasoned director of highly successful features, including his first film, *The Maltese Falcon* (1941), *The Treasure*

of the Sierra Madre (1947) and *The African Queen* (1952). He relished
the high-risk element of making movies for Hollywood, and could
treat actors with calculated sadism. While shooting *Moby Dick* (1956),
he came close to drowning his leading man, Gregory Peck, who, as
Captain Ahab in his death throes, was strapped to the side of a two-
ton rubber whale that pitched uncontrollably in gale force winds
generated by the special effects team. Huston felt a need to adapt
respected writers for the screen, from Herman Melville and
Tennessee Williams to Flannery O'Connor and James Joyce; and
Arthur Miller's drama clearly appealed to him in this way. But he was
also a director who rapidly lost interest in films that were not going
well, and he routinely gave little explicit direction to actors, depending on the chemistry of the shoot to create drama in front of his
cameras. All of this can be sensed in the risk-laden direction and
acting in *The Misfits*. What is also extraordinary is that this creator of
rugged, male-focused action films chose to put Marilyn Monroe's
Roslyn at the nominal centre of his film. Huston was the director
least likely to understand the nature of this role, or to bring out the
best in his by now fragile and deeply vulnerable female lead.

Miller had been working on the screenplay since 1957, but it was
still unfinished when shooting began in 1960, in the July heat of the
Nevada desert. Four years earlier, he had met an eccentric pair of
cowhands in Nevada, who hunted down some of the remaining wild
mustangs for sale to the slaughterhouse. The dramatist was struck by
these men and their degraded work, and drew on them for his
screenplay, which was to reveal 'our lives' meaninglessness and maybe
how we got to where we are' (Spoto 1993: 477). But, fatally, Miller
had a low opinion of writing for movies, and his commitment to *The
Misfits* was in fact a desperate personal gamble, since he was intending
to create the perfect vehicle for his wife, Marilyn Monroe, as a way of
regaining her affection and perhaps salvaging their marriage.

Miller's screenplay is frankly pretentious and often disjointed, drawing too heavily on the cult of psychoanalysis that pervaded American
film and culture in the late 1950s. The modern tragedy of broken
marriages, failed family life and solitude is painfully established in the
opening sequences, as in Roslyn's poignant tautology, before she goes
to appear in the divorce court proceedings – 'If I'm goin' to be alone
I want to be by myself.' Mothers recur throughout the film as figures
of loss, rejection and death, fathers as desperate and utterly deluded
about their children. The only functioning 'family unit' is the group
of mustangs that the cowboys finally isolate, a stallion, four mares and
a colt, which is destined for a pet-food plant. All of this would be too

close to melodrama, were it not for the desperate intensities with which the cast perform their roles. Inseparable from this is the moviegoer's compelling fascination with the lives of stars. *The Misfits* can be such an involving film because it incorporates this compulsion as an inescapable part of the attention we bring to the screen.

The Misfits was an ambitious and expensive risk, with a budget of three and a half million dollars, which it overshot by another half million. Huston wrote, 'The cast alone made *The Misfits* the most expensive black and white film – above the line – which had been made until then' (Leonard 1997: 239). The director could hardly have chosen a more unstable and demanding trio for the central roles than Monroe, Clark Gable and Montgomery Clift – and both direc-tor and his leads were in the grip of serious addictions that came near to destroying the entire production. Clift was intimidated by Gable, but could not respect his acting, which he considered limited. Gable had no time for Clift, as a product of the 'Method' school, yet he came to admire the younger actor's willingness to perform his own stunts. Despite being heavily dependent on drugs and alcohol, Clift was highly professional on set. Against Clift's 'Method' training, Gable simply said, 'I gather up everything I was, everything I am and hope to be. That's about it' (ibid.: 241). Monroe's technique, para-doxically, was nearer to that of Gable than Clift, calling on her own innate abilities and troubled history while relying heavily for support on her drama coach, Paula Strasberg. What her husband's screenplay could never allow her to display was her essential genius for comedy and the free spirit that the film had been intended to celebrate. Clift and Monroe, recognizing each other as lost souls, rapidly came to trust and depend on one another.

For Monroe, the experience of making *The Misfits*, her 28th and last completed film, could not have been more painful. Miller's script, begun in 1957 as a celebration of her qualities, now catalogued the tragic failures in her life. The scene introducing Roslyn Tabor shows Monroe struggling to learn lines before her appearance in the divorce court, and frames her from the outset as little more than an inept burlesque performer. She is being coached by Isabelle (Thelma Ritter), and the scene reproduces details and even lines from Monroe's own divorce case. She was persistently late on set, though with genuine justification, as Miller would pass rewritten scenes to her at the last possible moment.

Miller chose Gable as his wife's romantic lead because he was the actor she had idolized 'as my father' since she was a child. Gable did become a paternal figure, patiently reassuring her even as he became exasperated with her erratic behaviour. She was, in her turn, frustrated by the role her husband was creating for her, which she knew to be poorly conceived. At the dramatic climax of the mustang round-up, rather than arguing with the cowboys about what they have in mind for the horses, Roslyn is shown simply screaming hysterically. 'I guess they thought I was too dumb to explain anything, so I have a fit – a screaming, crazy fit. I mean nuts. And to think, Arthur did this to me' (Spoto 1993: 482).

Yet at a very painful level, the role of Roslyn is profoundly accurate as the representation of a compelling female icon, misrecognized for what she is by competing males who circle around her. As Monroe said, 'Everyone was always pulling at me, tugging at me, as if they wanted a piece of me ... God, I've tried to stay intact, whole' (ibid.: 483). Here too, *The Misfits* anticipates Godard, in his critique of screen femininity and the gender politics of its time.

On its release, *The Misfits* divided audiences, as well it might, but was praised by some critics: 'The theme with its implications of an essentially male savagery suits Mr Huston, and he has drawn extraordinary qualities from all his chief players' (Dilys Powell). Other, more puzzled responses described the film, not inaccurately, as a cowboy story for an arthouse theatre, or as an 'eastern western'. Others complained that nothing really happens in the film, but it is precisely the unmotivated series of random events where everything depends on the ordinariness of experience that brings the narrative close to French New Wave narration. As Roslyn remarks to Perce behind the saloon, 'Maybe all there is, is just the next thing.'

When Roslyn, Gay and Guido first dance in the unfinished house because so much seems at stake, a desperate intensity develops between them. Roslyn is worshipped by them as the only person who uniquely has 'the gift for life', but she is stricken by the tragedy of what unfolds around her: 'We're all dying, aren't we, all the husbands and all the wives.' At the end of the drunken evening, Roslyn goes outside and dances alone, while the other three look on. Monroe wrote to her analyst from a sanatorium shortly after the film was released, and commented revealingly on this scene: 'Did you see *The Misfits* yet? In one sequence you can perhaps see how bare and strange a tree can be for me' (Spoto 1993: 509).

All of the characters are vulnerable in their own, painful way, and none of them acts their true age. Gay hovers on the edge of becoming an old man, while Roslyn behaves with a girlish naivety. This is what becomes so painful about Isabelle's witless repetition of 'Dear girl' to Roslyn, and it is also what gives such poignancy to the only child who appears in the film, the boy-cowboy with the strangely blank gaze, perched on the bar during the bat-and-ball wager. When Perce is thrown from his horse at the rodeo, Clift conveys an absurd vulnerability that suddenly becomes an image of the madness of a nation, as 'Old Glory' streams in the background and a clown-faced cowboy hovers around him. *The Misfits* has failings, but also the power to haunt, as in the ominous final shot, when Roslyn and Gay drive into the night. She asks him, 'How do you find your way back in the dark?' He replies, 'Just head for that big star straight on. The highway's under it – it'll take us right home.' Miller's screenplay adds, 'They both keep their eyes on the star that shines above and beyond – the bright star of hope. FADE OUT.' But by now the ending is inseparable from the fate of its two stars, and the fiction of the movie is co-opted by the mythic truth of the screen god and goddess, both shortly to die.

Further reading

Maurice Leonard, *Montgomery Clift*, London, Hodder and Stoughton, 1997.
Donald Spoto, *Marilyn Monroe: The Biography*, London, Chatto and Windus, 1993.
David Thomson, *The New Biographical Dictionary of Film*, 4th edn, London, Little Brown, 2003.

NIGEL WHEALE

WEST SIDE STORY (1961)

[Production Company: The Mirisch Corporation/Beta Productions/ Seven Arts Productions. Directors: Jerome Robbins/Robert Wise. Screenplay: Ernest Lehman, based on the play by Arthur Laurents. Producer: Robert Wise. Music: Leonard Bernstein. Cinematographer: Daniel L. Fapp. Editor: Thomas Stanford. Choreographer: Jerome Robbins. Cast: Natalie Wood (Maria), Richard Beymer (Tony), George Chakiris (Bernardo), Rita Moreno (Anita), Russ Tamblin (Riff), Jose de Vega (Chino), Eliot Feld (Baby John), Susan Oakes (Anybodys), Gina Trikonis (Graziella), Carole D'Andrea (Velma), Ned Glass (Doc), Simon Oakland (Lieutenant Schrank), William Bramely (Officer Krupke).]

'"West Side Story" is the paradoxical peer of movie musicals – terrifying, yet an opulent blend of music and choreography, photography and ringing entertainment', Justin Gilbert wrote in his review of the film in 1961. Based on the successful Broadway musical first staged in 1957, a modern adaptation of Shakespeare's *Romeo and Juliet*, the musical expressed a number of ambivalences, about youth culture, social and urban change, high and low culture. Critics were divided about the film, some hailing it as a masterpiece lauding its choreography and pulsating rhythm, while others deplored the film's romanticization of the heterosexual couple and of the street gangs as well as the tensions between stylization and realism. In many ways, the stage musical and the film picked up on a subversive trend in the 1950s, on an emerging youth culture, and, with its unhappy ending, anticipated the edgier films of the late 1960s. At the same time, however, it remained committed to utopian (and romantic) thinking so typical of musicals.

West Side Story is an urban musical, a form that puts it in the context of films such as *42nd Street* (Lloyd Bacon, 1933), *On the Town* (Stanley Donen/Gene Kelly, 1949), *The Band Wagon* (Vincente Minnelli, 1953) and *Guys and Dolls* (Joseph L. Mankiewicz, 1955), and which may be distinguished from more rural, folkloristic musicals such as *Oklahoma!* (Fred Zinnemann, 1955) and *The Music Man* (Morton DaCosta,1962). The urban context for *West Side Story*, however, was very specific, referencing post-war urban renewal. After the overture, the film opens with a sequence shot on location in Manhattan, and we see the gangs run through a number of non-continuous spaces, including a heap of construction rubble. The latter is an indication that the film commemorates what was about to be destroyed: the tenements in the San Juan Hill neighbourhood, which were about to be razed to make way for the construction of the Lincoln Center for the Performing Arts (among others, home of the Metropolitan Opera). This replacement of working-class, ethnic neighbourhoods with a monument to high art – what was generally understood as slum clearance – was part of Robert Moses' plan for New York City. It was controversial not least because of the number of people it displaced. Another gesture towards a changing New York can be found in the rumble taking place under a highway overpass (represented by a set). Moses was also famous for razing blocks of apartments in order to make space for highways, in a misguided attempt to adapt New York City for the automobile. While the film is hardly a critique of Moses' policies, it nonetheless suggests that the restructuring of New York City created a number of deadly spaces.

Likewise, the film's take on New York City urban culture and its Puerto Rican inhabitants is ambivalent at best. The original idea for the musical had a different ethnic cast: located on New York City's East Side, the story was to be about Catholics and Jews feuding at Passover time. (A trace of Jewishness can be discerned in the Doc's Yiddish-inflected English, which casts the film's most reasonable character as a former immigrant.) During a stay in Hollywood, Leonard Bernstein and Arthur Laurents read about gang fights between Mexican immigrants and native-born Americans, and decided to relocate the story into New York City's Puerto Rican context (Garebian 1995: 30, 35). Immigration from Puerto Rico, which had been invaded by the United States during the Spanish-American War of 1898, whose inhabitants have US citizenship, but not the right to vote, surged in the 1950s. Since its release, the film has often been criticized for its stereotypical depiction of Puerto Ricans, which was not helped by the fact that apart from Rita Moreno as Anita (who was made to assume an over-exaggerated accent), the cast was mostly non-Puerto Rican, a fact the producers were trying to conceal with hair dye and make-up. Puerto Ricans protested early on, though the objections to the original stage musical had to do less with the depiction of Puerto Rican juvenile delinquents (or of Puerto Ricans as delinquents) than with the characterization of Puerto Rico in the song 'America' (ibid.: 138). Part of the ambivalent response to the film may have to do with the film's own ambivalence. Casting a conflict between ethnic strife and romantic love, the film's choreography of urban space is simultaneously celebratory and martial, as becomes visible, for instance, in the opening encounter between the Jets and the Sharks.

West Side Story combined these urban and ethnic contexts with a theme that had proven profitable for Hollywood in the 1950s: youth culture, more specifically juvenile delinquency. The 1950s in general saw an increased targeting of younger movie audiences, in part because cinema was now locked into competition with television, which turned out to be more family-oriented. By contrast, cinema now sought out niche markets (such as teenagers in drive-ins). Movie stars tapping into a newly emerging youth culture, such as James Dean or Elvis Presley, proved incredibly popular. *Rebel without a Cause* (Nicholas Ray, 1955) had definitely established juvenile delinquency as a sellable product. To some extent, *West Side Story* can be understood as the transposition of this issue into a more working-class, ethnic context. Coming several years after *Rebel*, and after a wave of popularizing the psychological theories of Sigmund Freud in Hollywood, *West Side Story* is very aware of the psychological contexts of juvenile delinquency. The most hilarious moment in this regard may be 'Officer Krupke', a musical number in which the Jets make fun of police officers, judges, psychotherapists and social workers. 'See them cops, they believe everything they read in the papers about us JDs. So that's what we give 'em, somethin' to believe in', Riff says. These self-consciously ironic moments provide a comic counterpart to the film's more romantic longings, and place the film in-between the melodramatic earnestness of films such as *Rebel without a Cause* and the more nihilistic scepticism of youth-culture films from the late 1960s, such as *Bonnie and Clyde* (Arthur Penn, 1967) and *Easy Rider* (Dennis Hopper, 1969).

West Side Story may thus be seen as a transitional film, originating in the 1950s and pointing toward a more youth-oriented film culture. This liminal status – and the ambivalences it entails – is crucially connected to its status as a musical. Rick Altman has argued that musicals are 'dual-focus' narratives, playing things against but also alongside each other. The most obvious version of such a dual focus may be the heterosexual couple – in *West Side Story* Tony and Maria – who get solos as well as duets. In a related issue, within musical criticism, the relationship between the musical numbers and the rest of the narrative has always been considered important. There are many different kinds of musicals – from the revue (which essentially strung together a series of musical numbers with little plot connecting them), to the backstage musical (where the stage setting justifies the inclusion of musical numbers), to the integrated musical (in which songs and dances advance plot and develop characters). Though not the first integrated musical, the original stage version of *West Side Story* was hailed as a landmark show, conceived around movement, with dances advancing plotlines even as the choreography allowed for interruptions, asymmetries and youthful freedom (Garebian 1995: 13).

West Side Story thus seemed to develop a musical form that was particularly good at staging and choreographing conflicts. One of these conflicts may well be the one between comedy and tragedy, irony and sincerity already mentioned in the discussion of the 'Officer Krupke' number. But other tensions abound, for instance, between realism (the location shots) and fantasy (the fantastically coloured and stylized sets). Indeed, part of the film's conflict is brought out through subtle uses of colour, as the gangs are colour-coded, with the Jets wearing clothes ranging from yellow to brown while the Sharks' clothing ranges from purple to red. In this context, Maria's clothing is particularly interesting to watch, because she goes back and forth between the two groups. The film's gorgeous colours, however, also gesture toward another conflict. On the one hand, by the 1950s, the film industry was investing in colour movies and wide-screen formats, so as to offer something more spectacular than the new televisual medium. On the other hand, the colour play during the overture also suggests another ambition. The film's solemn beginning reveals the high aspirations of film at the time – the attempt to become a high-brow art. The show's composer, Leonard Bernstein, son of Jewish immigrants, who had written a BA thesis titled 'The Absorption of Race Elements into American Music', was well known for his enthusiasm for American music, especially jazz, his eclecticism, and for mixing high and low, the classical and the vernacular (ibid.: 24). The film's overture, though, clashes with its lowly subject as well as with the graffiti at the end of the film.

At the same time, however, the musical's impulse often is to try to transcend and resolve such conflicts. Richard Dyer has argued that musical entertainment has a profoundly utopian dimension. Musical numbers, through representational and non-representational signs (such as colour, movement, etc.), seek to overcome limitations, for instance, replacing scarcity with abundance, exhaustion with energy, dreariness with intensity, fragmentation with community. In *West Side Story*, Tony's and Maria's romance – and duets – are part of the utopia – in 'Somewhere', Tony dreams of a 'place for us', 'peace and quiet and open air', and later he tells Doc about his fantasy of having 'lots of kids' with Maria in the country. But this place seems to play on the original meaning of utopia, a 'non-place'. This seems fairly conventional – conceiving of the nuclear family as utopian – and yet it is interesting that it does not exist in the film. One of the more intriguing minor characters is 'Anybodys', the girl who rejects conventional gender norms. She is thoroughly ridiculed, according to dominant sentiments of the time, but it is nonetheless worth asking to what extent the film registers, negotiates and responds to unstable or changing gender and sexual roles. ('My sister wears a mustache, my brother wears a dress', Riff sings in 'Officer Krupke'.) In addition to the question of gender utopia, the issue of national utopia may be most prevalent, staged as a disagreement between Puerto Rican men and women in 'America'. The song not only comments on the comparative merits of the two 'islands' – Puerto Rico and Manhattan – but also registers profound ambivalence about US consumerism – and capitalism more generally – because of how racism and unequal access are structured into the system. Because utopia always seems elsewhere in *West Side Story*, it becomes easier to read social issues against the grain – the film proposing the critique of gender or national norms as utopian. It is this ability to play both sides – to champion simultaneously critique and affirmation – that makes it one of the greatest American musicals.

Further reading

Richard Altman, *The American Film Musical*, Bloomington, IN, Indiana University Press, 1987.

Hillary Ballon and Kenneth T. Jackson (eds), *Robert Moses and the Modern City: The Transformation of New York*, New York, Norton, 2007.

Thomas Patrick Doherty, *Teenagers and Teenpics: The Juvenilization of American Movies in the 1950s*, Philadelphia, PA, Temple University Press, 2002.

Richard Dyer, 'Entertainment and Utopia', in Bill Nichols (ed.), *Movies and Methods*, Vol. II, Berkeley, CA, University of California Press, 1985, pp. 220–32.

Keith Garebian, *The Making of* West Side Story, Toronto, ECW Press, 1995.

SABINE HAENNI

BONNIE AND CLYDE (1967)

[Production Company: Warner Brothers. Director: Arthur Penn. Screenwriters: David Newman and Robert Benton. Cinematographer: Burnett Guffey. Music: Charles Strouse. Editor: Dede Allen. Cast: Warren Beatty (Clyde Barrow), Faye Dunaway (Bonnie Parker), C.W. Moss (Michael J. Pollard), Gene Hackman (Buck Barrow), Estelle Parsons (Blanche Barrow), Denver Pyle (Sheriff Frank Hamer).]

When first released in 1967, *Bonnie and Clyde* was a critical failure and achieved only mediocre box office sales. Even then, however, it appealed to those who embraced 1960s counter-culture in the wake of post-war social conformity and political unrest sparked by the conflict in Vietnam which cast a cloud over the entire decade. The following year, Penn's film was reassessed for its aesthetic and thematic innovations, and went on to achieve great critical acclaim and commercial success. Reappraised by most as a work of ground-breaking importance, it was also nominated for ten Academy Awards, winning for best supporting actress (Parsons as Blanche) and best cinematography for Guffey. It is now widely regarded as one of a handful of films that marked a significant turning point in US cinema's approach to form and content, at a time when the control of the Hollywood industry began to shift from producers to directors.

Working at a time of renewal in US narrative film-making, Penn was looked upon as one of those: 'young, wilful and maverick [US] directors having their own way and making fresh pictures that entertained millions while whispering to them about the true state of the nation' (David Thomson, in Williams and Hammond 2006: 252).

However, while *Bonnie and Clyde* is now valued for having heralded a 'Renaissance' (King 2002: 12) period for Hollywood cinema as an art form, harking back to the pre-studio days of innovation, it struggled in its initial stages to attract funding. Indeed, Warner Brothers – perhaps recognizing its potential as a gangster movie – only came on board when Warren Beatty became involved as its star and producer.[1]

The film's status as a gangster movie is worth considering as, like many belonging to that genre, it is loosely based on the true story of a villainous gang and used events of the past to set up a critique of the present. The real criminals were more brutal than their screen counterparts, but they became legendary nevertheless and much of the area where the film was shot was still known 30 years later as Barrow County. The gang became famous for rampaging through the mid-West, looting banks and causing havoc. The terrible effects of the Wall Street Crash (1929) and Great Depression that ensued were made more acute in this region by famine. Many families saw their homes and farms repossessed by banks, and the smaller banks were then forced to close. While the movie's references to the 1930s are explicitly made, an investigation of similar concerns regarding the oppression by the establishment of the poor and otherwise marginalized of the 1960s is implied. Moreover, if the protagonists are taken as representing the romantic but doomed heroes who claim to act on behalf of all society's outcasts, their tragic demise confirms the film's ideological stance, indicating 'a recognition of the dark forces that threaten the more utopian or idealistic aspirations of 1960s social movements' (ibid.: 18).

Bonnie and Clyde perplexed some and delighted others for its constantly surprising shifts of tone, from light-hearted banter, domestic squabbles and intimate moments, to shocking and apparently heartless acts of intense and aestheticized violence. It fascinated many for daring to draw inspiration as much from the stylistic experimentation of European cinema as from its own Hollywood predecessors. The influence of the Italian neo-realist movement of the late 1940s and 1950s, for example, is confirmed by the choice of 'real' locations, the use of local people as cast members, a predilection for hand-held camerawork and point-of-view shots, and an overall emphasis on manufacturing an 'authentic' look via naturalistic lighting strategies. Perhaps even more obvious is the impact of the French New Wave on this film, as Penn draws upon that movement's innovations with shooting, editing and *mise-en-scène*. Indeed, an overt homage is paid early on to Jean-Paul Belmondo's iconic character, Michel, from Godard's *A Bout de Souffle* (1959) via the costume, posture and props adopted by Beatty as Clyde Barrow in his first main scene with Dunaway and Pollard at the gas station.[2]

The use of the jump cut device that was key to the New Wave style is noticeable from the very opening when Bonnie is introduced in her small and cluttered bedroom, preparing herself for yet another dull stint working as a waitress. Here, the fragmentary editing technique seems to suggest 'restlessness, edginess and a palpable sense of sexual hunger or longing' (King 2002: 12). Bonnie is clearly desperate to escape her humdrum life, and the frosted windows, bars on the bedstead, shadows across her face, all serve as symbols of the entrapment she feels.[3] Later on, in particular during the adrenaline-fuelled shoot-out sequences between the Barrow gang and the police, an even more disruptive cutting style is used that is reminiscent of the Soviet montage techniques of the 1920s. With close-up shots of blood-sullied bespectacled victims, an explicit reference is made to Eisenstein's powerful *Battleship Potemkin* (1925), another important film about resisting authoritarian oppression.[4]

Thematically, the film offers a bold critique of the manipulation of reality by the mass media, alongside a concern for the dangers of celebrity culture. We see how the drama of their life on the run is heightened for Bonnie and Clyde by reading reports of their supposed deeds in newspapers. The pair, with their fellow misfits, are given new meaning and motivation when they see that they have been labelled the 'Barrow gang' by the press, and then feel it their duty to live up to that name. The tragedy of this situation is emphasized towards the end when Clyde shows genuine contentment after Bonnie has immortalized him through her poem about their adventures together which is published by the papers.

Further debate was provoked by the film's vivid portrayal of apparently pointless acts of violence (at a time when sensitivities about the Vietnam War were particularly acute), and for its depiction of villains as romantic heroes to be commended for taking the side of the impoverished victims of the corporate priorities of the banking system. The film suggests that neither protagonist is really involved in armed robbery for the money itself, but that both are instead caught up in a rebellious struggle against alienation and conformity, and motivated by a desire for freedom and respect. In order to strengthen this position of sympathy, the popular Robin Hood myth is referenced by making it clear that the primary targets of their attacks are the banks that are repossessing the homes and businesses of the poor farmers and their (black) workers. Meanwhile, the irreverent depiction of the authorities (the police, in particular) as incompetent and cowardly, at one point turning back from a car chase when the gang cross into another county, prevents the audience from taking their side too easily. The vengeful Sheriff Hamer, desperate to regain respect after being taunted and tortured by the gang, comes under particular attack for his obsession with status and pride.

The film highlights a concern for the complexities of identity formation in several ways. The opening scene begins with close-ups of Bonnie pouting at and preening herself in the mirror, and she quickly and carefully reinvents herself as the gangster's moll. Meanwhile, frequent references are made to the importance of photography in the modern world as a way of constructing and responding to a sense of self that is constructed largely by others. As Liora Moriel has suggested, this film is important not just for its approach to violence and society but also for its concerns with the 'fluidity of social constructions such as identity, family and race' (in Friedman 2000: 148). The protagonists' shared yearning for a strong family unit of their own elicits further sympathy for their situation. This is emphasized by the brotherly bond between Clyde and Buck (more a father figure), the warmth they show towards the youngest member of their gang, C.W. Moss (as if their child), and the touching scene during which Bonnie is briefly reunited with her beloved mother.

The film uses its articulation of violence as a means to develop the identities of its main characters. It takes quite a complex approach to the relationship between violence, gender and sexuality. For example, it highlights and then distorts the meaning of the quite obvious phallic symbols (matchstick, bottle, gun) that Clyde uses to seduce Bonnie when he first meets her, confusing her shortly afterwards by declaring himself to be useless as a 'lover boy' and hinting at an ambiguous sexuality. Throughout, Clyde seems desperate to prove his status as a macho man, and uses his gun to do so, but even his efforts to become the fearless armed robber are often thwarted in almost ridiculous ways.

Bonnie is also complex as the main female character: sexually provocative and aware of her own power over men, she is at the same time vulnerable, child-like and desperate to be loved. She appears deeply hurt by Clyde's initial lack of interest in her sexually, and also by his reluctance to share any intimate moments with her. She is contrasted with Blanche, the shrill-voiced, self-righteous preacher's daughter (Clyde's sister-in-law) who is scared of everything and demands protection. Their differences are first made clear when Blanche shies away from being photographed, while Bonnie poses with excessive confidence in front of one of their stolen cars, holding a gun and pretending to smoke Clyde's cigar. By the end, however, Bonnie has largely renounced her more 'masculine' traits. In the final scene, her fascination with a delicate porcelain figure distances her from the gun-toting criminal of old and instead 'speaks to her growing domestication and desire for a new identity, one in accord with more traditional female roles' (Friedman 2000: 72).

The film of *Bonnie and Clyde* both reflected and played its part in the cultural, social and political unrest of the time. It crossed boundaries and broke new ground from a stylistic and an ideological point of view, forcing its spectator to question the usual patterns of identification with its murderous (anti-)heroes. While its sexual politics may resort to a position that reifies the structures of patriarchy, it is fair to assert that this film deserves its place in cinema history for changing the shape of Hollywood forever; as Carr reminds us, 'Few movies since *Bonnie and Clyde* have had such a profound impact on [mainstream popular] culture or have generated as intense and passionate a debate' (in Friedman 2000: 72).

Notes

1 When the genre system was first established and studios began to specialize in niche areas, Warner Brothers developed its reputation as a producer of high quality, crowd-pleasing gangster movies, such as those starring James Cagney.
2 The film was first considered by both Jean-Luc Godard and François Truffaut before being offered to Penn.
3 Geoff King does argue, however, that this is still very much a film in the Hollywood mould in which style, however innovative, is subordinate to narrative, and which draws on the old frontier mythology that was central to movies of the classical Western genre.
4 See the famous Odessa Steps sequence in *Battleship Potemkin*.

Further reading

Steven Alan Carr, 'From "Fucking Cops!" to "Fucking Media!": *Bonnie and Clyde* for a Sixties America', in Lester D. Friedman (ed.), *Arthur Penn's Bonnie and Clyde*, Cambridge, Cambridge University Press, 2000.

Lester D. Friedman, *Bonnie and Clyde*, London, BFI, 2000.

Geoff King, *New Hollywood Cinema: An Introduction*, London and New York, I.B. Tauris, 2002.

Liora Moriel, 'Erasure and Taboo: A Queer Reading of *Bonnie and Clyde*', in Lester D. Friedman (ed.), *Arthur Penn's Bonnie and Clyde*, Cambridge, Cambridge University Press, 2000.

Linda Ruth Williams and Michael Hammond (eds), *Contemporary American Cinema*, New York, McGraw-Hill, 2006.

SARAH BARROW

NIGHT OF THE LIVING DEAD (1968)

[Production Company: Image Ten. Director: George A. Romero. Producers: Russell W. Streiner and Karl Hardman. Screenwriters: George A. Romero and John Russo. Cinematographer: George A. Romero. Editor: George A. Romero. Music: Stock music from the Capitol Hi-Q music library. Make-Up: Hardman Associates, Inc. Special Effects: Regis Survinski and Tony Pantanello. Cast: Duane Jones (Ben), Judith O'Dea (Barbara), Karl Hardman (Harry Cooper), Russell Streiner (Johnny), Marilyn Eastman (Helen Cooper), Keith Wayne (Tom), Judith Ridley (Judy), Kyra Schon (Karen Cooper).]

Here's how the important American film industry periodical *Variety* greeted *Night of the Living Dead* upon its original release in 1968:

> Until the Supreme Court establishes clearcut guidelines for the pornography of violence, *Night of the Living Dead* will serve nicely as an outer-limit definition by example ... [the film] casts serious aspersions on the integrity and social responsibility of its Pittsburgh-based makers, distrib Walter Reade, the film industry as a whole and exhibs who book the pic, as well as raising doubts about ... the moral health of filmgoers who cheerfully opt for this unrelieved orgy of sadism.
>
> (quoted in Lowenstein 2005: 154)

And yet by 1970, *Night of the Living Dead*'s director, George A. Romero, was traveling from Pittsburgh to New York to host a screening of his film at one of America's most prestigious temples of high culture, the Museum of Modern Art. This extraordinary transformation from 'orgy of sadism' to modern art only begins to hint at the power of *Night of the Living Dead*: it is not just one of the most successful and influential horror films ever made, but one of the most significant independent American films of any kind.

From today's vantage point, it is easy to see the evidence of *Night*'s success and influence. How many films, let alone films produced on a shoestring budget (reportedly $114,000) far from Hollywood without any recognizable names in its cast or crew, can claim the kind of legacy that belongs to *Night* in the international realm of popular culture? This legacy includes Romero's own increasingly ambitious and sophisticated series of sequels (*Dawn of the Dead* [1979], *Day of the Dead* [1985], and *Land of the Dead* [2005] thus far), the remakes of *Night of the Living Dead* (Tom Savini, 1990), *Dawn of the Dead* (Zack Snyder, 2004), and *Day of the Dead* (Steve Miner, 2008), the campy variation *The Return of the Living Dead* (Dan O'Bannon, 1985) and its own sequels, numerous homages and offshoots that range from the suspenseful *28 Days Later* (Danny Boyle, 2002) to the hilarious *Shaun of the Dead* (Edgar Wright, 2004) to Sam Raimi's wonderfully berserk series begun with *The Evil Dead* (1981), an entire subgenre of gruesome Italian cannibal/zombie films like *Cannibal Holocaust* (Ruggero Deodato, 1980) and *City of the Living Dead* (Lucio Fulci, 1980), books such as John Skipp and Craig Spector's horror anthology *Book of the Dead* (1989), video games like *Resident Evil* (Capcom, 1996) that have become the basis for comic books and films in their own right, and even the long-form music video for Michael Jackson's 'Thriller' (John Landis, 1983).

The matter of *Night*'s status as a landmark in independent American cinema is a more complicated subject, but finally just as undeniable. Hollywood's success has always been rooted in the skillful manipulation of familiar genres and stars to deliver what has been broadly construed as 'entertainment' to as wide a public as possible. Films that depart from this mission of entertainment, opting instead for art or politics or education, have usually been relegated to the ranks of foreign, documentary, exploitation, avant-garde, or independent cinema. What *Night* accomplished so successfully that it can be considered a precedent for many films that followed was its melding of a popular genre (a marker of entertainment) onto a set of independent, anti-establishment aesthetics and politics (a marker of art). Of course, this is not to say that *Night* was the first or the only American independent film to accomplish this feat, but in the post-classical era of American film dating roughly from 1960, its model has been a particularly forceful one.

A number of social, historical, and industrial factors contributed to *Night*'s phenomenal success. Part of the aforementioned transformation in the film's reception as sadistic in 1968 and artistic in 1970 has to do with the fact that these years were some of the most turbulent in American history. The space between 1968 and 1970 exposed the American public to such traumatic events as the My Lai massacre in Vietnam, the assassination of Martin Luther King, Jr., and the killings of anti-war student demonstrators at Kent State University by the Ohio National Guard. Shattering events like these crystallized the national turmoil surrounding the Vietnam War and drove home a sense of America in deep crisis, perhaps even on the verge of self-destruction. In this chaotic social climate, what once looked like pornographic violence in *Night* now seemed closer to political commentary. For example, the American critic Elliott Stein, in his 1970 review of *Night* published in the British film journal *Sight and Sound*, suggested the film's possibilities for political allegory when he compared the film's walking corpses who crave the flesh of the living to President Richard Nixon's 'silent majority' (quoted in Lowenstein 2005: 154). If America was eating itself alive metaphorically during the Vietnam era, then *Night* made that metaphor literal. In one of the nation's darkest moments, *Night* showed America to itself in ways few other films dared.

Among the daring aspects of *Night* is its casting of Duane Jones, an African American actor, in the lead role of Ben. Ben is the film's central protagonist, the leader inside a country farmhouse where a group of seven people struggle to survive an onslaught by 'ghouls' that have risen from the dead to eat the living ('zombie' is not a term used within the film, but it has become attached to *Night* subsequently). The strength, courage, intelligence, and resolve displayed by Ben are something rare to find in lead film roles for blacks even today, never mind in 1968. Indeed, the fact that *Night*'s critical redemption followed the film's pairing on a double-bill with a slavery drama (*Slaves* [Herbert J. Biberman, 1969]) suggests that *Night*'s racial subtexts were crucial for its reception as 'art'. Romero completed the film prior to King's assassination, but *Night* did not reach audiences until afterwards. So Ben's demise at the end of the film, when he is shot by a posse of white militiamen who 'mistake' him for a zombie, inevitably evokes for viewers the often violent resistance faced by the Civil Rights movement, including lynchings and of course, assassination.

Ben's murder concludes *Night* on a truly devastating note. For Ben, a character that we have rooted for throughout, to survive the awful ordeal of the zombies only to be shot by his 'saviors', is the final blow in the film's steady assault on our desires for reassurance that things are going to be OK. This grim sense of a world so damaged and dangerous that the only destiny imaginable for its 'heroes' ends with an early, violent death is a sentiment shared by a number of American films during the Vietnam era that proved particularly resonant with younger audiences identifying with the counterculture. In this light, *Night*'s kindred spirits are films such as *Bonnie and Clyde* (Arthur Penn, 1967), *Easy Rider* (Dennis Hopper, 1969), and *Joe* (John G. Avildsen, 1970). All of these films capture the counterculture's belief that the establishment is not just something to rebel against, but something bent on destroying them – a belief substantiated all too vividly in Vietnam and at Kent State. So it is not surprising that *Night* became a sensation as a 'midnight movie', a film watched by younger audiences at times and places bound to foster a sense of countercultural community, even 'cult' adoration. In New York, for instance, *Night* played at midnight continuously (with the exception of several weeks) 'for over two years, from May 1971 through mid-July 1973' (Hoberman and Rosenbaum 1983: 126).

Surely part of *Night*'s cult appeal had to do with its notorious presentation of graphic gore. But the film's most graphic scenes, when the zombies feast hungrily on human intestines and assorted body parts, are relatively brief and few. There are other disturbing images (including a rotting corpse and a mother stabbed to death by her zombie daughter), but given the disturbing, sometimes bloody news footage from Vietnam reaching American living rooms through television as well as the garish colour spectacles of graphic violence pioneered in earlier exploitation films such as *Blood Feast* (Herschell Gordon Lewis, 1963) and taken to operatic heights in contemporary mainstream hits like *Bonnie and Clyde* and *The Wild Bunch* (Sam Peckinpah, 1969), *Night*'s shock value can hardly be attributed to the sight of gore alone. What distinguishes *Night*'s graphic violence and sets it apart as particularly upsetting is that it is embedded so matter-of-factly within a low-key, low-budget, black-and-white, nondescript, western Pennsylvanian reality that refuses to surrender to flights of fancy. Certainly the film's premise about a mysterious plague that reanimates the recently deceased, possibly instigated by radiation from a space probe returned from Venus, participates in the typically fantastic hallmarks of the horror and science fiction genres (Romero was especially inspired by Richard Matheson's classic SF novel *I Am Legend* [1954]), but *Night*'s dogged preference for the ordinary over the extraordinary is not very typical at all.

In fact, one of the most striking aspects of *Night*'s ordinariness is its investment in the unspoken and the unacknowledged. Barbara

(Judith O'Dea), the first character we meet during the film's opening in a graveyard, is so traumatized by an encounter with a zombie who attacks both her and her brother that she spends the rest of the film nearly comatose, speaking only in rare outbursts. Ben's race is never referred to by anyone, even though the steadily escalating disputes between Ben and the shifty white father/husband Harry Cooper (Karl Hardman) are shot through with unspoken racial tensions. But even Harry, easily the film's most irritating and exasperating character, clearly suffers from his own unarticulated fears: that his daughter will die from wounds inflicted by a zombie, that he will fail as a father and a husband in the eyes of his wife. Tom (Keith Wayne) and Judy (Judith Ridley), the film's young lovers, are barely granted a brief, exceedingly awkward moment of romantic confession before they burn alive together in a botched escape attempt. The ways that Judy and Helen Cooper (Marilyn Eastman) tend to the incapacitated Barbara and Karen Cooper (Kyra Schon) suggest the tentative outlines of a female community, perhaps even the stirrings of limited feminist identifications, but again, these connections remain almost entirely implicit.

Finally, the film's concluding scenes transpire as a series of bitter, unspoken ironies. Ben, the last survivor, must finally seek refuge from the zombies by barricading himself in a basement, the very act he condemned repeatedly as suicidal when Harry advocated it during their earlier arguments over plans of action. And of course, Ben's death at the hands of his would-be rescuers, his fate as a corpse indistinguishable from the zombies he battled against so strenuously, leaves the audience shellshocked over the greatest silence of all: none of the characters whose struggles we have just witnessed has lived to tell the tale. In this way, as in so many others, *Night of the Living Dead* refuses to allow the daylight comforts of normality to return. This may well be a nightmare from which we cannot awaken, or perhaps no nightmare at all – the film's 'living dead' might be understood ultimately as 'living history'.

Further reading

Paul R. Gagne, *The Zombies That Ate Pittsburgh: The Films of George A. Romero*, New York, Dodd Mead, 1987.

J. Hoberman and Jonathan Rosenbaum, *Midnight Movies*, New York, Harper and Row, 1983.

Adam Lowenstein, *Shocking Representation: Historical Trauma, National Cinema, and the Modern Horror Film*, New York, Columbia University Press, 2005.

John Russo, *The Complete* Night of the Living Dead *Filmbook*, Pittsburgh, PA, Imagine Inc., 1985.

Tony Williams, *The Cinema of George A. Romero: Knight of the Living Dead*, London, Wallflower Press, 2003.

Robin Wood, *Hollywood from Vietnam to Reagan ... and Beyond*, New York, Columbia University Press, 2003.

ADAM LOWENSTEIN

THE WILD BUNCH (1969)

[Production Company: Warner Bros-Seven Arts. Director: Sam Peckinpah. Producer: Phil Feldman. Cinematographer: Lucien Ballard. Editor: Lou Lombardo. Cast: William Holden (Pike Bishop), Robert Ryan (Deke Thornton), Ernest Borgnine (Dutch Engstrom), Edmond O'Brien (Freddie Sykes), Warren Oates (Lyle Gorch), Ben Johnson (Tector Gorch), Jamie Sánchez (Angel), Emilio Fernández (General Mapache), Bo Hopkins (Clarence 'Crazy' Lee), Alfonso Arau (Lieutenant Herrera), Sonia Amelio (Teresa).]

From the very beginning *The Wild Bunch* produced strong and passionate reactions. During a preview in Kansas City in 1969, 60 per cent of the audience had negative reactions to it; one irate woman wrote to her Congressman who in turn wrote to Jack Valenti, head of MPAA (The Motion Picture Association of America). Still, some 20 per cent of the audience rated the movie as excellent or outstanding. That the producers went ahead with the film had much to do with the crisis in which Hollywood found itself, and with the fact that the viewers who liked the film were predominantly in their late teens and early twenties. While it didn't gross as much as some other quintessential films of the late sixties – such as *Bonnie and Clyde* (Arthur Penn, 1967) and *Easy Rider* (Dennis Hopper, 1969) – like these latter films, *The Wild Bunch* simultaneously captured a historical moment and profoundly influenced future generations of filmmakers. Not just famous for its level of violence, *The Wild Bunch* revised the myth of the Western, reflected on the difficulty of (male) community and solidarity, reframed Mexican-American politics, and commented on the advance of modernization and the effects of capitalism.

The violence for which *The Wild Bunch* – and Sam Peckinpah's films in general – has become famous cannot be quite understood outside the context of the late 1960s. Major changes, transformations and upheavals occurred while the film was being shot on location in Mexico, from March to June 1968. The Production Code, which had regulated what could be shown on screen and what was deemed unacceptable, was revised in 1966 and in November 1968 replaced by the Code and Rating Administration (CARA), which installed the ratings system, giving *The Wild Bunch* an R-rating. That *The Wild Bunch* could get away with an R-rating – rather than an X-rating – was at least partially connected to the social and political violence occurring in American streets. While the film was being shot, Martin Luther King, Jr. and Bobby Kennedy were assassinated (in April and June 1968 respectively). Right before shooting for the film had started, in March 1968, American soldiers massacred over 300 unarmed Vietnamese, including women and children, at My Lai, a story that broke in November 1969, after the film had been released. As Vivian Sobchack has pointed out, the incredible violence that erupted on the screens in the late 1960s reflected the general social climate, from urban riots, to the images of death and violence in Vietnam that appeared on the evening news, to anti-war protests. The emergence of 'ultraviolent' movies can thus be understood as a way of reflecting, negotiating and transforming the social violence of the late 1960s.

While reviewers were divided about the effects of violence when *The Wild Bunch* first came out – middle-brow critics were appalled while intellectuals loved the film (Waddle 1994: 366) – more recent critics have tended to agree with Peckinpah himself that the violence in the film conveys the sense of 'horror and agony' inherent in violence (Prince 1998: 33). Critics of the film usually presume its focus on frequently violent action: 'No one [in the film] thinks ... they all just act', Wheeler Winston Dixon writes.[1] Such a focus on violent action seems justified by the film's unprecedented numbers of cuts. Peckinpah was much influenced by the films of Akira Kurosawa. In a careful analysis of all of Peckinpah's films, Stephen Prince has isolated three types of montage that translate violence into a filmic language: (1) slow-motion inserts, as in the opening massacre, that aestheticize violence but can also be understood as the human body's loss of control over its actions or as a way of slowing down – and paying tribute – to the last moments of somebody's life (Prince 1998: 63; Seydor 1997: 192); (2) extended montages using cross-cutting; and (3) poetic or psychological montages that are connected to Peckinpah's use of flashbacks – such as when Deke is captured at the bordello – in *The Wild Bunch* (Prince 1998: 67–73). Part of the problem of translating violence into an aesthetic language has to do with how it turns violence into a commodity, making it available for (excited) consumption. But Peckinpah, Prince argues, tempers that possibility by complementing the aesthetics of violence, by also showing what emotional pain violence inflicts, and by producing moments of ironic and intellectual distance.

In this sense, violence in *The Wild Bunch* can be understood as joining the era's critique of US society, a critique that was often manifested in the cinema's attempt to revise – and thus critique – mythological histories, in this case, the Western. Many classical Hollywood Westerns were set between 1865 and 1893 – between the end of the Civil War and the moment when Frederick Jackson Turner famously declared the frontier 'closed' – and featured conflicts between 'civilization' and 'wilderness', in which a righteous cowboy often helped stabilize law and order – 'civilization' – in an emerging Western settlement. While many so-called 'adult' Westerns of the 1950s often took a more skeptical view, *The Wild Bunch* pushed things to an altogether different level. Like other films from the period invested in revising notions of masculinity, *The Wild Bunch* dismantles the myth of the Western hero, as its characters are aging, frequently incompetent, and unethical (working for whomever pays best). At the same time, there are remnants of an ethical code – 'He gave his word', Pike says, and 'That ain't what counts! It's who you give it to', Dutch angrily responds – and the characters' flashbacks investigate their depth of character as well as their morality. Set in 1913, during the Mexican Revolution, the characters themselves are painfully aware of the passing of the 'old' – or mythological – West, something they often comment on and that is visually brought out most poignantly when the cowboys have their first encounter with an automobile.

The film's revision of the Western formula extends well beyond a critique of the genre and the mythological history attached to it – it can also be used to comment on larger political, social, and economic issues. For instance, we can understand it as a complex and ambivalent commentary on the American war in Vietnam – as a so-called 'Vietnam Western'. Thus, the savage robbery and killing of innocent civilians that open the film can be understood as an 'essentially impotent outrage and despair' about the US involvement in Vietnam.[2] Such a reading becomes more complex when we consider how the film's final, extended massacre appears to reaffirm violent military intervention. An economic, rather than political avenue of interpretation is opened up by the importance of the railroad in the film. As a corporation hiring bounty hunters, the railroad represents 'a narrowing of possibilities', as experienced by Thornton, for instance, a sense of 'entrapment', 'arbitrary violence', and 'fateful inevitability'. 'The film's violence is capitalist violence', Michael Bliss has provocatively argued.[3]

If the film's commentary on difficult contemporary issues – such as Vietnam and capitalism – is complex and ambivalent, then its more apparent object of engagement – the US relationship with Mexico – seems even more vexed. Set during the Mexican Revolution, much of this history remains absent from the film, most notably revolutionary leader Pancho Villa and the United States government, which occludes not only the revolutionary struggle, but also the complex US involvement with a military dictatorship – the ways the US had helped General Huerta come into power in 1913, even if they later refused to recognize him as a legitimate leader. Instead of revealing the complexity of the political situation, the film sets up two key Mexican locations, the village where Angel, a Mexican member of the gang, comes from, and Agua Verde, a village under the command of Mapache, an ally of General Huerta who terrorizes Angel's village. While Agua Verde is seen as brutal, Angel's village is understood as primitive, a lush place where toddlers play and youngsters dive into the water. Things get even more complicated after Mapache tortures and ultimately kills Angel, when the gang transfers its political loyalties from Huerta to the oppressed villagers, deciding to fight their former patron, even if such a shift remains full of problems because motivations remain unclear and because it leaves most people dead.

The film has even more unsettling aspects. Critics have often noted how the film seems to attack its viewers, leaving them no safe vantage point from where to observe the action, the characters, and the setting, instead pulling them in different directions. One of the more unsettling techniques used in the films can be found in the moments of unrestrained laughter, for instance, after the gang escapes across the border and rests in a small Mexican settlement, only to fight about shares and to discover they had been set up. Laughter here comes after a tense moment of confrontation – between the generations, between Americans and Mexicans – the danger that the group and camaraderie may 'fall apart'. The scene ends with a tenuous resolution to stick together – one of the main obsessions and difficulties in the film – and the laughter registers the discomfort attending such sticking together. In this context, the film's ending, after Sykes says, 'It ain't like it use to be, but it'll do', and romantic music is mixed with superimpositions of the dead laughing, may be one of the most difficult sequences to read.

While *The Wild Bunch* is important for both its aesthetic accomplishment – the ways in which it uses editing, slow motion, allegorical images, etc. – and for its social commentaries, its most complicated legacy might concern the history of screen violence. When the film was restored and re-released in 1994, it got an NC-17 rating (introduced in 1990) before the original R-rating was reinstated because no new footage had been added (Seydor 1997: 147–8). Upon the film's original release, Martin Scorsese was one of the film's avid viewers whose aesthetics of violence was much influenced by *The Wild Bunch*. Likewise, the film – as well as Peckinpah's other films – broke crucial ground for the representation and aestheticization of violence for filmmakers such as Quentin Tarantino and Oliver Stone. Some critics worry that while Peckinpah's screen violence was a reaction to the social violence of the period – and was thus not only justified but had an ethical and moral component – today's screen violence seems decontextualized, disconnected from any urgent social, political, and cultural issues, and thus potentially not only meaningless but hurtful. The current debates surrounding screen violence – which sometimes too easily assume that we know what effect screen violence has on spectators – certainly confirm the importance of the issue. While *The Wild Bunch* may offer no solution, it can nonetheless sustain a profound engagement and conversation about a crucial contemporary issue.

Notes

1 Wheeler Winston Dixon, 'Re-Visioning the Western: Code, Myth and Genre in Peckinpah's *The Wild Bunch*', in Stephen Prince (ed.), *Sam Peckinpah's* The Wild Bunch, Cambridge, Cambridge University Press, 1999, p. 173.
2 Robert Torry, 'Therapeutic Narrative: *The Wild Bunch, Jaws*, and Vietnam', *The Velvet Light Trap*, Vol. 31, Spring 1993, p. 27.
3 Michael Bliss, '"Back Off to What?" Enclosure, Violence, and Capitalism in Sam Peckinpah's *The Wild Bunch*', in Stephen Prince (ed.), *Sam Peckinpah's* The Wild Bunch, Cambridge, Cambridge University Press, 1999, pp. 107–8, 124.

Further reading

Michael Bliss (ed.), *Doing it Right: The Best Criticism on Sam Peckinpah's* The Wild Bunch, Carbondale, IL, Southern Illinois University Press, 1994.
Edward Buscombe, 'The Western', in Geoffrey Nowell-Smith (ed.), *The Oxford History of World Cinema,* Oxford, Oxford University Press, 1996, pp. 286–94.
Christine Gledhill, 'The Western', in Pam Cook and Mieke Bernink (eds), *The Cinema Book,* 2nd edn, London, BFI, 1999, pp. 147–56.
Stephen Prince, *Savage Cinema: Sam Peckinpah and the Rise of Ultraviolent Movies*, Austin, TX, University of Texas Press, 1998.

—— (ed.), *Sam Peckinpah's* The Wild Bunch, Cambridge, Cambridge University Press, 1999.

Paul Seydor, *Peckinpah: The Western Films, a Reconsideration,* Foreword by David Weddle, Urbana, IL, University of Illinois Press, 1997.

Vivian C. Sobchack, 'The Violent Dance: A Personal Memoir of Death in the Movies', in Stephen Prince (ed.), *Screening Violence,* New Brunswick, NJ, Rutgers University Press, 2000, pp. 110–24.

David Weddle, *'If They Move ... Kill 'Em!': The Life and Times of Sam Peckinpah,* New York, Grove Press, 1994.

SABINE HAENNI

SWEET SWEETBACK'S BAADASSSSS SONG (1971)

[Production Company: Yeah. Director: Melvin Van Peebles. Producers: Jerry Gross and Melvin Van Peebles. Screenwriter: Melvin Van Peebles. Cinematographer: Robert Maxwell. Music: Earth, Wind & Fire and Melvin Van Peebles. Cast: Simon Chuckster (Beetle), Melvin Van Peebles (Sweetback), Hubert Scales (Mu-Mu), Mario Van Peebles (Young Sweetback), John Amos (Biker).]

'A Baad Asssss Nigger is Coming Back to Collect Some Dues', with these provocative words, Melvin Van Peebles ended his third feature film, *Sweet Sweetback's Baadasssss Song.* This somewhat tongue-in-cheek coda, equal parts political and aesthetic threat, became the defining moment for African American cinema during the 1970s. Most often considered the model for 'blaxploitation', or Hollywood's attempt to capitalize on the popularity of narrative focusing on African American gangsters, pimps, and drug dealers, *Sweetback* was a trendsetter as well as a product of larger national and international filmmaking trends itself; its style and subject matter as much indebted to the French New Wave as it was to the Black Arts Movement. The film also was the product of Van Peebles' experiences and vision, and in order to gauge its place in cinema history it's important to understand how creator, aesthetics, and politics combined for box office success.

Melvin Van Peebles began making films in France during the 1960s. After a stint in the Air Force and assorted jobs in San Francisco, Van Peebles moved to Amsterdam in 1959, where he enrolled in the University of Amsterdam. It was at this point that Melvin Peebles became Melvin 'Van' Peebles. During the 1960s, Van Peebles moved to France, where he supported himself by writing novels and performing (singing, dancing, acting). His debut in filmmaking came when he adapted one of his novels, *La Permission*, for the screen with the help of a grant from the French government. The resulting film, *Story of a Three-Day Pass*, tells of an African American soldier stationed in France who meets a white Frenchwoman during a three-day furlough. The affair is soon discovered by white members of the soldier's unit, and his future in the military is jeopardized as a result. While the film's story verged on the conventionally melodramatic, its style evidenced influences from the French New Wave and Italian Neorealism. Shot on location with a hand-held camera, *Story of a Three-Day Pass* featured jump cuts, direct address, and fantasy sequences disrupting the linear flow of the narrative. In story and structure, it was a product of its time and place as well as a precursor of what would come.

Van Peebles returned to the United States in 1967 when *Story of a Three-Day Pass* was screened as part of the San Francisco Film Festival. Based on the success of this film, the director was contracted to work with Columbia Pictures (legend has it that Columbia executives were initially unaware that he was African American), where he directed and scored *Watermelon Man* (1970), a satire about a white advertising executive who wakes up one day to discover that he has become a black man. While the film's subject matter was timely – American viewers were familiar with Civil Rights struggles and Black Power rhetoric – the film earned only a modest return in its first year, making approximately $1.5 million dollars on a budget of $1 million. One possible reason for the film's disappointing box office might be due to *Watermelon Man*'s experimentation with style, including jump cuts and the use of colour filters for symbolic impact, which was still relatively innovative for American mainstream cinema. Perhaps more important, however, was that *Watermelon Man* required that viewers take the point of view of an African American man – albeit a successful middle-class businessman – a narrative shift that was almost unheard of at this point in American film despite Sidney Poitier's efforts to change the face of American film heroes.

Next came *Sweet Sweetback's Baadasssss Song*. Van Peebles' third film was a hybrid; the product of the director's experiences with and exposure to innovative and self-conscious European Art Cinema and the more conventional Hollywood mainstream. Most directly influenced by the director's experimentation with form and narrative structure, the film also was enabled by his involvement with Columbia Pictures: Van Peebles used his salary from *Watermelon Man* to fund his next project. The film is at one and the same time an experimental independent feature with massive box office appeal.

Sweetback is legendary for its innovative approach to production and marketing – it was produced, directed, edited, and scored by Van Peebles, who also performed in the lead role. The film was made on a budget of approximately $500,000, from a combination of sources, including Van Peebles' personal funds and last-minute investments from African American celebrities like Bill Cosby. Production costs were kept to a minimum by using non-professional actors (most notoriously the director's son, Mario, as the young Sweetback who is initiated sexually by an adult prostitute) and a non-union crew masquerading as a porn production. Once released, the film received an 'X' rating, which Van Peebles used to buoy the box office through clever marketing (claiming on posters, for example, that the rating was given by an 'all white jury'). Rental income was supplemented by the sale of a companion soundtrack album and 'making-of' book. Made on a tiny budget, *Sweetback* became one of the highest grossing films of the year, with most sources estimating a box office of between $5–15 million.[1]

The film's plot is fairly simple. Unofficially adopted by prostitutes as a child, Sweetback (Van Peebles) grows up performing odd jobs and sex acts in a Watts brothel. When the LAPD is in need of somebody for a police line-up, Sweetback is 'volunteered' by his boss after he's coerced into doing so by police detectives. On the way to the precinct, the police pick up Mu-Mu, a young black revolutionary, whom they beat (initially while he's still attached to Sweetback with handcuffs). During Mu-Mu's thrashing, Sweetback turns on the cops, beating both unconscious. This moment is presented as Sweetback's political awakening. It is also the beginning of Sweetback's flight from the police – action that consumes the remainder of the narrative, puts Sweetback in touch with other residents of the black community, and maps out certain areas of urban and rural Southern California. During his flight, Sweetback sleeps with a number of women, beats two more cops, and leaves the city, famously promising to come back to collect some dues.

While the plot is relatively straightforward, the film's form is more experimental, the product of budgetary constraints and Van Peebles' continuing interest in cinematic reflexivity. The film's narrative structure provides the first indication that *Sweetback* was breaking new ground (at least in the United States). The narrative is elliptical, following Sweetback's flight through the city and its surroundings. While Sweetback spends the majority of the film running from the law, he doesn't seem to get anywhere, and the film's repetition of shots of Sweetback in flight supports this interpretation. Moreover, the film's famous coda leaves the narrative unresolved, a rarity at this point in Hollywood filmmaking, which tended to provide audiences with films with straightforward and satisfying endings. Like his earlier films, Van Peebles used a combination of direct address, jump cuts, montage sequences, superimpositions, and colour filters as a self-conscious means of creating a reaction in spectators. The soundtrack, an often asynchronous combination of music by Van Peebles and the then-unknown Earth, Wind & Fire, acted as an aural counterpoint to the film's visuals, and often functioned in a similar manner as montage sequences, providing audiences with an Eisenstein-like collision of sound and image.

The film was shot on location in and around the Watts section of Los Angeles and this, in combination with the use of hand-held camera and non-professional actors, supported *Sweetback*'s claim (in its opening shots) that it starred the community. More important, community support for Sweetback in the film sent a message of solidarity to its audiences. Sweetback, in the tradition of a Staggerlee, was the people's hero: he fought back in the face of skewed justice, and the community came to his aide with food, shelter, and transport out of the city. *Sweetback*'s experimental moments actually served to forward this message. Late in the film, for example, there appears a montage sequence of different people answering whether they know Sweetback's whereabouts. In each instance, the answer is no, but the overall effect suggests unity.

Not surprisingly, *Sweetback* sparked heated debate upon its release. For viewers still reeling from the assassinations of John F. Kennedy, Martin Luther King, Jr., Malcolm X, and Robert Kennedy, and the violent urban insurrections that followed in cities like Los Angeles, Detroit, and Newark, New Jersey, the film directly embodied (and in some scenes, visually echoed) the frustration, pain, and fear of American race politics. But unlike more mainstream – or politically neutered – Hollywood products about race inequities (such as the 'message movies' of the previous decade), *Sweetback* offered a more assertive alternative in its characterization of its eponymous hero: Sweetback fought back, the first time an African American character did so in a film with nationwide release.

The debate over *Sweetback* normally fell between two poles. Identified as 'revolutionary' filmmaking by Van Peebles, an attempt to 'de-colonize' his audience's minds, the director argued that Sweetback's mythic qualities, sexual virility, and political agency empowered African American audiences.[2] This view was supported by Huey Newton of the Black Panthers.[3] An equally common viewpoint, often voiced by the black middle class (in the pages of *Ebony*, for example), criticized that very same violence, sexism, and the film's insinuation that a revolution could succeed through sexual dexterity and violent action.[4] Here, the film's echoing of the images of recent urban insurrections (burning cruisers, for example) was seen as counter to Civil Rights advocacy.

While these debates continued over the next few years, their focus shifted to what would be *Sweetback*'s more immediate legacy: its influence on Hollywood's investment in blaxploitation film. During the late 1960s the film industry was financially struggling, the result of a number of factors, including lagging attendance as people moved to the suburbs, the increasing popularity of television, and a rising youth audience hungry for more unconventional (less staid) film fare. After a number of costly flops, such as Robert Wise's *Star!* (1968), industry executives were looking for projects that offered high returns for little risk.[5] Additionally, the industry was coming under fire from African American groups, primarily the Hollywood branch of the NAACP, for its dismal hiring record for African American personnel. *Sweetback* offered the perfect model for Hollywood: a low risk, high gain, and easily repeated formula. Moreover, the film's box office suggested the profitability of previously underexplored target audiences, particularly African American urban youth audiences.[6] Starting with *Shaft* (Gordon Parks, Sr., 1971), an action film featuring Richard Roundtree as Private Detective John Shaft, the industry began releasing films featuring African American (mostly) male outsiders – pimps, drug dealers, and a few private detectives – 'sticking it to the man'. The blaxploitation cycle lasted roughly until 1975, when Hollywood, sparked by Steven Spielberg's *Jaws*, moved on to other models of profitable filmmaking. For a few years, however, Sweetback existed in blaxploitation.

Sweetback's immediate legacy may have been one of controversy and cooptation, but its reputation as one of the most important American films of the 1970s still stands. The film is a clear example of American, and African American, film narrative and style in transition. Breaking away from political and aesthetic conventions, the film provided a blueprint for socially- and politically-committed filmmaking that was also profitable. By drawing upon international filmmaking movements, not the least of which was the French New Wave and Italian Neorealism, Van Peebles provided a workable approach to low-budget filmmaking; a model that was used by Hollywood in the 1970s, but which was resurrected to much longer-lasting effect in the 1980s when a younger generation of African American filmmakers, Spike Lee and Robert Townsend, for example, used Van Peebles' approach to 'guerrilla' filmmaking as inspiration for their own independent features. Furthermore, *Sweetback*'s unconventional narrative structure, cinematography, and editing proved that American audiences were ready for more demanding, more self-conscious filmmaking. In all these ways, Sweetback continues to collect his dues.

Notes

1 Actual box office figures vary. *Variety* lists the first year's gross at approximately $5 million, while www.imdb.com suggests a figure closer to $15 million. Van Peebles, in various interviews, has estimated that the film earned $10 million. See also 'Big Rental Films of 1971', *Variety*, 5 Jan. 1972, p. 9.

2 Quoted in James P. Murray, 'Running with *Sweetback*', *Black Creation*, Vol. 3, No. 1, Fall 1971, p. 10.

3 See Newton's commentary on the film in *The Black Panther* 6, 19 June 1971.

4 Lerone Bennett and Don L. Lee, 'The Emancipation Orgasm: Sweetback in Wonderland', *Ebony*, September 1971, p. 108. For a detailed overview of the critical responses to the film, see Jon Hartmann's 'The Trope of Blaxploitation in Critical Responses to *Sweetback*', *Film History*, Vol. 6, No. 3, 1994, pp. 382–404.

5 *Star!* was made for $14 million. The film earned a mere $4 million during its first year of release, suggesting that audiences were no longer interested in big-budget musicals.

6 American independent cinema began exploiting target markets in the 1950s, especially teens with expendable income (a result of post-war affluence). While studios had been aware of the African American segment of the box office since the 1920s, it did not actively seek to capitalize on black audiences until the 1970s. For more on early exploitation practices, see Thomas Doherty, *Teenagers and Teenpics: The Juvenilization of American Movies in the 1950s*, Philadelphia, PA, Temple University Press, rev. 2002, and Eric Shaefer, *Bold! Daring! Shocking! True: A History of Exploitation Films, 1919–1959*, Durham, NC, Duke University Press, 1999.

Further reading

Manthia Diawara (ed.), *Black American Cinema*, New York, Routledge, 1993.

Thomas Doherty, *Teenagers and Teenpics: The Juvenilization of American Movies in the 1950s*, Philadelphia, PA, Temple University Press, rev. 2002.

Ed Guerrero, *Framing Blackness: The African American Image in Film*, Philadelphia, PA, Temple University Press, 1993.

Paula J. Massood, *Black City Cinema: African American Urban Experiences in Film*, Philadelphia, PA, Temple University Press, 2003.

Mark Anthony Neal, *Soul Babies: Black Popular Culture and the Post-Soul Aesthetic*, New York, Routledge, 2002.

Eric Shaefer, *Bold! Daring! Shocking! True: A History of Exploitation Films, 1919–1959*, Durham, NC, Duke University Press, 1999

PAULA J. MASSOOD

THE GODFATHER (1972)

[Production Company: Paramount Pictures. Director: Francis Ford Coppola. Screenplay: Mario Puzo and Francis Ford Coppola, based on the novel by Mario Puzo. Producer: Albert S. Ruddy. Cinematographer: Gordon Willis. Editors: William Reynolds, Peter Zinner. Music: Nino Rota. Cast: Marlon Brando (Don Vito Corleone), Al Pacino (Michael Corleone), James Caan (Santino 'Sonny' Corleone), Robert Duvall (Tom Hagen), Diane Keaton (Kay Adams), Talia Shire (Connie Corleone Rizzi), Gianni Russo (Carlo Rizzi), John Cazale (Fredo Corleone), Simonetta Stefanelli (Appollina Vitelli Corleone), Lenny Montana (Luca Brasi), Richard Castellano (Peter Clemanza), Richard Conte (Emilio Barzini), Tony Giorgio (Bruno Tattaglia), Al Lettieri (Virgil 'the Turk' Sollozzo), Salvatore Corsitto (Bonasera), Al Martino (Johnny Fontane), Alex Rocco (Moe Greene).]

'I believe in America', the opening line of the first *Godfather* film famously goes. Released in 1972, when Hollywood was barely coming out of a big financial crisis, directed by a mostly unknown Francis Ford Coppola, *The Godfather* became one of the highest grossing films of its time. It also became a social phenomenon, often quoted and referred to in casual interactions, spawning two sequels (*The Godfather, Part II* was released in 1974 and *The Godfather, Part III* in 1990) and a TV mini-series that combined the first two films in chronological order (1977). It is said to have altered the self-image of the Mafia. And it became a crucial film for scholars to think about the function and effects of mass culture in general.

Despite the success of such late 1960s films such as *Bonnie and Clyde* (Arthur Penn, 1967) and *Easy Rider* (Dennis Hopper, 1969), which included an unprecedented amount of violence and sexuality, tapped into the counter-cultural movement, and showed Hollywood how to live through a major cultural revolution, by the early 1970s the industry was still going through a major box office crisis.

Unemployment reached an all-time high in March 1970, a staggering 42.8 per cent.[1] *The Godfather* signalled the beginning of Hollywood's emergence out of this crisis. In many ways, the film is part of a number of socially progressive films from the late 1960s and early 1970s, when a desperate Hollywood gave more flexibility to directors who promised to tap into the mood of the time and especially into the new youth market (Hollywood's redefined audience). Ironically, however, *The Godfather* also signaled the beginning of a new era in Hollywood marketing, fully achieved with cinema events such as *Jaws* (Steven Spielberg, 1975) and *Star Wars* (George Lucas, 1977), 'calculated blockbusters [that] are massive advertisements for their product lines' (Schatz 1993: 32) and that appeal to a wide mass audience. It may be because it is suspended between these two poles – a critical cinema of the late 1960s and early 1970s and the mainstream blockbuster – that *The Godfather* remains so universally popular.

While *The Godfather* is an aesthetically much more conventional film than *The Godfather, Part II,* it nonetheless can be understood as a combination of European art film and American commercial cinema. At the very least, the film is characterized by a very careful aesthetic style. Many have characterized Coppola's aesthetic as theatrical, as defined by *mise-en-scène* – a subtle adaptation of theatrical features into cinematic language that allows actors to showcase their talent. Who could forget, for instance, the look on Kay's (Diane Keaton's) face in the very last shot of the film, as the door closes on her in medium close-up? Or the close-up of Bonier (Salvatore Corsitto) in the very first shot of the film, as he pronounces his faith in America, before the camera begins to zoom out to reveal the back of Don Vito Corleone (Marlon Brando)? Or the magisterial handling of the bright, outdoor space of the wedding and the dark, indoor office in the opening sequence, that establishes Don Corleone's power over both, while also revealing the tension between a joyous social group and a secretive individualism?

Beyond working with actors and *mise-en-scène*, Coppola also manipulates conventional narrative. The sensational effect of Jack Woltz, the studio head, discovering his prized race-horse's head in his bed, is achieved through both *mise-en-scène* (the incongruity/surprise of a horse's head in a bed) and narrative. The entire sequence in Hollywood is marked by narrative ellipses that leave out crucial information – that Jack Woltz changed his mind after checking out Tom Hagen and invited him to his mansion, that Tom Hagen dropped his pleasant behaviour and had the horse killed. William Simon has argued that these missing turns in plot increase the surprise, and make us into active spectators. One editor, who would be fired from the film and who may have been motivated by selfish reasons, complained that Coppola had 'no idea what continuity means' (Browne 2000: 30). Such editing that tweaks classical continuity, is also audible in the film's soundtrack, worked on by Walter Murch, who would go on to create the field of sound design, using multi-channel sound tracks for the first time in *Apocalypse Now* (Coppola, 1979). When Michael (Al Pacino) shoots Sollozzo at Louis' Italian-American Restaurant, for instance, the noise of the elevated train is less realistic and more an indication of Michael's state of mind, an effect that disassociates him from his surroundings (see Jarrett and Murch 2000).

At the same time, *The Godfather*'s thrust is not only aesthetic but also social. Like other critical films from the period, it is critical of America, especially American politics and American capitalism. In a *Playboy* interview conducted after *The Godfather, Part II* came out, Coppola declared,

> Like America, Michael began as a clean, brilliant young man with incredible resources and believing in a humanistic idealism. Like America, Michael was the child of an older system, a child of Europe. Like America, Michael was an innocent who had tried to correct the ills and injustices of his progenitors. But then he got blood on his hands.

Coppola then went on to suggest that the main characters 'could have been the Kennedys'. In this sense, *The Godfather* becomes a 'horror-story statement' about where American politics and American capitalism could go (Browne 2000: 181).

It is no coincidence that *The Godfather* revised the gangster genre, for the original gangster films from the 1930s (such *as Scarface* [1932]), being produced at the height of the Great Depression, were likewise understood as allegorical treatments – and indictments – of the excesses of American capitalism, with the gangster cast as a capitalist gone bad. In this context, it is good to remember that even the early gangster films' attitude toward the gangster were ambivalent – both critiquing and glorifying him. Nonetheless, one of the biggest differences between the early gangster films and the Mafia films starting in the 1970s has to do with the fact that the descendants of immigrants were now directing the films. Unlike *Scarface, The Godfather* often gives us Michael's point of view (as in the restaurant shooting). And the family, dysfunctional at best in *Scarface,* now assumes a crucial function, so that the gangster film has effectively been fused with the family melodrama. And the family, we should note, is not only defined by blood, but can be asserted via adoption, marriage or employment.

The influential cultural critic Fredric Jameson has taken *The Godfather*'s mixing of the crime film with the family melodrama as a starting point to reflect on the function of mass culture more generally. According to Jameson (1992), mass culture simultaneously serves two functions, appealing to a utopian wish fulfillment while also performing an ideological operation. *The Godfather,* on the one hand, contains a pointed critique of American capitalism, uncovering the violence and deterioration of family and social life attending its development: 'I wanted to destroy Michael' (and by extension capitalism), Coppola said of the final image of Michael Corleone in *The Godfather, Part II*, which shows a successful Michael sitting utterly alone, abandoned by everybody (Browne 2000: 181). On the other hand, the substitution of the Mafia and the extended Sicilian-American family for big business allows the film to fantasize about a utopian, social collectivity – the possibility of the survival of a complex familial organization. This utopia becomes most apparent in the brightly lit Sicilian sequences and the operatically staged family rituals that take place in the US. Nonetheless, a closer examination of these sequences also reveals more complexity. For one thing, the repetition of family rituals invites us to compare them with each other, possibly asking us to diagnose a decline – or at least a transformation.[2] For another, as Thomas Ferraro (1993) has argued, family, violence and business are so intricately linked that they cannot be disassociated from each other. The Americanization of the strong-willed Appollina (the first wife), and her eventual demise, as well as the cross-cutting between the baptism of Connie's son and a series of killings in *The Godfather's* climactic scene make this abundantly clear. Family business is bloody business.

One of the more troubling effects of mid-century family life has to do with the ways in which it mobilizes (consciously or unconsciously) a gender politics that already seemed outdated at the time of the film's release. We have already mentioned the film's ending with the exclusion of the wife from the male sphere of decision. Kay, of course, is Michael's non-ethnic wife who sometimes asks a few questions too many, especially about Michael's business. Intriguingly, Appollina may be the most interesting female character, while Connie often seems all too masochistic. We would do well to remember that *The Godfather* was released during the height of second-wave feminism. It is thus hard not to understand *The Godfather* as a reaction to – and negotiation of – the women's movement. In fact, something similar could be said about the film's ethnic politics. In the wake of the Civil Rights movement, Malcolm X and the Black Panthers, in the wake of race riots in American cities, *The Godfather* almost seems to embody 'the wish for an all-white militant group'.[3] An all-white male, militant group.

The Godfather had all kinds of (sometimes strange) effects. For one thing, it is said to have captured the *myth* of the Mafia exceptionally well. As Alessandro Camon has pointed out, the Mafia itself based its image on a myth. Its advocacy of a mysterious masculinity, a paradigm of 'power balanced by fairness, virtue, and control', seemed to dovetail well with efforts in the 1970s to construct an alternate masculine image (Browne 2000: 63). But the film itself changed the Mafia, which became much more media-conscious, with dons transforming themselves from inconspicuous characters to celebrities, locking themselves into a cycle in which media and crime feed each other. (By the early twenty-first century, media-conscious terrorists often replaced the media-conscious mafiosi.) On the level of the film industry, *The Godfather* showed the way to a different future: by the late 1970s, Hollywood would be dominated by well-calculated blockbusters that advertised a series of related products and that appealed to as wide an audience as possible. The financial success of *The Godfather* paved the way for this development, although it was not entirely in this paradigm yet. (That *The Black Godfather* – a lowly blaxploitation precursor to *American Gangster* [2007] – was produced in 1974 suggests that film entrepreneurs were still thinking in terms of niche marketing as a way out of the economic slump.) Coppola himself went a somewhat different path: the 1974 sequel to *The Godfather* was more resolutely innovative in style, and is often called an art film, not least because of how it messes with chronological story-telling. While less extremely successful at the box-office than *The Godfather*, the sequel cemented Coppola's reputation as a director – and the emergence of the director as a star – to which we owe today's reverence for directors as well as the fascination with the 'director's cut' and directorial DVD commentary.

Notes

1 Jon Lewis, 'If History Has Taught Us Anything … Francis Coppola, Paramount Studios, and *The Godfather, Parts I, II* and *III*', in Nick Browne (ed.), *Francis Ford Coppola's* The Godfather *Trilogy*, Cambridge, Cambridge University Press, 2000, p. 23.

2 Naomi Greene, 'Family Ceremonies: or, Opera in *The Godfather* Trilogy', in Nick Browne (ed.), *Francis Ford Coppola's* The Godfather *Trilogy*, Cambridge, Cambridge University Press, 2000, p. 138.

3 Vera Dik, 'The Representation of Ethnicity in *The Godfather'*, in Nick Browne (ed.), *Francis Ford Coppola's* The Godfather *Trilogy*, Cambridge, Cambridge University Press, 2000, p. 96.

Further reading

Nick Browne (ed.), *Francis Ford Coppola's* The Godfather *Trilogy*, Cambridge, Cambridge University Press, 2000.

John G. Cawelti, 'Myths of Violence in American Popular Culture (1975)', in *Mystery, Violence and Popular Culture,* Madison, WI, University of Wisconsin Press, 2004, pp. 152–72.

Thomas J. Ferraro, 'Blood in the Marketplace: The Business of Family in *The Godfather* Narratives', in *Ethnic Passages: Literary Immigrants in Twentieth-Century America,* Chicago, University of Chicago Press, 1993, pp. 18–52.

Fredric Jameson, 'Reification and Utopia in Mass Culture', in F. Jameson, *Signature of the Visible*, New York, Routledge, 1992, pp. 9–34.

Michael Jarrett and Walter Murch, 'Sound Doctrine: An Interview with Walter Murch', *Film Quarterly*, Vol. 53, No. 3, Spring 2000, pp. 2–11.

Thomas Schatz, 'The New Hollywood', in Jim Collins, Hilary Radner, and Ava Preacher Collins (eds), *Film Theory Goes to the Movies*, New York, Routledge, 1993, pp. 8–36.

William Simon, 'An Analysis of the Structure of *The Godfather, Part One'*, *Studies in the Literary Imagination*, Vol. 16, No. 1, Spring 1983, pp. 75–89.

SABINE HAENNI

CHINATOWN (1974)

[Production Company: Paramount Pictures. Director: Roman Polanski. Producer: Robert Evans. Screenwriters: Robert Towne, Roman Polanski (uncredited). Suggested by Tod Robbins' story 'Spurs'. Cinematography: John A. Alonzo. Editor: Sam O. Steen. Music: Jerry Goldsmith. Cast: Jack Nicholson (Jake Gittes), Faye Dunaway (Evelyn Cross Mulwray), John Huston (Noah Cross).]

Chinatown is about corruption and greed; it's about Manifest Destiny and the control of nature; it's about voyeurism; it's about the mythology Hollywood generates about its own past; it's about enduring structures of tragedy; it's about the movies. Borrowing from *Oedipus Rex* and film noir detective thrillers from the 1940s, Chinatown mythologizes critical developments in the history of Los Angeles. It has become a master text for filmmakers who want to make period movies about corruption, Los Angeles, and real estate.

Despite continued resonance and many imitations, it is hard to imagine that *Chinatown* could have been made at any period in film history other than the moment when it was made. In the late 1960s and early 1970s, American filmmakers were stretching the boundaries of what could be shown or implied on screen. When the rating system went into effect in 1968, the Motion Picture Association of America (MPAA) acknowledged that the Production Code, which had policed the visual and moral universe of Classical Hollywood since 1934, had ceased to be enforceable.[1] After 1968, American filmmakers were able to tell stories about official corruption and the failure of law enforcement. They were able to represent sex and violence on-screen more explicitly. They were able to deal with taboo topics like incest.

Although it is a period thriller, *Chinatown* reflects the political concerns of the early 1970s, notably the emerging environmental movement and the protest movements for Civil Rights and against the Vietnam War. The arrival of more flexible boundaries of film narrative coincided with a cultural moment when narratives of official corruption and official conspiracy had exceptional resonance. Released less than two months before President Richard Nixon resigned, *Chinatown* was interpreted by critics of the time as an environmental movie and a conspiracy movie. The Vietnam War and Watergate had spawned a degree of mistrust for government and corporate America in particular that would have been inconceivable for middle-of-the-road Americans during the patriotic 1940s or the conformist 1950s. The assassinations of President John F. Kennedy in 1963, Civil Rights leader Martin Luther King, Jr. in 1968, and US Senator and Presidential candidate Robert F. Kennedy in 1968 were widely interpreted as conspiracies in which powerful forces in government and the military might have participated. As Americans became aware of how the FBI meddled in protest movements, and of how the CIA meddled in affairs of other states, conspiracy theorizing went mainstream.

The early 1970s was also a major auteurist period in Hollywood cinema. The French film critics associated with film journal *Cahiers du Cinema* in the 1950s invented the *auteur* theory to explain how directors like John Ford, Howard Hawks, and Alfred Hitchcock, working within the production-line system of the Hollywood studios, managed to make genre pictures that bore the authorial stamp of their director. The concept of the *auteur* has also come to be associated with directors who manage to exert vertical control over their films' productions, from script to final cut.

When several of the *Cahiers'* critics, including Jean-Luc Godard and François Truffaut, became the filmmakers of the French *nouvelle vague* (New Wave), they made low-budget, independent films, often inspired by Hollywood genre work. Like other French critics before them, they noticed a particular trend in American cinema from the 1940s and 1950s: black and white films, often low budget, with a visual style that borrowed from German Expressionism, and a universe of moral ambiguity that was at odds with the moral clarity associated with Hollywood, which the French had dubbed *film noir*. They joined other influential European directors of the early 1960s – including Italy's Michelangelo Antonioni and Frederico Fellini and Sweden's Ingmar Bergman – in making films that embodied a directorial vision. In the 1970s, their American apostles – including Martin Scorsese, Francis Ford Coppola, and Woody Allen – found themselves able to do the same thing, even when making big budget, star-driven, studio-financed productions. Roman Polanski, a filmmaker born in Paris, raised and educated in Poland, who has produced films in many countries, found this environment hospitable during his brief Hollywood career.

Chinatown was released one year before the publication of Laura Mulvey's landmark essay 'Visual Pleasure and Narrative Cinema'. Mulvey argues that the pleasures available to spectators of Hollywood narrative film are founded on voyeurism. Few movies thematize voyeurism as explicitly as *Chinatown*. Detective Jake Gittes is always peeping in a window, taking illicit photographs, ignoring signs that say 'Private' or 'No Trespassing'. At these moments the camera is often right behind Gittes's shoulder, taking us where we are not supposed to go, showing us what we are not supposed to see. Nevertheless, *Chinatown* is about the failure of vision, about Jake's failure to make sense of what he sees. In this, as in many other ways, *Chinatown* makes plain its debts to that primal detective story: *Oedipus Rex*.

After *Chinatown's* opening credits have finished rolling, the first thing we see is a black and white photograph of a man and woman, outdoors, mostly clothed, having sex. As the camera pulls back, we see several other stills of the same couple, in a variety of sexual poses. The only sound is a series of groans that get louder with each photo. The photos are slightly out of focus and are shuffled quickly through someone's hands. As viewers, we construct a story about sex acts captured on film, without the participants' knowledge. The camera pulls back to reveal an office filmed in colour, a man who has hired a private detective to find out if his wife is having an affair, and the detective whose photographs confirm the husband's suspicions. The groans are not those of man enjoying the voyeuristic pleasure derived from homemade pornography; they are the groans of a cuckolded husband. The office furnishings, the detective's suit, the photo of Franklin Roosevelt on the table by the liquor cabinet indicate that we, as viewers, have left 1974 behind and entered the 1930s.

The black and white photographs stand in for the movie that follows. We begin in a black and white world, a world familiar to viewers of classic detective thrillers. The photographs indicate that we have entered a different visual and moral universe. This movie will show us things the 1940s movies could not even suggest. *Chinatown* repeatedly alludes to *The Big Sleep*, Hawks's 1946 adaptation of Raymond Chandler's novel. The plot of *The Big Sleep* is famously incomprehensible, in part because the Production Code made it impossible to even hint at the portions of the novel that deal with homosexuality and a lending library of pornographic books.

Gittes resembles Phillip Marlowe, the detective in the Chandler novels and the movies based on them. Like Marlowe, Gittes insults people; tangles with the police; gets beaten up; traverses the Los Angeles basin in an automobile; moves up and down the social ladder. He even uncovers some version of the truth. Gittes is different in crucial ways, however. Marlowe has a highly developed code of ethics which includes a policy against doing marital work. Marital work, which largely means providing (or manufacturing) evidence of adultery, is Gittes's 'métier'. Gittes is not above manipulating clients (or sleeping with them). Mostly, Gittes thinks he's smarter than he is. He acts like a movie detective but turns out to be a movie detective who can't stage manage his own case well enough to protect the innocent and bring the guilty to justice.

This period thriller has two parallel plots: one about public corruption, one about private corruption. The two plots intersect in the character of Noah Cross, played by John Huston, whose performance is one of the terrifying pleasures of *Chinatown*. From the 1940s through the 1980s, Huston was one of Hollywood's most respected directors. His directorial debut, the 1941 adaptation of Dashiell Hammett's *The Maltese Falcon*, is the archetypal noir detective thriller. The plot of *The Maltese* Falcon, like the plot of *Chinatown*, is set in motion when a woman asks a detective to follow a man. In both movies, the woman is playing a part.

The events of the public corruption plot are loosely based on the machinations undertaken by politicians and businessmen in the early twentieth century to secure the water that would make it possible for Los Angeles to expand, to supplant San Francisco as the major city on the West Coast, and to make wealthy capitalists even wealthier, particularly if they invested in Southern California real estate. Horace Mulwray is loosely modelled on William Mulholland, Los Angeles's legendary superintendent of water. Mulholland became superintendent in 1887 when the city's water was managed by a private company under a lease agreement that expired in 1902. His career as an employee in the city's department of Water and Power ended in 1929, after a dam collapsed, killing over 400 people. In between, he is credited with (or blamed for) inventing modern Los Angeles. He was instrumental in securing the rights to Owens River Water in 1905. He oversaw the construction of the aqueduct which opened in 1913 and carries water 233 miles, from the Owens Valley in the foothills of the Sierra Nevada, south to Los Angeles.

Chinatown is often credited with teaching non-Californians about the history and mythology of the Los Angeles water wars. Joan Didion refers to *Chinatown* when she writes about the 'The false droughts and artful title transactions that brought Northern California water south'.[2] Very early in her biography of her grandfather, Catherine Mulholland attempts to settle scores with 'uninformed' outsiders who see 'One fictional and melodramatic movie ... as a kind of documentary work on the history of Los Angeles' or 'a clever parable on the greed and ambition of an upstart town.'[3] Abraham Hoffman begins his history of the controversy over Owen Valley Water with a presumably apocryphal anecdote about an employee at the Los Angeles Department of Water and Power who claims that the movie is 'totally inaccurate' because 'There was never any incest involved.'[4]

Incest and rape are, of course, at the centre of the private corruption plot. The horror of these crimes is revealed late in the movie, when we learn that Horace's alleged girlfriend is actually his wife's sister/daughter. Cross's rape of his daughter, and his probable future rape of his daughter/grand-daughter, reads as a metaphor for other kinds of rape, particularly the rape of the land. Read through the lens of Los Angeles mythology, incest functions as a metaphor for dangerously intimate relationships between business, government, and criminal activity, relationships that make it possible for real estate development to supersede all other priorities.

Chinatown is often cited as one of the first neo–noir films: one of a series of films that translates the visual style and moral universe of 1940s *noir* to a world filmed in colour; a world where the sex, violence, and systemic corruption implicit in earlier *noir* films can be represented explicitly. Since 1974, filmmakers have repeatedly mined Robert Towne's screenplay and Polanski's film for plot and visual imagery. The most flagrant imitation is the live action meets animation thriller comedy *Who Framed Roger Rabbit* (Robert Zemeckis, 1989). In Noah Cross's place, *Roger Rabbit* gives us a cartoon villain who melts like the witch in the *Wizard of Oz*. The film ends with a cloying song and dance number performed by cartoon characters. More typical is *LA Confidential* (Curtis Hanson, 1997), which replaces moral ambiguity with self-righteousness. *LA Confidential* begins with crowd-pleasing violence and ends with a villain shot in the back in the name of justice. These films fail to confront audiences with the terrifying inevitabilities of a Sophoclean tragedy, or the moral emptiness of a man like Noah Cross.

If *Chinatown* could not have been made a few years earlier, it is just as difficult to imagine it being made more than a few years later. *Star Wars* (George Lucas, 1977) and Ronald Reagan reignited the market for stories that made Americans feel good about themselves. Incest lost some of its power to shock. Movie studios became less inclined to grant directorial control to filmmakers that might depress audiences, saving the big bucks for films like the first *Star Wars* trilogy and the *Indiana Jones* trilogy. Hollywood may be still haunted by *Chinatown*, but finds it preferable to market happy endings.

Notes

1 Thomas Doherty, *Pre-Code Hollywood: Sex, Immorality, and Insurrection in American Cinema 1930–1934*, New York, Columbia University Press, 1999, pp. 343–5.
2 Joan Didion, 'Times Mirror Square', in *After Henry*, New York, Simon and Shuster, 1992, pp. 222–3.
3 Catherine Mulholland, *William Mulholland and the Rise of Los Angeles*, Berkeley, CA, University of California Press, 2000, p. 4. Catherine Mulholland's biography, which treats Mulholland as a hero, makes a point of responding to the many aspersions cast on her grandfather's life work. It is, however, the most detailed account of his life.
4 Abraham Hoffman, *Vision or Villainy?: Origins of the Owens Valley-Los Angeles Water Controversy,* College Station, TX, Texas A&M University Press, 1981, p. xiii. About the history of the Los Angeles Aqueduct, see also William Kahrl, *Water and Power: The Conflict over Los Angeles' Water Supply in the Owens Valley,* Berkeley, CA, University of California Press, 1982.

Further reading

John G. Cawelti, '*Chinatown* and Generic Transformation in Recent American Film', in Barry Keith Grant (ed.), *Film Genre Reader III*, Austin, TX, University of Texas Press, 2003, pp. 227–45.

Paul Cronin (ed.), *Roman Polanski Interviews*, Jackson, University Press of Mississippi, 2005.

Mike Davis, *Ecology of Fear: Los Angeles and the Imagination of Disaster*, New York, Metropolitan Books, 1998.

James Morrison, *Roman Polanski*, Urbana, IL, University of Illinois Press, 2007.

Laura Mulvey, 'Visual Pleasure and Narrative Cinema', in Constance Penley (ed.), *Feminism and Film Theory*, New York, Routledge, 1988, pp. 57–68.

John Orr and Elzbieta Ostrowska (eds), *The Cinema of Roman Polanski: Dark Spaces of the World,* London, Wallflower Press, 2006.

ELLIOT SHAPIRO

TAXI DRIVER (1976)

[Production Company: Bill/Phillips, Columbia Pictures and Italo/ Judeo Productions. Director: Martin Scorsese. Screenwriter: Paul Schrader. Cinematographer: Michael Chapman. Music: Bernard Herrmann. Editors: Tom Rolf and Melvin Shapiro. Cast: Robert De Niro (Travis Bickle), Cybill Shepherd (Betsy), Jodie Foster (Iris) and Harvey Keitel ('Sport').]

This film offers an intense portrayal of a man on the edge who spends more and more of his time detached from the world in the borderlands between sanity and madness before becoming, in his own words, 'a man who could not, a man who would not take it any more'. Often the locations in which we find Travis Bickle mirror his alienated psychological state. Enclosed within his taxi he cruises a dark, noir-like urban realm of dirt and squalor cut off from that world, observing it in a disengaged, distant fashion. In his bleak, grey flat, again eschewing contact with human society, he exists with few comforts, observing life on a TV screen, unable to sleep and therefore unable to gain any respite. When he is with his fellow drivers, he remains disconnected and removed, existing within his thoughts and, ironically, wary of all those who might be seen as outsiders.

We follow Travis constantly, spending much more time with him than any character in the film would ever wish to, and because of this (fulfilling our role as audience), we attempt to identify with him; but the activities he engages in are often alienating, the things he says ominous and doom-laden ('Some day a real rain will come and wash all this scum off the streets'), and his looks to camera are scary, so that we find it impossible to empathize with him. His presence within the film has been compared to that of the brooding Ethan Edwards in *The Searchers* (Ford, 1956), a man who lives on the margins of society and yet feels he has a responsibility as a moral guardian for that society. Like Ethan, Travis has returned home as a defeated war veteran: both have taken part in a war that has split the United States into two diametrically opposed camps.

Our relationship with Travis at the screen interface demonstrates exactly why he is such a loner. He is not easy to be with; mono-syllabic and frequently rather embarrassing, we wish to turn away from him as almost everybody else in the film seems to, and yet we cannot because we are held in position as a viewer growing increasingly uncomfortable, but also as a voyeur aware that Travis' repressed anger is certain to erupt at some point. The camera allows us to look away as he phones Betsy, moving to the emptiness of the dull corridor, but still we cannot escape. Our embarrassment in listening to his painfully stilted words becomes if anything more intense since with little of visual note in the screen and with our attention drawn to the words by the obvious camera movement we concentrate on them even more. The glance away that we have been permitted only serves to intensify the extent to which we wish to escape his claustrophobic world. The most intense relationship in the film is thus successfully constructed as being between the main character and the viewer.

This is an examination of an altogether darker mind than that of Charlie (Harvey Keitel), the central character in Scorsese's *Mean Streets* (1973), but the focus on a single male character and his search for redemption remains. Here the cross (of the crucifix) which is such a recurring image in that earlier film is etched into the end of bullets by Travis. There is also the same symbolic use of mirrors as a looking into the self but on an altogether more frightening level. Most disturbingly, at one point Travis appears to talk directly to us when supposedly addressing himself in a mirror, positioning us as the outsider whom he sees as a moral threat and wishes to violently confront. We are both his mirror image or other self, drawn on with him towards the denouement we know is surely coming, implicated in his actions and unable to escape being part of what is to happen, and also the enemy within himself and the world around him that he is (and we know he is) preparing to exorcise. Steadily he cuts himself off from the world and his psychological deterioration is paralleled in the deteriorating state of his room until he symbolically kicks over the television, both his last line of communication with the outside world and the epitome of the cold, faceless world of the city (and of Western society).

For Travis, the urban life of New York is a vision of hell; vibrant reds, oranges and yellows flash across the predominant darkness of the screen like the glow from some subterranean inferno. To him, the people who live here, the 'pimps', the 'whores' and all the others, are 'scum'. The 'garbage and trash of the sidewalks' is literally there but this is also his metaphorical summation of the inhabitants of this netherworld. At a further level it is like a jungle: 'All the animals come out at night,' he tells us. The device of the diary enables him to talk directly to us, further drawing us into his inner world as a confidante, and further reinforcing what the camera has already been telling us that the key relationship in this film is going to be between us and this increasingly deranged character that nobody (and certainly not us) is able to help.

The climax carries extreme violence and much of the negative critical reaction to the film focused on Scorsese's moral stance toward this bloodbath, claiming it was portrayed as a positive, cleansing ritual that redeemed Travis' character. Indeed, within the context of the narrative the blood-letting does seem to be in some way to be therapeutic.[1] But *Taxi Driver* is more complex than such a simplistic interpretation would suggest. De Niro appears in nearly every scene and we see nearly everything through his character's skewed vision, but this does not mean we can necessarily identify Travis' views and perspectives on life with those of Scorsese or anybody else involved in the film-making process.

Public concern with the shock of this powerful visual representation of violence ironically gives expression to the confused morals in modern life to which the film draws our attention. The real shock should not be that someone with such a fragile grip on sanity would tip over the edge but that he should then become a hero, heralded in the newspapers for his stand as a vigilante. This is the ultimate expression of the degradation of the society portrayed in the film. The failure to be shocked by this truly disturbing aspect of the narrative while vehemently condemning the visual representation of what is merely an inevitable outcome within such a world crystallizes the misguided value system of the society receiving the film.

The power of our experience throughout is produced from the coming together of script, camerawork and performance. For example, the scene that involves Scorsese's cameo performance as 'Man Watching Silhouette' is one in which we seem to be offered a momentary escape from our close confinement with Travis; and yet we find ourselves thrown into an altogether darker perspective on the world than even that offered by the central character. Dressed in black and with black hair and beard, Scorsese offers us a portrait of a human being embodying the cold distance of absolute satanic evil. We are once again trapped within the claustrophobic space of the taxi as camerawork, performance and dialogue harmonize to create a less than harmonious vision of society. The utter viciousness of Scorsese's cameo role as the husband who is being cheated on but who is about to exact a terrible vengeance is actually, as a result of its use of a male linguistic code of misogyny, more brutal than the climactic bloodbath involving Travis.

For Travis, women are either, blonde and beautiful and to be set upon a pedestal as with Betsy (Cybill Shepherd) or, delicate and vulnerable and therefore to be protected as with Iris (Jodie Foster). Like Charlie in *Mean Streets*, Travis has difficulty understanding women but where Charlie dances in his imagination with the black stripper, Travis takes the idealized female with him to watch the male fantasy of woman in a porn movie, thereby associating himself with the very aspects of the street he claims to despise and emphasizing the male confusion. Betsy, he says, 'appeared like an angel out of this filthy mess', but by the end of their relationship he states, 'I realized now how she was like all the rest, cold and distant – women for sure.' The difficulties men find in understanding women is a theme for Scorsese, as it is throughout Western (male-dominated) culture: women are either beautiful goddesses to be worshipped or vulnerable prizes to be protected, and ultimately usually deceptively cold and deadly. Scorsese's cameo role in this movie highlights this same theme. But perhaps the most worrying aspect of this strand of the narrative comes at the end of the film when Betsy appears to get into Travis' cab and is seemingly attracted to this man who has become a hero.

The ending in fact resolves nothing but, with Travis once more cruising the streets, potentially leaves the whole scenario to be played out again in a never-ending loop. Once more, as in *Mean Streets* but to a greater degree, the final sequences leave us with unanswered questions. In a way there is a classic resolution with the hero winning the day, and yet what sort of hero is this? And what sort of society can create a hero of such a person? The nature of both the city and society would seem to be unchanged. Did Travis lose his sanity and has it now been restored? What is certain is that the film refuses easy answers. In that sense, it is true to the noir tradition; this remains a dark world without traditional values that cannot be changed and within which men and women are destined to play out the same scenarios in an unending cycle.

Note

1 The ritual slaughter of domesticated sheep and cattle clearly played an important role in the ceremonies of 'primitive' societies and folk tales abound of people who, depressed by the narrowness of their world, find some release in maiming farm animals.

Further reading

Peter Brunette (ed.), *Martin Scorsese: Interviews*, Jackson, University Press of Mississippi, 1999.
Pete Fraser, *Taxi Driver*, London, York Press, 2000.
Paul Schrader, *Taxi Driver:* Screenplay, London, Faber and Faber, 2000.
Amy Taubin, *Taxi Driver*, London, BFI, 1998.

JOHN WHITE

KILLER OF SHEEP (1977)

[Director: Charles Burnett. Screenplay: Charles Burnett. Cinematography: Charles Burnett. Editor: Charles Burnett. Cast: Henry G. Sanders (Stan), Kaycee Moore (San's wife), Angela Burnett (Stan's daughter), Jack Drummond (Stan's son).]

Killer of Sheep is a key American film for both aesthetic and historicopolitical reasons. Aesthetically, it is a beautifully poetic rendering of life. Historically and politically, the film marks a defining moment in African American film and aligns black cinema with Third Cinema and international liberation struggles.

The opening scene of *Killer of Sheep* depicts a young boy being castigated, scolded, berated, and beaten by his parents for not standing up for his bullied brother. The young boy is indifferent, the dialogue and acting harsh. This scene is followed by some of the most beautiful footage of young African American boys in American film history. This sequence is elegiac in its imagery and in the life against adversity that the unfolding film depicts. Thus begins *Killer of Sheep*. Shot in 1973 and released in 1977, *Killer of Sheep* approximates the story of Stan (Henry G. Sanders), a slaughterhouse worker, living in the desperate, vain urbanity of Los Angeles' Watts neighbourhood. The narrative is meandering, comprised of vignettes, rambling situations, lingering, contemplative shots of characters in motion, in silence, in happiness, sadness and despair. Through this indirect telling of Stan's story, the film reveals itself to be about not only Stan, but also about the existential crisis of African Americans living and thriving in poverty.

Much screen time is given to children: the opening scenes of young boys playing in abandoned lots or by train tracks; young girls jumping rope in alleys; young boys testing their stamina by daring each other to do small feats of endurance (like who can stand on his head the longest); or poignant scenes like Stan's young daughter, seated in the floor, playing with her dolls, while singing, in her child's language, Earth, Wind and Fire's 'Reasons'. On the one hand, these scenes are rare cinematic instances of African American children, as children, playful and carefree; on the other hand, there is a violence to the play, as the play is survival in some of the harshest of circumstances and environments.

Narratively, these scenes serve to frame and buttress scenes of adults. The adult scenes are more structurally composed through action and dialogue. In addition, the adult scenes are often accompanied by music that provides narration or evocative interpretation of the events taking place. These scenes depict Stan's everyday efforts to survive. The scenes of Stan with friends, in his home, on family outings, and the accompanying scenes of other community members give the viewer the options and the mediating circumstances in Stan's life. What is revealed in these scenes is a blues aesthetic: the content and framing of the scenes (the narrative events, the dialogue and action, the performances and the music) present strategies in Stan's life and the lives of his community, strategies for the comprehension and continuity of life in the face of adversity. Indeed, the film is an aesthetic avowal of these strategies of life as accomplishments of and testaments to survival.[1]

In and through this blues aesthetic, we see that Stan's survival, as portrayed through his interactions with his friends, family, and community, is bittersweet, at times incomprehensible, fleetingly pleasurable, and tragicomic at best. As a protagonist, Stan synecdochally represents the entire African American filmic community. As such, Stan is proud, defiant, and resourceful in the face of poverty, and at the same time, burdened to the point of sexual dysfunction by his predicament. Nowhere is this more apparent than in the scene where Stan and his wife (Kaycee Moore) quietly slow dance in their living room. We see, between the two, the longing for intimacy, and the difficulty of it, as Dinah Washington narrates with the music and lyrics of 'This Bitter Earth' ('This bitter earth, well, what fruit it bears').

In this scene, as in many others, the austerity of the *mise-en-scène* and visuals is reminiscent of Neo-realism. At the same time, much of the exchanges between and among the adults are shot in an observational mode, giving the film an experimental, ethnographic sensibility. The alternation between the documentary and the aesthetic, the use of non-professional actors and improvised and mimetic performances, and the use of natural lighting and ambient sound provide the viewer with precise, accurate depictions of Stan's very human condition. Furthermore, the pacing of the editing, which is elliptical and methodical, allows for extended scenes of the mundane, the banal, and the quotidian. The expressive use of close-ups, the high-contrast black and white cinematography, the oblique camera angles, and the languorous, fluid camera work invite the viewer to reflect upon and appreciate the lives of the characters presented on-screen.

As mentioned above, scenes of Stan's interactions with his family and friends are framed by scenes, often random, of children at play. Each given sequence of children, followed by adults, is an episode in Stan's life. Each episode is punctuated by a scene from the slaughterhouse. With the same alternation between the documentary and the aesthetic used to depict children and adults with such lyricism and grace, the slaughterhouse scenes are rendered graphic in the disquieting monotony of the labour that is shown: the corralling of the sheep, the slaughter of the sheep, the cleaning of the accoutrement, the removal of aprons and gloves, the clocking out at the end of the shift. As revealed in the sequence of children, adults, slaughterhouse, the metaphor of the 'killer' and the 'sheep' is strikingly apparent, if not fatalistically clear.

The significance of *Killer of Sheep* lies not only in the poetic delivery of an image of African Americans, but also in what this delivery reveals of the social and cultural relations and conditions under which African Americans and others like them live. *Killer of Sheep* and Charles Burnett are associated with a group of African American filmmakers trained at the University of California at Los Angeles in the early 1970s called the LA Rebellion.[2] The name of the group of filmmakers is taken from the Watts Riot of 1965. The group emerged alongside various cultural-nationalist movements, like the Black Power Movement, the Black Arts Movement and Pan-Africanism and allied themselves with Third Cinema movements and national liberation struggles in Africa, Asia, and Latin America.[3] With regard to the milieu of cultural nationalism, the filmmakers of the LA Rebellion were part of an African American cultural renaissance specifically aimed at directly addressing the economic, educational, political, social, and cultural needs of African Americans. This included the use of cultural production, such as literature, the visual arts, theatre, film and performance art, to promote cultural history and critique. An immediate site of critique for the LA Rebellion was the tradition of Hollywood filmmaking and the standard representations of African Americans in this tradition. Furthermore, in keeping with the tenets of Third Cinema, which were informed by the Marxism of Franz Fanon and Amilcar Cabral, in particular, the LA Rebellion filmmakers used filmmaking and cinema as a tool for enlightenment and social and political activism, emphasizing and directly addressing colonialism, decolonization, labour, the working class, and the class struggle.

Alongside films like *A Child of Resistance* (Haile Gerima 1972), *Bush Mama* (Gerima 1974), and *Passing Through* (Larry Clarke 1977), *Killer of Sheep* ushered a radical challenge to existing images of African Americans in American cinema. LA Rebellion films stressed experimentation in narrative and content and shifted away from the Hollywood and black cinema emphasis on the middle class. With *Killer of Sheep* and the focus on the quotidian, the use of vernacular, and depictions of community, we see what would otherwise be called 'country' black folk. With this image, indeed, we see the lives of African Americans living in Watts as displaced, rural, and migratory. This image is counter to those of the usual Hollywood productions, the saint-like films of Sidney Poitier or the escapist fantasies of Blaxploitation. The image of the folk in *Killer of Sheep* is even different from that of the black independent tradition initiated by the work of Oscar Micheaux in that it is a shift away from the black middle class and the struggle for assimilation. The figures of the film's Watts community are working class, unable to be assimilated, dispossessed, and displaced. Herein lies the political and historical value of the film: without patronizing, the film is an uncompromising examination of the oppressed lives and struggles of Stan and his community.

The recognition of *Killer of Sheep* as a key American film not only appreciates the aesthetic worth of the film, but also acknowledges the importance of the film and the LA Rebellion to the development of black cinema. *Killer of Sheep* marks a turning point in the way of seeing African Americans, which can still be felt today in the films of directors like Spike Lee, John Singleton, Allen and Albert Hughes, and others.

Notes

1 For more discussion of the blues aesthetic and cultural production in a blues idiom, see Murray (1997).

2 Other LA Rebellion filmmakers include Haile Gerima, Larry Clark, Pamela Jones, Ben Caldwell, Julie Dash, Barbara McCullough, and Alile Sharon Larkin.

3 For a history and cultural contextualization of the LA Rebellion, see Masilela (1993). For Third Cinema, see Pines and Willemen (1989); Solanas and Getino (1997); Espinosa (1997).

Further reading

Julio Garcia Espinosa, 'For an Imperfect Cinema', in Michael T. Martin (ed.), *New Latin American Cinema*, Volume 1, *Theory, Practices, and Transcontinental Articulations*, Detroit, Wayne State University Press, 1997, pp. 71–82.

Ntongela Masilela, 'The Los Angeles School of Black Filmmakers', in Manthia Diawara (ed.), *Black American Cinema*, New York, Routledge, 1993, pp. 107–17.

Albert Murray, *The Blue Devils of Nada: A Contemporary American Approach to Aesthetic Statement*, New York, Vintage, 1997.

Jim Pines and Paul Willemen (eds), *Questions of Third Cinema*, London, BFI, 1989.

Fernando Solanas and Octavio Getino, 'Towards a Third Cinema: Notes and Experiences for the Development of a Cinema of Liberation in the Third World', in Michael T. Martin (ed.), *New Latin American Cinema*, Volume 1, *Theory, Practices, and Transcontinental Articulations*, Detroit, Wayne State University Press, 1997, pp. 33–58.

KEITH M. HARRIS

STAR WARS (1977)

[a. k. a. *Star Wars, Episode IV: A New Hope*. Production Company: Lucasfilm/20th Century Fox. Director: George Lucas. Screenplay: George Lucas. Cinematography: Gilbert Taylor. Sound Designer: Ben Burtt. Music: John Williams. Editors: Richard Chew, Paul Hirsch, Marcia Lucas, T. M. Christopher (special edition). Production Sound Mixer: Derek Ball. Dolby Stereo Sound Consultant: Stephen Katz. Cast: Mark Hamill (Luke Skywalker), Harrison Ford (Han Solo), Carrie Fisher (Princess Leia Organa), Peter Cushing (Grand Moff Tarkin), Alec Guinness (Obi-Wan 'Ben' Kenobi), Anthony Daniels (C-3PO), Kenny Baker (R2-D2), Peter Mayhew (Chewbacca), David Prowse (Darth Vader), James Earl Jones (Darth Vader, voice), Phil Brown (Uncle Owen), Shelagh Fraser (Aunt Beru).]

When you've been in the business of studying films for a few years, you take your duties for granted as you would in any other job –

until new acquaintances ask you about it. When people ask exactly what it is that I do, their next question inevitably takes one of two forms: *What made you decide to do* that? Or, *What's your favourite film?* These are reasonable questions, but they startle me because no particular film or viewing experience sent me marching to the graduate school catalogues to seek my fortune. I chose this profession because it seemed a natural extension of my interests in literary interpretation and in the histories of such mass cultural media as comic books, movies, television, and video games, not because the profession chose me.

Yeah, right. That's what I've been telling myself for a long time, but at last I see that I've been repressing the true answer. After mumbling responses about post-war French cinema and Hollywood film noir and Gloria Grahame and Luis Buñuel for years, I've finally come to terms with my professional primal scene: My epiphany happened in 1977 when I was 9 years old, watching a summer blockbuster that my small-town single-screen theatre screened one season late because it had held over *Smokey and the Bandit* for 20 weeks. That blockbuster was *Star Wars*, and it is my favourite film of all time.

Why did it take me so long to admit this to myself? The best reason I can come up with is that the original *Star Wars* is a world-class guilty pleasure for a serious film scholar. For one thing, it's not as original as we imagined it was three decades ago. There isn't much new about the story or the presentation of Luke Skywalker's development from whiny farm boy into galactic freedom fighter. The plot cobbles together – some would say plagiarizes – snippets from sources as diverse as Tolkien's swords-and-sorcery epic *The Lord of the Rings*; Frank Herbert's science fiction classic *Dune* with its desert-bound moisture farmers (Tatooine, anyone?) and spice-trade intrigue; and even Joseph Campbell's nonfiction book *The Hero With a Thousand Faces* (1949), a work of comparative mythology inflected by Carl Jung's theory that all cultures cast human maturation as a mythical journey from anti-social naïveté to public heroism. For influences on the visual style of *Star Wars*, one need look no further than Stanley Kubrick's *2001: A Space Odyssey* (1968) with its massive but plausible-looking space stations, courtesy of Douglas Trumbull's detailed plastic miniatures and groundbreaking process photography.

But writer and director George Lucas cast his genre-poacher's net wider than fantasy, myth, and science fiction. He showed his effects team aerial combat sequences from Hollywood war movies to demonstrate the shot setups and pacing he wanted for the

Millennium Falcon's battle with imperial TIE fighters. Thematically, Lucas drew upon the obsession with honour, duty, and the spoils of loyalty and betrayal found in post-war Japanese *chanbara* (swordplay) films, especially the epics directed by Akira Kurosawa. Lucas's eclecticism was hardly unique. His generation of 'movie-brat' directors, which included his friends Francis Ford Coppola, Brian De Palma, and future *Raiders of the Lost Ark* collaborator Steven Spielberg, learned their trade not by the traditional means of Hollywood apprenticeship, but by becoming movie omnivores. They grew up watching classic films on late-night television and in big-city art house theatres, and wound up attending film schools like Lucas's own University of Southern California that offered courses on global film history as well as on production. The references *Star Wars* sweeps together probably seemed as natural to Lucas and his cohort as they seemed incoherent and unprofitable, at first, to the executives at 20th Century-Fox. If not for Fox executive Alan Ladd Jr's faith in Lucas's 'kiddie film', the studio would have abandoned this expensive, uncategorizable project without looking back.

Before you start berating those industry stuffed-shirts for their lack of vision, please bear in mind that the 'old' Hollywood generation had been burned by big ideas too many times not to play it safe. As witnesses to expensive flops in the recent past (such as *Dr. Doolittle, Darling Lili,* and *Cleopatra,* the epic that nearly sank Fox in the early 1960s), studio chiefs took note of the surprise success of the no-frills countercultural film *Easy Rider* in 1967 and placed smaller piles of their investors' chips on personal films about anti-heroes dealing with everyday obstacles. Once Coppola's *Godfather* films (1972 and 1974) and Spielberg's horror-thriller *Jaws* (1975) became mega-hits, Hollywood seemed to be turning another corner, back toward the straightforward, goal-oriented plots and more formulaic filmmaking procedures of its past, but no studio felt compelled to rush to the blockbuster model just because a couple of extraordinary films had done extraordinary business. Rather, *Star Wars* earned its position in Hollywood history by demonstrating the earning potential of a new kind of formula film, the 'high-concept' blockbuster. Its success helped convince studio executives that they had to reorganize their business model if they hoped to reap the unparalleled profits generated by the blockbuster phenomenon.

Though it differed in obvious ways from its immediate predecessors in blockbusterdom, *Star Wars* also incorporated key elements from *The Godfather* and *Jaws*: the epic sweep of history-making conflict and the changes it wreaks, the American family as a locus of this conflict, and suspense and surprise techniques borrowed from crime movies, Hitchcock's suspense thrillers, and horror films. Lucas was as familiar with the theme of intergenerational discord as he was with science fiction. His USC thesis film, a sci-fi short titled *THX-1138* (re-shot as a feature-length film in 1971), chronicles a man's attempt to escape a post-apocalyptic society that dehumanizes its citizens. In Lucas's breakthrough film, *American Graffiti* (1973), two guys from the high school class of 1962 spend a final night drag-racing through their hometown and wrestling with doubts about their departure for college the next day. Frustrated by the cuts that MCA/Universal forced him to make to *American Graffiti*, Lucas demanded final cut rights on *Star Wars* and has gotten, or taken, those rights ever since. His legendary commitment to overseeing his projects at every stage already showed through in his establishment of Lucasfilm Ltd to produce *Star Wars* (the Fox studio merely fronted production money and distributed the film), and Industrial Light and Magic (ILM), the in-house special effects unit which founding head John Dykstra quickly made the most sought-after effects company in Hollywood.

What no one predicted was that Lucas's reboot of the science fiction genre, a film so disrespectful of the genre's conventions that its first title screen sets the scene not in the future but '[a] long time ago, in a galaxy far, far away', would garner such critical admiration and viewer fanaticism that it would gross more than one hundred million American dollars (1977 dollars, mind you) by the end of the summer – before the Burt-Reynolds-drunk Majestic Theater in Centerville, Iowa, had even bothered to bring the movie to my attention. However unoriginal its plot and premise, however unintentionally awkward its dialogue, the film succeeded then (and still grips viewers now) because it simultaneously surprised us with its unexpected juxtapositions of diverse elements and bathed us in the aura of straightforward, plot-driven filmmaking – something most viewers had not experienced in a new-release moviehouse, to paraphrase Ben Kenobi, for a long, long time. That mixture of the familiar and the unfamiliar certainly caught the attention of my father, whose interest was piqued largely by John Williams's orchestral score. A life-long opera buff who spent a winter's worth of Saturday afternoons taping radio broadcasts of Wagner's Ring Cycle with his reel-to-reel, my dad was smitten with Williams's use of musical leitmotifs to emphasize the entrances of characters like Luke and Leia and to reflect plot turns and mood shifts by modulating these themes as necessary. The classical score, inspired by Kubrick's use of classical masterworks in *2001*, instantly turned Williams into an industry star himself. It's difficult now to watch starships on a movie screen without hearing the sweep of strings or the hammer-blasts of trombones, even if only in our imaginations.

I couldn't have put any of that into words in 1977, of course. I had no idea that Hollywood had ever experienced a business-model crisis, or that Lucas's dialogue made his actors want to throttle him, or that practically the only things that distinguished *Star Wars* from Kurosawa's *The Hidden Fortress* (1958) were, first, that the central comic duo consisted of androids R2-D2 and C-3PO instead of Japanese peasants, and second, that Lucas was not able to convince *Fortress* star Toshiro Mifune to play Obi-Wan. What captivated me about the film back then was its level of *definition*. No movie I had seen outside a Disney feature presented such clear and vivid heroes – young, attractive, squabbling idealists accompanied by the grandfatherly Kenobi (an unself-consciously noble Alec Guinness) – and grotesque villains with names like Darth Vader and Grand Moff Tarkin (played by British B-movie vampire killer Peter Cushing) who spouted bwa-ha-ha bad guy lines like 'There'll be no escaping us this time' as slimily as did Ming the Merciless in the old *Flash Gordon* serials (from which *Star Wars* also borrows). It kept up an unrelenting level of tension as Luke, Princess Leia, and Han improvised their way out of the Death Star space station and then returned to destroy it. It developed a world, or a galaxy rather, in which smart-mouthed 'droids and humongous starships looked so grungy and were treated with such nonchalance that they seemed as plausible as my dad's Impala station wagon. Speaking for the kid I was, who dreamed of being either a cartoonist or a superhero in a town where neither aspiration meant much to anybody else, a story about a frustrated kid who dreamed as fervently of escape from being misunderstood as he did of escaping to the stars seemed the height of verisimilitude.

Star Wars's low-tech high-tech aesthetic may in fact be *its* key innovation. Scuttling the *science* of science fiction and permitting the fantasy elements to dominate allows the film's special effects to thrill and convince us more completely than they could have if Lucas had stuck to the gospel of 'hard' science fiction preached by fiction writer Larry Niven in the 1970s. Dykstra constructed his starships out of spare parts from hundreds of model cars and planes, aged them artificially with grease, grime, and dents, and filmed them using an electronically-timed motion control system that he and ILM essentially invented for the movie. By synchronizing the models' movements exactly to the background shots into which they would later be matted, Dykstra imbued 'ships' no larger than a foot or two in length with a solidity and kineticism more convincing than any computer-generated starship I have seen since. This aesthetic makes *Star Wars* an important bridge between the warts-and-all realism of 1970s Hollywood and the future-grunge look of the action-blockbuster era, especially visible in such films as *Alien* and *Aliens*, *Blade Runner,* the *Terminator* films, *Total Recall,* and *The Matrix.* Lucas's technologized galaxy seemed to reflect American culture's alternating smugness and anxiety about its scientific achievements. Machines could draw moisture from the sands of Tatooine and cool a movie theatre on a summer afternoon, but they could also destroy a planet at a whim, a worry as close to Americans' minds as the Cold War and its hottest hotspot, the recently abandoned Vietnam conflict.

Indeed, Lucas's mass-culture obsessions led him to make a personal film that coincidentally appealed to the growing conservatism of post-Vietnam political culture in the US. *Star Wars* changed the industry by making book on spectacle and simplicity while echoing the political means by which conservative politicians tried to 'heal' the wounds of an ambiguous and humbling war: a hard turn to the political right, to an ideology that divided the planet into the light and dark sides of the Force as definitively as Lucas divided up the galaxy. When US President Ronald Reagan called the Soviet Union an 'evil empire' and dubbed his administration's never-realized nuclear deterrent blueprint 'Star Wars', no one who paid close attention to the film's simplistic image of political conflict should have been surprised.

Lucas's fortune-making decision to retain the rights to all *Star Wars* marketing, including everything from action figures to pyjamas, strikes me now as a crass betrayal of the idealist ethos he represented for me as soon as I knew his name. And I get angry along with scholar Will Brooker when he chastises Lucas for banishing the original release versions of *Star Wars* and its first two sequels, *The Empire Strikes Back* (1980) and *Return of the Jedi* (1983), by refusing to re-release them to theatres or the home market since he foisted digitally 'enhanced' Special Edition versions of the films on the public in the late 1990s. Sure, Lucas invented these characters and concepts and stories, but what gives him the right to change or efface the labour of the actors and crew who helped craft the film into the hit it became, or to ride herd over the historical importance of how these films initially looked and sounded? (To be fair, I must note that Lucas eventually capitulated to fan pressure and appended the original versions to the most recent Special Edition DVD sets.) In the late 1970s, however, whatever monies Lucas collected from the mounds of toys that Kenner produced for Lucasfilm seemed to me more than his just desserts. I wasn't even envious of his own intergalactic empire, built on billions of bits of painted plastic doomed to be dropped from car windows or lost in furniture cushions forever; the original *Star Wars* action figures weren't things I *wanted* so much as *necessities* akin to Nacho Cheese Doritos or my bicycle. Without plastic effigies of Luke, Leia, Vader, and the 'droids near me as totems, my frustrated dream of proving myself a deep, sensitive hero would have become unbearable. Like most proper nerds, I suspect, but unlike the majority of *Star Wars* fans, I completely identified with Luke, shunned bad-boy Han Solo for his similarities to the anti-intellectual bullies I encountered in middle school, and wanted Princess Leia for my very own with all the proto-erotic, preadolescent angst that a 9-year-old hetero boy could muster, no matter how closely her hairdo resembled twin cheese Danishes.

That's my confession, dear reader. But tell on me at a cocktail party and I'll deny everything, shriek something about the glories of *Citizen Kane* or Antonioni, and accuse you of remaining a closet Wachowski Brothers fan even after *Speed Racer* crashed and burned. Please, then, let this be our secret, OK? I'll keep mum if you will.

Katherine Fusco provided invaluable research assistance for this essay.

Further reading

'"Star Wars": The Year's Best Movie', *Time*, 30 May 1977, pp. 54–6+.

Gary Arnold, '"Star Wars": A Spectacular Intergalactic Joyride', *Washington Post*, 25 May 1977, p. B1.

Peter Biskind, *Easy Riders, Raging Bulls: How the Sex-Drugs-and-Rock-'N'-Roll Generation Saved Hollywood,* New York, Simon & Schuster, 1998.

Will Brooker, *Using the Force: Creativity, Community, and 'Star Wars' Fans,* London, Continuum, 2002.

Owen Gleiberman, 'Empire of Fun [review of 'special edition' re-release of *Star Wars*]', *Entertainment Weekly,* 31 January 1997, pp. 32–3.

Matt Hills, '*Star Wars* in Fandom, Film Theory, and the Museum: The Cultural Status of the Cult Blockbuster', in Julian Stringer (ed.), *Movie Blockbusters,* London, Routledge, 2003, pp. 178–89.

Derek Johnson, '*Star Wars* Fans, DVD, and Cultural Ownership: An Interview with Will Brooker', *Velvet Light Trap,* Vol. 56, Fall 2005, pp. 36–44.

David A. Kaplan, with Adam Rogers and Yahlin Chang, 'The Force is Still with Us [report on 'special edition' re-release of *Star Wars*]', *Newsweek*, 20 January 1997, p. 52.

Jack Kroll, 'Fun in Space', *Newsweek*, 30 May 1977, p. 60.

'Murf', 'Star Wars', *Variety*, 25 May 1977, n. p.
Justin Wyatt, *High Concept: Movies and Marketing in Hollywood*, Austin, TX,
University of Texas Press, 1994.

PAUL YOUNG

APOCALYPSE NOW (1979)

[Production Company: Zoetrope Studios. Director and producer:
Francis Ford Coppola. Screenwriters: John Milius and Coppola.
Cinematography: Vittorio Storaro. Music: Carmine Coppola and
Coppola. Editing: Lisa Fruchtman, Gerald Greenberg and Walter
Murch. Cast: Marlon Brando (Colonel Walter E. Kurtz), Martin
Sheen (Captain Willard), Robert Duvall (Lieutenant Colonel
Kilgore), Frederic Forrest (Jay 'Chef' Hicks), Sam Bottoms (Lance B.
Johnson), Albert Hall (Chief Phillips), Laurence Fishburne (Tyrone
'Clean' Miller), Dennis Hopper (photojournalist).]

Heavily indebted to Joseph Conrad's novella *Heart of Darkness*, it
might be argued this film wears its literary credentials rather too pre-
tentiously. When we first meet Dennis Hopper's photojournalist character,[1] for example, he seems to attribute godlike stature to Kurtz
(Marlon Brando) partly on the basis that he quotes lines from T.S.
Eliot's *The Love Song of J. Alfred Prufrock*; hardly the most likely piece of
verse to be quoted by a US army officer who in the late 1960s/early
1970s has set himself up as a small-time, ultra-authoritarian dictator
deep inside South-East Asia. When we eventually meet Kurtz himself,
there is further use of Eliot's verse; this time perhaps more appro-
priately from *The Hollow Men* but still rather lacking in originality.[2]

But it is not the range of literary allusions, from the placing of a
copy of James Frazer's *The Golden Bough* on Willard's bedside table
during the opening to the photojournalist scuttling from Kurtz's
presence towards the end reciting the final words from *The Hollow
Men*: 'This is the way the world ends / Not with a bang but a whim-
per', that makes this an important film. These somewhat forced
attempts to express profound insights into the wider nature of the
human experience are probably the weakest part of the whole. The
most interesting aspect of this film is the way in which it offers, just
four years after the fall of Saigon, a complex set of responses to the
American experience of Vietnam.

In Conrad's book, the narrator, Marlow, takes the reader ever
deeper into the depths of the late nineteenth-century European

colonial enterprise, on a journey that operates as a metaphor for an examination of the (dark) heart of man:[3] in *Apocalypse Now*, we follow our narrator, Willard, as he is drawn with fatalistic inevitability ever further into an exploration of the American imperialist venture in Vietnam and Cambodia. Through him, we experience both the historical realities of this particular war and its psychological ramifications for those individuals (and maybe a whole society) ensnared in the on-going nightmare of that moment. Both Marlow and Willard move towards a mysterious man called Kurtz who seems to offer the possibility of some insight into not only the particular expansionist enterprise under examination but also the psychological (even the spiritual) state of man. Both the novella and the film move towards their culmination in the final words of Kurtz, 'The horror, the horror', and both abandon the reader to their own devices to decide the significance (if any) of these words.

Apocalypse Now utilizes a very basic episodic narrative with no great sense of new complications or developments – we are simply and inevitably moving towards the climactic rendezvous with Kurtz. A sequence of events may occur which reveals an ever stronger sense of the madness at the heart of the American GIs' experience of Vietnam but these are merely sights along the way. A lieutenant colonel, Kilgore (Robert Duvall), who loves 'the smell of napalm in the morning' leads a helicopter charge scudding across the sky to the sound of Wagner's *Ride of the Valkyries*;[4] troops at an army base riot at the sight of the tantalizing glimpses of home offered by Playgirls during a surreal 'girlie' stage show; soldiers in a forward base surrounded by Viet Cong and abandoned by their commanders survive in a drug-induced haze; and in between, a routine search of a sampan results in the slaughter of an innocent Vietnamese family by inexperienced, nervous US 'kids' abroad. There is no connection between these events other than that they occur during Willard's journey towards Kurtz. And this sense of a disjointed, dislocated picaresque narrative is entirely fitting for a film about the madness of war and the insanity of man.

However, despite this episodic approach, there is some sense of steady incremental change as the story progresses. We move from daylight and vast tracts of open water at the start of the journey towards an ever-narrowing funnel of a river, ever more night-time episodes, and ever darker and more death-filled events. Not only that, but Willard and those who are unfortunate enough to find themselves accompanying him into the jungle darkness lose their innocence in a remorseless delving ever deeper into their self and away from 'civilization'. For Willard, this culminates in a shot of him emerging at night from a swamp, half-naked and with his face blackened, on his way towards carrying out the ritual slaughter of Kurtz.

In one sense, Willard might be said to kill his alter ego, in another he plays the endgame as Kurtz seems to require it to be played, but in a further narrative sense, he simply operates as the traditional hero who successfully reaches the inner cave where the final test must be endured and emerges triumphant and therefore able to return to the world changed but also ritually cleansed. What this has to say about the American experience in Nam, about war in general (and about the human condition) is open to interpretation.[5] If, as Kurtz asserts, he has seen through to the purity of action that is required in order to win such a war, then in showing this as unacceptable to the US authorities the film might be seen to be critical of the armed forces (and perhaps a democratic country) that was not prepared to go far enough. However, Willard's comment, that he can see no method in what Kurtz is engaged in, positions him as the restorer of not only order but also reason (and therefore, sanity).

In keeping with the episodic nature of the whole, the initial exposition phase effectively operates as a self-contained short film. Jim Morrison's lyrics playing over images of a verdant jungle devastated by the explosive intrusion of human technology followed by a scene in a claustrophobic hotel room effectively brings together the external socio-political world and the interior human psychology. And these dual aspects of the film come together in the superimposed image of the jungle fires playing around Willard's head. The war and its effects are inescapable. Willard's response as he peers between the slats of the blind, 'Saigon: shit', represents at several levels what within a few years of the deployment of troops came to be the dominant American response to Vietnam. Our guide is immediately disconcertingly positioned as observing this place but yet cut off from it and unable to comprehend it. We begin with a contradiction which is also a statement: 'This is the end.' This film is in its entirety going to be about 'the end': the end of civilization, the end in terms of the death of the individual, and most of all, the end in terms of a reaching of the extremes of human experience.

The resolution phase too 'works' in the same way; from the moment Willard reaches Kurtz's kingdom, we find ourselves in a section from the whole that has its own sense of narrative structure with its own exposition, development, complication, climax and resolution phases. The only element holding the whole together is the presence of Willard, just as Marlow is the only link maintaining any sense of coherence within Conrad's *Heart of Darkness*. This is entirely appropriate: the creative impulse behind both the film and the novella is the idea that the only thing enabling any sense to be made of the world at large is the connectedness achieved through the individual consciousness (and storytelling).

To be more critical, this film is American-centred and highly masculine in its outlook.[6] However, this would be to criticize it for what it is not rather than to recognize it for what it is, to judge it in terms that are beyond its terms of reference. This is a key US film because it attempts to deal with a national disaster that was at the time very recent. That it explores this period in such a way as to convert a naïve (if not idiotic) foreign policy into a heroic if doomed effort to come to some understanding of the human condition might be a valid criticism; but the fact that it does this at precisely this point in American history demonstrates the strength of the US desire to see its efforts prevail and to envision even its failures as Hollywood, even epic, in scale.

This film is a reflection of complex contradictions found in the US in the period, and not simply, as some commentators have suggested, a condemnation of the war. In its bold approach, it embodies the emergence into the cultural arena of the confidence of a younger generation taking on the perceived failings of their parents. It attempts to confront the arrogance of US foreign policy and yet remains firmly and confidently US-centred in its offering of solutions. The sequence showing Kilgore's attack on the Vietnamese village is entirely conventional in Hollywood terms in its use of sound and cinematography to engender an atmosphere of gung-ho excitement; and yet it also employs the powerful juxtaposition of the cut to the peace, tranquillity and innocence of the village that is about to be attacked. We are given a full-on Hollywood experience only to end in the shadows of a cave with a madman searching for truth in an insane world ('Horror has a face and you must make a friend of horror'; 'To kill without judgement because it is judgement that defeats us'). It is not just that war is pointless and inhumane (and yet horribly human), but that there is something sick at the very heart of man; and this evil cannot be escaped but only faced and accepted.

Notes

1 Several photojournalists simply disappeared into the jungle in South East Asia in the period US forces were operating in the region. One of them, Sean Flynn, as the son of actors Errol Flynn and Lili Damita, had a

slightly higher profile than the others. He worked in both Vietnam and Cambodia, but was captured in Cambodia by the Viet Cong or Khmer Rouge in 1970 and is believed to have been killed in 1971.

2 Kurtz reading from *The Hollow Man* was added during shooting and was not in the original script from Milius.

3 There are few representations of women in the film. The Playboy 'chicks' 'choppered' in and then swiftly out of the first American base visited on the Mekong are conventional sex objects, and the disembodied, taped female voice playing at the death of 'Mr Clean' is that of the other traditional female figure of the mother.

4 The handmaidens of Odin who in Old Norse mythology rush into the confusion of battle on horseback and with swords drawn in order to carry off those selected for death; who are then taken to Valhalla as heroes.

5 See Frank P. Tomasulo, 'The Politics of Ambivalence: *Apocalypse Now* as a Prowar and Antiwar Film', in Linda Dittmar and Gene Michaud (eds), *From Hanoi to Hollywood: The Vietnam War in American Film*, New Brunswick, NJ, Rutgers University Press, 1990, pp. 145–58.

6 See the shot of the hand caressing the missile slung on the side of a helicopter as Kilgore's attack commences.

Further reading

James Clarke, *Coppola*, London, Virgin, 2003.

Eleanor Coppola, *Notes: On the Making of 'Apocalypse Now'*, London, Faber, 1995.

Peter Cowie, *The 'Apocalypse Now' Book*, London, Faber, 2000.

Linda Dittmar and Gene Michaud (eds), *From Hanoi to Hollywood: the Vietnam War in American Film*, New Brunswick, Rutgers University Press, 1990.

JOHN WHITE

BLADE RUNNER (1982)/BLADE RUNNER: THE DIRECTOR'S CUT (1992)

[Production Company: Warner Brothers. Director: Ridley Scott. Screenwriters: Hampton Fancher and David Peoples. Cinematographer: Jordan Cronenweth. Music: Vangelis. Cast: Harrison Ford (Rick Deckard), Rutger Hauer (Roy Batty), Sean Young (Rachael), Daryl Hannah (Pris), Edward James Olmos (Gaff), William Sanderson (J.F. Sebastian), Brion James (Leon Kowalski).]

Ridley Scott decisively changed the way we view the near future with *Alien* (1979) and *Blade Runner* (1982, 1992). Scott's films were perfectly judged for their times. George Lucas's *Star Wars* (1977) had drawn cinema audiences back to watching science-fiction features, which by the mid-1970s had become a genre that appeared to have no future on the big screen. Lucas re-cast sci-fi as a narrative offering epic thrills accompanied by the reassuring conventions of an earlier Hollywood moment. Steven Spielberg's *Close Encounters of the Third Kind* (1979) and *E.T., the Extra Terrestrial* (1983) triumphantly combined science fantasy with the director's own comforting, family-values aesthetic. But Scott's two contributions to the newly popular genre posed darker and deeper questions: what is within us that wishes to lock E.T. and the Alien in a room together, just to see what might happen?

Paul M. Sammon's *Future Noir: The Making of Blade Runner* (1996) is an exhaustive account of the film's creation, and a salutary reminder of the monumental complexities involved in shooting a major Hollywood feature. A multitude of talents and commitments has to combine successfully, and it seems invidious to focus on a single role or individual. But everyone who contributed to *Blade Runner* agreed it was the commitment and vision of its director that brought the film as we see it to the screen.

Ridley Scott was born in South Shields, Tyne and Wear, England, in 1937. He was one of the first students to attend the Royal College of Art's newly established film school in the late 1950s. After a spell in New York, he joined the BBC where he worked first as a set designer, and ultimately as a director for successful crime series such as *The Informer* and *Z-Cars*. In 1967, he moved into commercial advertising, going on to produce and direct over 2000 ads. His first feature film was *The Duellists* (1977), based on a story by Joseph Conrad. Conceived by Scott as a variant on the 'Western' and made for a mass audience, *The Duellists*, to the director's chagrin, was restricted on release to the art-house circuit, where it achieved limited but critical success, being highly praised for its visual flair. Scott's mainstream break-through came with *Alien* (1979), which confirmed his genius for creating complex visual environments that powerfully articulate the emotional world of their inhabitants.

In each of his films, perhaps revealing his art school origins and subsequent work in advertising, Scott controls art direction in all its aspects. His aim is to achieve a complex 'layering' of image; for Scott, 'a film is like a seven-hundred-layer layer cake' (Sammon 1996: 47). This visual complexity certainly contributed to *Blade Runner*'s eventual success. On its first release, the film did only moderately well at the box office, and critical response was confused. But again, the moment was propitious. The increasing use of video-players in the home meant that, for the first time, viewers could pause and re-run sequences from feature films at will, and the semiotic richness of *Blade Runner* seems to have invited this kind of scrutiny. When Deckard interrogates Leon's snapshot of his hotel room via Esper, the state-of-the-art police computer which, according to the film's production notes, enables 'investigators to search a room without even being there' (ibid.: 146), he was anticipating our paranoid world of contemporary surveillance, and the ways in which we now interact with virtual, digitized environments. In this scene, Deckard becomes a metonymy for the obsessive *Blade Runner* fan, pausing and poring over the imagery of each shot in the film, if not indeed a metaphor for the avid gaze of every engaged cinema audience, which has always dreamt of truly entering the illusory world before them.

Like *The Duellists*, *Blade Runner* is that rare film, a successful adaptation from an existing literary property. Philip K. Dick can quite accurately be described as a 'visionary' SF author – he experienced intense, altered states, in one of which he was convinced he was speaking with God. Dick's novel, *Do Androids Dream of Electric Sheep?* (1968), was in part a response to the corrupting influence of American involvement in Vietnam, then at its peak. But Philip K. Dick's radical unease with the world had older roots. While researching for his novel *The Man in the High Castle* (1962), which describes an America where National Socialist Germany and imperial Japan have won the Second World War, Dick came across the testimony of SS guards at death camps in Poland. One described how, to their annoyance, the soldiers were 'kept awake at night by the cries of starving children' (ibid.: 16). Dick became obsessed – not too strong a word – with the thought that any individual might begin to lose supposedly innate emotional responses to the point where they could not properly be described as 'human' any more. He explored this perception in short stories and novels over three decades, and linked it to a closely related worry: the possibility of creating perfect 'simulacra' through faultless replication. Where would true authenticity be located, in a world of perfectly copied objects and persons?

The combination, in *Blade Runner*, of Dick's existential concerns about the nature of the human essence, and Scott's complex visual intelligence, was again fortuitous. The film appeared at a transitional moment in the rarefied world of academic critical theory, where structuralist preoccupations with sign theory and semiotics from the 1960s and 1970s, under critique from deconstruction and gender-based analyses, were combining with the emergent disciplines of film and cultural studies. *Blade Runner* became one of the most rewarding 'film texts' through which to negotiate a transition from semiotics, via deconstruction and gender studies, to the emerging agenda of 'the postmodern', and whatever lay beyond (Žižek 1993). Scott's *'future noir'* seems to have judged the mood of its time astutely and, consequently, also became a key source of inspiration for William Gibson's novel *Neuromancer* (1984), masterpiece of the Cyberpunk generation. Following the release in 1992 of *Blade Runner: The Director's Cut*, widening interest in the film seemed to elide and fuse all distinctions between 'high' and 'mass-popular' forms of discursive attention. More recent attempts to discuss *The Matrix* in terms of current theory are facile by comparison.

One of the ways *Blade Runner* intrigues the audience is in its combination of a reassuringly familiar convention that is placed in a new and disconcerting context. Where Lucas and Spielberg evoked the values of classical Hollywood features to engage audiences, Scott characteristically drew on a darker heritage. Rick Deckard (Harrison Ford) is immediately recognizable as a 'gumshoe', a freelance detective straight out of 1940s Hollywood. Deckard's job description, as in the film title, was found by the screenwriter, Hampton Fancher, in a minor work by William Burroughs, who in turn may have taken it from Victorian underworld slang. As the hired assassin of desperate and dangerous androids, Deckard is a 'blade runner' in several senses, not least that he is himself poised dangerously on the knife's edge.

The replicants Deckard must destroy are 'intensified people', in crucial ways more human than the creatures of mere flesh-and-blood inhabiting Los Angeles of 2019. The brevity of the androids' (four-year) life-span gives them a sense of urgency and a pathos that are missing from the mundane lives of ordinary humanity. This vulnerability is quickly established with the first replicant, Leon (Brion James); constructed as no more than a brutal, low-grade operative, he is in search of the mother and childhood he never experienced, as if he feels the lack of the humanity denied him through his manufacture. Roy Batty, the Blake-quoting 'combat model' machine, has an admirable and insatiable desire for, precisely, 'more life'. Rutger Hauer, playing Roy, very acutely acted a kind of childish innocence through his role, which he described as 'this four-year-old thing' (Sammon 1996: 131).

Film theory has long recognized that female roles in cinema are constructed in markedly different ways to their male counterparts. There are no significant women's roles in *Blade Runner*, though Zhora, Pris and Rachael (Joanna Cassidy, Daryl Hannah, Sean Young), the three female-type soft machines, as 'intensified women', are supremely self-possessed and athletic, and in Rachael's case, a certain notion of femininity engineered to the extreme. Deckard's relation to the three replicant females becomes increasingly tortured as he destroys the first two and falls in love with the third. The manufactured perfection of the replicants perhaps seems even more thinkable now than it was in the early 1980s, given the startling twenty-first-century developments in DNA manipulation and gene therapy.

It seems entirely appropriate that there are 'essentially five different theatrical/video/laser disc cuts of *Blade Runner* which have been seen by the general public' (ibid.: 394), and all of these contribute to the endless play of 'undecidable' readings and response (Bukataman 1997: 82). The most widely circulated versions are the initial 1982 'International Cut' release, and the 1992 'Director's Cut', which was, in truth, another compromise between Scott and the studio. The two versions differ in ways that serve to cast doubt on the status of the central character: is it possible that Rick Deckard is also a replicant? The first version of the film was accompanied by a dominating voice-over, narrated by Deckard, in part a tribute to the jaundiced interior commentaries of 1940s film noir, in part a response to anxieties that the film's plot was too opaque and required explanation. This was removed in the second, 1992 release, rendering the action immediately more enigmatic. The first version's final escape sequence, in which Deckard and Rachael fly to the freedom of a far northern wilderness, and when Deckard reveals that Rachael has no 'termination date', was also removed in the later version.

The most troubling addition to the *Director's Cut* is Deckard's enigmatic dream vision of a unicorn, which he experiences after he has analysed Leon's snapshot. In the closing moments of the film, Gaff, Deckard's mysterious fellow blade runner, leaves a third and final origami creature where Rachael and Deckard must see it as they are about to leave; it is a unicorn. By this point Gaff has come to seem more like Deckard's handler than simply another operative. Deckard picks up the foil sculpture, smiles wryly, and nods. Is he acknowledging that Gaff knows his most private thoughts and day-dreams because they too are implanted? There is an earlier, perhaps more troubling moment when Gaff again mysteriously appears, immediately after Roy dies, and when he congratulates Deckard, saying, 'You've done a man's job, sir.' This too could be read as an 'authenticity test', in that replicant Deckard has succeeded in doing the work of a man.

Here *Blade Runner* echoes Shakespeare's *King Lear*, when the villainous Edmund is seeking to have Cordelia, Lear's daughter, murdered. The otherwise anonymous individual who agrees to commit this final tragic crime of the play says simply, 'If it be man's work I'll do it' (5.3.40). He strangles the innocent daughter, proving that such atrocities are indeed the work of men. Rick Deckard is an 'undecidable' role, perhaps more, perhaps less than 'a man', but since he is the tragic hero of the movie, we have followed and identified with him as an individual. In the final moments, this serves to turn all the questions back on ourselves: to what extent have we too become not much more than replicated beings?

Further reading

Scott Bukataman, *Blade Runner*, BFI Modern Classics, London, BFI, 1997.
Paul M. Sammon, *Future Noir. The Making of 'Blade Runner'*, London, Orion Media, 1996.
Slavoj Žižek, 'I or He or It (the Thing) Which Thinks', in *Tarrying with the Negative: Kant, Hegel, and the Critique of Ideology*, Durham, NC, Duke University Press, 1993.

NIGEL WHEALE

ALIENS (1986)

[Production Company: 20th Century Fox. Director: James Cameron. Screenwriters: Dan O'Bannon, Ronald Shusett, David Giler, Walter Hill and Cameron. Cinematographer: Adrian Biddle. Music: James Horner. Editor: Ray Lovejoy. Cast: Sigourney Weaver (Ellen Ripley), Carrie Henn (Rebecca 'Newt' Jorden), Michael Biehn (Cpl. Dwayne Hicks), Lance Henriksen (Bishop), Paul Reiser (Carter Burke), William Hope (Lt. Gorman), Bill Paxton (Cpl. Hudson), Jenette Goldstein (Pt. Vasquez).]

The fact that a film is part of a franchise can often detract from its individual strengths, with the sum seeming greater than the parts. That is until you encounter the *Alien* franchise where the second film *Aliens* (Cameron, 1986) rises far above the others. Setting the roadmap for sci-fi films for decades, Cameron offers not only a story well told and an adrenaline-fuelled special effects-filled romp, but also a film reflecting the corporate US society that produced it.

From the moment Ellen Ripley (Sigourney Weaver) is woken from the nightmares of a 50-year stasis and fears of alien impregnation, Cameron ceases to consider possible futures; instead he mirrors an American past and reflects on an uncertain present (an American present that has drawn into sharper focus today, allowing the film to have resonances for the contemporary audience). The story of a military 'rescue mission' that becomes embroiled in a deadly fight for survival despite its strength of technology and firepower, is one that enables this film to symbolize the latter half of the twentieth century.

Aliens was produced against a backdrop of right-wing politics and international conflict. The US was in the grip of Reaganomics with corporate America allowed free rein under the presidency of former actor Ronald Reagan, and in many respects international policy was determined by the financial interests of big business. Simultaneously, Reagan was playing hardball with his Soviet counterparts, Yuri Andropov and later Mikhail Gorbachev, in the final throes of the Cold War. America's ruthless and corrupt business approach to politics was seen in the Iran-Contra affair where it was revealed to be selling arms to Iran (a state it deemed a pariah) in order to fund the anti-communist Contras in Nicaragua. This political background can be seen in the philosophy of *Aliens'* Weyland-Yutani Corporation, embodied in Paul Reiser's portrayal of the über-sleazy corporate executive Carter J. Burke.

The nature of corporate America and its potential for destruction are central to the themes of *Aliens*. 'The Company' choose to ignore the dangers of the killer species discovered by the crew of the Nostromo in the first of the franchise films, *Alien*, and greed drives them to 'terraform' the planet, sending colonists to profit from this virgin territory. Ripley is dismissed as a fantasist as her story of the alien is seen as a risk to their corporate strategy and territorial expansionist aims. It is only when contact is lost with the colonists, that Ripley is put to company use as an advisor to the heavily armed Colonial Marines dispatched to 'deal' with the problem (perhaps the first film moment showing the true nature of the politico-corporate relationship in which a nation's military might is used to defend the interests of its business community).

The model for the marine incursion is undoubtedly the invasion of Grenada (1983), where the US military machine was employed in 'regime change' on a small Caribbean island. The model for its failure comes in part from the US peacekeeping mission to Lebanon where despite its military power, America was unable to contend with the 'alien' tactics of a guerrilla civil war. The second model for the disastrous marine operation comes in the Soviet occupation of Afghanistan (1979–89) where, again, a militarily advanced and numerically superior power suffered from the determination of an 'alien' culture. While undoubtedly the Vietnam War was in the back of Cameron's mind, there were clearly more current world events that were affecting the thematic development.

Ripley is often heralded as a feminist icon. Barbara Creed identifies the first film of the franchise as a key feminist text in her examination of the monstrous feminine,[1] while Carol Clover cites it as a central text in a feminist revision of the horror film.[2] Ripley is an empowered woman within the corporate world, but whether this was an expression of the advances of feminism, or an industrial tactic of reinventing a genre to appeal to particular audience segments (a trend evidenced through other films of the period such as *Working Girl* (Mike Nichols, 1988), *The Terminator* (James Cameron, 1984), *Outrageous Fortune* (Arthur Hiller, 1987), and *Near Dark* (Kathryn Bigelow, 1987), is debatable. Ripley's character could easily be transposed to a male with no effect on the delivery. Her 'adoption' of the child colonist Rebecca 'Newt' Jorden (Carrie Henn) is often presented as the feminizing of the lead role, but this is little more than the standard protectionist approach of the traditional hero. Cameron is not above utilizing the opportunities presented for voyeurism; not only is there a fetishizing sequence early in the film where Ripley's underwear clad body is segmented in lingering close-up, but she spends much of her time running around in a vest, with the same sexualizing purpose utilized in placing Bruce Willis in a vest in *Die Hard* (John McTiernan, 1988).

It is, perhaps, telling that many Hollywood films of the 1980s dealt with the authorities' inability to deal with new threats, and certainly in *Aliens*, the marines are seen as traditional American GIs who are gung-ho in their belief in their own superiority and firepower. Cameron makes a concession to the times by including a female marine (Private Vasquez, played by Jenette Goldstein) but falls into predictability by having her played as butch, with an inferred lesbian sexuality. A further concession comes when Vazquez is given the traditionally male role of self-sacrifice in order to save the rest of her team and the mission; injured and cut off, dragging her injured superior with her, she waits until the aliens are on top of them before detonating a grenade, saving Lieutenant Gorman and herself from impregnation, and killing several aliens.

The marines bring their doom upon themselves by not understanding their enemy and arrogantly ignoring intelligence in the form of the advice from their 'advisor' (Ripley), the only one to have survived contact with the aliens. Arriving on the planet, they find the missing colonists corpses cocooned in an alien 'nest' where they encounter a newly born alien 'chest-burster'. They immediately reveal their inability to adapt strategically to emerging threats by using a traditional approach (overwhelming firepower) to destroy the 'chest-burster', and in doing so stir the mature aliens in the nest who decimate their troop. It does not take a leap of imagination to draw parallels back to the Vietnam War and also (perhaps prophetically) forward to Iraq. The very location of the alien 'nests' (under the primary heat exchangers of the nuclear reactor) prevent the marines using their superior weaponry and render them impotent, offering a chilling foreshadowing of the situation in urban Iraq where much of the US military's weaponry became ineffective or impossible to use (without catastrophic 'collateral damage' and political fallout). It is not without note that when the solution to the 'bug hunt' is to 'nuke' the facility, Burke raises the 'substantial dollar value' of the facility and the political damage to all of their careers if they cause the Company such expense.

The marines are forced into a haphazard retreat where they are continually attacked from all sides, and their force is slowly eroded. Their fallback position of extraction is undermined when an alien accesses their escape vehicle and kills the pilot (another under-estimation of the enemy, this time leading to a special effects laden set-piece action sequence), leaving them to barricade themselves into the colonist's nuclear power station complex, surrounded by an unstoppable enemy. They retreat from the alien environment of the nest to the perceived safety of the familiar but discover (when the aliens come crashing through the floors and ceilings) that the security of their own world is soon overcome by an enemy that does not fight by the same rules, and does not have a concept of unacceptable casualties (this overwhelming, unstoppable wave of enemy fighters is a clear reference to the US experience in Vietnam).

Trapped in an unstable nuclear complex (another reflection of the fears of the time), the truly horrific immorality of corporate America is revealed through the actions of company-man Burke, who seals Ripley and Newt in a Medi-lab with two 'face-huggers', determined to get a 'sample' of the alien life-form back through quarantine and into the Company's research and development programme. To Burke, the aliens are not an enemy to be exterminated, but an opportunity, a resource to be exploited, no matter what compromises are needed. His character is a parallel to Lieutenant-Colonel Oliver North whose role in the Iran-Contra scandal rocking US politics at this time revealed the government's needs-led view of morality. Like North, Burke continues to promote the Company's interests even when his own duplicity is revealed; and his predilection towards self-preservation by playing one side off against another presents another commentary on the state of the US nation at that time. Equally interesting is the position the surviving members of the mission are placed in when deciding what to do with Burke, offering an insight into democracy's ineffectiveness when under threat – the decision on Burke is never made as the survivors come under sustained attack. Burke's mantra was surely that of members of the Reagan administration when their duplicity was uncovered, and of course the pressing demands of the 'attacks on democracy' prevented any significant decision on their fate.

Other than the relationships between the marines (the actors playing these parts all underwent British Special Air Service training – except for William Hope playing Lieutenant Gorman whom Cameron was determined should lack any bond with the rest), it is the female relationships that are the focus of the film. Ripley is maternal towards Newt, but the question is whether this is representative of the mothering instinct of woman or the selfishness of grief (Ripley's daughter died during her time in stasis). Newt is seen as fiercely independent and self-sufficient, surviving the alien attacks on the colonists, and it is only when she softens and accepts help from Ripley and the marines that she faces true peril, when Vasquez's noble suicide blows her down an airshaft and into alien captivity.

Cocooned, Newt's situation provokes Ripley to risk a rescue, one that brings her into her first direct confrontation with the Alien Queen. Here, in order to save her 'child', Newt, Ripley 'murders' the Queen's embryonic 'children' in their eggs, and so enrages the Queen that she attacks. Taking Newt back to the assumed safety of the orbiter, Ripley is forced to fight the Alien Queen to protect Newt. Mounted into a cargo 'power-loader' Ripley delivers the oft-quoted line 'Get away from her, you bitch', and is met with a screeched reply of 'pure lethality'[3] making a clear character distinction between the two 'mothers'. There is no small irony in the fact that Ripley saves herself and Newt from the Queen by using advanced technology provided by the Company.

Aliens begins with Ripley waking into a corporate nightmare, and ends with her taking Newt into restorative stasis, though, of course, with the unanswered question of whether Newt was impregnated when cocooned. The Company's plans defeated, democracy saved, and a franchise ready to replay the same battle on a different battle-ground next time, the ending presents the audience with a metafictional revelation of *Aliens'* commentary on corporate Hollywood's commentary on corporate America's take on US democracy and the military's own franchise.

Notes

1 Barbara Creed, *The Monstrous-Feminine: Film, Feminism, Psychoanalysis*, London, Routledge, 1993.

2 Carol Clover, *Men, Women, and Chainsaws: Gender in the Modern Horror*, Princeton, NJ, Princeton University Press, 1992.

3 James Cameron, *Aliens* first draft screenplay, accessed on http://www.godamongdirectors.com/scripts/aliens2.shtml

FREDDIE GAFFNEY

BLUE VELVET (1986)

[Production Company: De Laurentiis Entertainment Group. Director: David Lynch. Producer: Fred Caruso. Screenwriter: David Lynch. Cinematographer: Frederick Elmes. Editor: Duwayne Dunham. Music: Angelo Badalamenti. Cast: Kyle MacLachlan (Jeffrey Beaumont), Isabella Rossellini (Dorothy Vallens), Dennis Hopper (Frank Booth), Laura Dern (Sandy Williams), Hope Lange (Mrs. Williams), Priscilla Pointer (Mrs Beaumont), George Dickerson (Detective John Williams), Frances Bay (Aunt Barbara), Ken Stovitz (Mike), Brad Dourif (Raymond), Jack Nance (Paul), Dean Stockwell (Ben), J. Michael Hunter (Hunter), Jack Harvey (Tom Beaumont), Dick Green (Don Vallens), Fred Pickler (The Yellow Man), Philip Market (Dr Gynde).]

One of the most important American films of the 1980s, *Blue Velvet* has bewildered and divided audiences since its release. A mystery film that hardly bothers to solve its crime, a teenage love story with sadomasochism, a film that completely remakes the meaning of the songs on its needle-drop soundtrack, *Blue Velvet* seemed completely original to most moviegoers when it appeared in 1986. The film has proven so influential that one could say it changed the tone of a certain kind of US cinema, broadening the art film beyond the domain of European filmmakers and preparing the way for the American independent films to come in the 1990s.

At first, the film inspired either lavish praise or outrage and disgust. While some critics gushed about the film's greatness (J. Hoberman, Pauline Kael), others found its violence unredeemable (Roger Ebert). Initial theatrical audiences famously squirmed in their seats, yelled at the screen, or walked out in droves, even while others sat transfixed and dumbstruck. *Blue Velvet* is that rare thing: a film that has the genuine ability to shock and haunt the viewer. In the context of the

1980s, *Blue Velvet* stood out; its moderate success at the box-office demonstrated that a segment of the commercial audience in the US would occasionally be receptive to challenging material. In the context of the 2000s, it has become clear that this is one of the more accomplished American films of the past few decades, a film that is trickier than it seems.

To the uninitiated (or analysis-averse), film criticism sometimes seems redundant, an exercise in rehashing what already appears so obvious. Lynch himself encourages this sort of untutored attitude, always attributing his method to intuition. When speaking of his films, he has said, 'I don't know what a lot of things mean. I just have the feeling that they are right or not right.' [1] However, Lynch's films are anything but naïve; in fact, they virtually cry out for interpretation. While many things in *Blue Velvet* seem plain and clear, this bluntness is in fact one of Lynch's techniques, and it is anything but simple. The film opens with a famous montage of happy small-town life complete with white picket fence, bright red and yellow flowers, and waving fireman, only to descend into the dirt and insects swarming underneath the neatly mown grass. Thus, in the first four minutes, the film announces that it will unearth the dark underbelly of American life. In case we didn't get it, the film's protagonist Jeffrey Beaumont says later: 'I'm seeing something that was always hidden.'

This kind of symbolic obviousness is a signature Lynch trait, and once one understands that this film can and should be read flatly, what feels disquieting begins to look quite logical. Dorothy wears a wig: she is deeply uncomfortable, and wants to disguise herself. A bird holds a worm in its mouth at the film's conclusion: Sandy's sunny dream-world perspective has won out, but the dark side is still present. These heavy-handed symbols reflect Lynch's interest in banality and naïveté. But despite the obviousness, there is still that uneasy feeling, and this is the important thing: the film's effect. If 1980s audiences were already well able to interpret obvious meanings in film, today's audiences are even more suspicious of such blatant symbols. *Blue Velvet* works with its audiences' knowing gaze, enticing us in with familiar images, and then disorienting us by making those familiar images seem strange. In more ways than one, *Blue Velvet* disturbs with its peculiar explicitness.

Despite these moments of apparent transparency, and perhaps because of its powerful effect, *Blue Velvet* (like all of Lynch's work) has been subjected to many different interpretations, and a veritable cottage industry of Lynch analysis has sprung up over the decades. Depending on who one reads, *Blue Velvet* is a critique of American suburban life, or it demonstrates the Freudian concepts of the Oedipus Complex or the Primal Scene, or it enacts violence against women, or it depicts a child's eye dream of sexuality, or it is a brilliant example of postmodern cinema, replete with references to film history and popular culture – and so forth. And certainly, *Blue Velvet* is a postmodern film, filled with references to film noir (with its moodiness, crime, and a mysterious woman at the centre of the plot) and to other films (*The Wizard of Oz* [Victor Fleming, 1939], *Night of the Hunter* [Charles Laughton, 1955], and *It's a Wonderful Life* [Frank Capra, 1946]). Despite these influences, however, *Blue Velvet* manages not to feel like an empty exercise in referentiality, but instead it creates an effect that is powerful and distinct. Part of the film's singular importance is due to the way it resonates with so many cultural hot points – and yet despite all this, it still holds together as a tightly woven, formally brilliant film.

So: the film unearths the dark underbelly of small-town American life, yes, but there is more to it than that. Rather than locating its crime and horror in an outside location, the film finds the dark side at home, in Lumberton, literally in the family garden. *Blue Velvet*'s reinterpretation of familiar places (home), familiar stories (the crime film or film noir), and familiar characters (the small-town boy, the girl next door) makes banal things look perverse. As several writers have pointed out, this is precisely a dramatization of the uncanny: making the familiar look unfamiliar. A phantasm of American family-values ideology, *Blue Velvet*'s sunny small-town world has been dubbed 'Lynchtown' by critic Michel Chion, and it can also be found in several of Lynch's other works, especially his 1990–91 television programme *Twin Peaks*. It is well known that the places Lynch dramatizes are often amalgams of his childhood home – Spokane, Washington, in particular. But Lynchtown is more an imagined place than a real place; Lynch masterfully exploits the cinema's ability to create uncanny locales that feel one step removed from reality, and the point seems to be this: in Lynchtown, despair is all the more horrible because it is found at home. What's more, the evil in *Blue Velvet* is not merely personified by the town psychopath Frank Booth, who rapes and kills and cuts off ears; the same drives are also revealed inside Jeffrey, who, like Frank, hits Dorothy during sex. 'You're like me', Frank says to Jeffrey, and this is the truth that makes Jeffrey cry.

For years, the film was vilified by feminists for its depiction of violence against women – and from a certain perspective, rightly so, for the film does not apologize for its characterization of Dorothy Vallens, a woman who is brutally abused, and seems to enjoy it. The film has been criticized for dramatizing all the masculine biases of the Oedipal dynamic: Dorothy functions primarily as a spectacle (she performs in a nightclub, she is spied on by Jeffrey), and she embodies every cliché about mysterious, incoherent femininity. Sandy, on the other hand, may be intelligent and just as interested in solving the crime as Jeffrey, but she is so buttoned-up and square that she functions as Dorothy's opposite, the other half of the film's all-too-familiar binary construction of woman as either virgin or whore. On the other hand, this too can be interpreted as part of the film's encounter with the familiar – the virgin/whore dynamic is not questioned by the film, for certainly *Blue Velvet* makes no pretence at political consciousness, but rather this familiar constellation serves as the stable ground of stereotype, if you will, that allows the film to take its viewer into forbidden realms of sexual desire and dread.

The question remains, however, whether *Blue Velvet*'s use of familiar, even clichéd, motifs is ironic or sincere, and this point of tension is where the film most seems to confound its audience in the current moment. Many viewers today feel that the film's depiction of the sunny side of life (the neatly mowed lawns, Sandy's dream about the robins) is merely a parody, and they find the mechanical bird with the worm at the end of the film to be a mocking joke that subverts the conservatism of this robotically happy world. However, some critics have questioned this interpretation, arguing instead that while the film does contain some irony, it is mostly sincere, that Sandy's dream of robins is not a parody but a genuine alternative to the horror of Dorothy's life. At least one film scholar has perceptively tied this sincerity-in-irony tone to a post-punk aesthetic that conjoined the profane and the sincere: 'Lynch's films were among the first to move beyond postmodernism's ironic, parodic appropriation of historical genres and narrative conventions ... to this day readings of Lynch as "ironic" persist because irony has become the dominant form of reading in [our] culture.'[2] In other words, even though one can easily interpret *Blue Velvet*'s happy ending as ironic, it might be more intriguing to instead consider the implications of the film's potential sincerity. Again, such a reading privileges Lynch's interest in clichés, banality, and improper fantasies. As irony moved into the mainstream by the 1980s, Lynch was already way ahead of the irony game; although there is currently much disagreement on this point, it has become apparent to some viewers today that this is a film that disturbs with its sincerity.

Finally, one cannot discuss this film without mentioning its sound track. From the moment Jeffrey Beaumont first discovers the severed ear in a vacant lot, this film announces itself as concerned with sound. Sound effects are hugely important in this film, but even more innovative is the film's use of music. Pop music soundtracks had become increasingly common since late 1960s films such as *The Graduate* (Mike Nichols, 1967) and *Easy Rider* (Dennis Hopper, 1969) made them popular. In the 1980s, films such as *The Breakfast Club* (John Hughes, 1985) and *Pretty in Pink* (Howard Deutsch, 1986) used pop music to quickly evoke a teenage emotional landscape; in these films, the audience is moved in synch with the music. In contrast, *Blue Velvet* uses music against the grain, so to speak, evoking a familiar mood in order to reinterpret it. When Ben sings 'In Dreams', for example, the wistful sadness of the melody and lyrics take on a sinister, sexually ambiguous element due to Dean Stockwell's amazingly inscrutable performance. Lynch did not invent this technique, but borrowed it from Kenneth Anger's seminal experimental film *Scorpio Rising* (1964), which had revolutionized the use of pop music in film decades earlier. *Blue Velvet* uses songs from a previous era, a practice that is much more common now than it was in the 1980s (see *The Squid and the Whale* [Noah Baumbach, 2005], or any of Wes Anderson's films). All the major songs in *Blue Velvet*, in fact, were popular in 1963 when Lynch was 17 years old, which adds to the film's strange sense of nostalgia. While most movies today still use music as an ancillary element, a backdrop that merely accompanies the visuals, *Blue Velvet*'s music is anything but subordinate to the images; rather, Lynch uses music as a discrete component that is just as crucial in shaping the film's meaning as the visuals. This use of pop music as counterpoint has rarely been equalled in commercial American cinema.

Notes

1 Laurent Bouzereau, '*Blue Velvet:* An Interview with David Lynch', *Cineaste*, Vol. 15, No. 3, 1987, p. 39.
2 Nicholas Rombes, 'Blue Velvet Underground: David Lynch's Post-Punk Poetics', in Erica Sheen and Annette Davison (eds), *The Cinema of David Lynch: American Dreams, Nightmare Visions*, London, Wallflower Press, 2004, p. 72.

Further reading

Michael Atkinson, *Blue Velvet*, London, BFI, 1997.
Michel Chion, *David Lynch*, trans. Robert Julian, 2nd edn, London, BFI, 2006.

Lynne Layton, '*Blue Velvet:* A Parable of Male Development', *Screen*, Vol. 35, No. 4, Winter 1994, pp. 374–92.

David Lynch, *Lynch on Lynch*, ed. Chris Rodley, London, Faber and Faber, 1997.

JENNIFER PETERSON

SEX, LIES, AND VIDEOTAPE (1989)

[Production Company: Outlaw Productions. Director: Steven Soderbergh. Screenwriter: Steven Soderbergh. Cinematographer: Walt Lloyd. Music: Cliff Martinez. Editor: Steven Soderbergh. Cast: James Spader (Graham Dalton), Andie MacDowell (Ann Bishop Mullany), Peter Gallagher (John Mullany), Laura San Giacomo (Cynthia Patrice Bishop).]

sex, lies, and videotape has come to be seen as a paradigm of independent filmmaking through its use of long takes, real locations and emphasis on relationships dissected in dialogue-heavy scenes and because it was directed, edited and written by one person, making it a fairly clear example of *auteur* filmmaking. Its reputation is also bound up with that of the Sundance Film Festival – then known as the US Film Festival.

While *sex, lies, and videotape* is now perceived as the archetypal Sundance film, this was not the case at the time. The Sundance Institute (a 'not-for-profit' organization set up by Robert Redford to help independent filmmakers develop projects) was more associated with a style of independent cinema which dealt with politics and social issues often set in areas ignored by the mainstream – the Mid-West, Northern and Southern states. The regional emphasis, coupled with what to critics was often a tedious, 'politically correct' worthiness, led to the term 'granola' films which appealed to a niche, politically-engaged, older audience. Whether the festival was changing and *sex, lies, and videotape* was a symbol of this or whether the success of the film – critical and commercial – forced a change at the festival and therefore within the wider context of independent cinema is debatable. Evidence for the latter argument is found in the difficulty the producers of the film faced getting it accepted for the competition and in the fact that it won the Audience – not the Grand Jury – Prize. (It was also true that the festival was close to bankruptcy and needed to attract more commercial distributors if it was to make a profit.)

The institutional context of independent films in the late 1980s was very different to the current situation of global conglomerates with an 'independent' arm (e.g. Time Warner's New Line, Universal's Focus Features). The few independent producers operating in the 1980s existed outside of the studio system and either went bankrupt or moved into distribution – acquiring the rights for completed films. The division between independent and mainstream film was still apparent during this period: *sex, lies, and videotape* is often cited as one of the films which helped to blur the distinction.

In contrast to contemporary 'independent major' films, it is tempting to consider the 1980s as a golden age of committed independent cinema (in some respects this is true with the emergence of directors like Jim Jarmusch, Spike Lee, John Sayles). However, even then the label 'art film' was seen as extremely detrimental to a film's possibility for distribution. Independent films gained attention and exhibition at festivals and art-house cinemas in cities but rarely found wider distribution. One catalyst for change in independent film marketing and distribution was Miramax – a distribution company founded by Bob and Harvey Weinstein who recognized the potential crossover appeal of a certain style of independent filmmaking (e.g. *Pulp Fiction, Clerks, The Crying Game*). Their strategy of marketing to a mainstream youth audience can be seen in the campaign for this film which exploited the sensational nature of the title and the suggestion of 'adult' material in a way which may have misrepresented the actual subject matter. Instead of only showing at art-house screens in New York and Los Angeles, *sex, lies, and videotape* was released on over 500 screens across the country. Their strategy made the company successful but some critics, actors and filmmakers accused Miramax of watering down the independent sector, making it indistinguishable from Hollywood 'product'.[1]

In addition to the new distribution context of independent cinema, the success of this film can also be attributed to subject matter and characters. The themes – desire, alienation and repression – embodied the emerging post-feminist identity politics of the period with the emphasis on gender and sexuality. The social and political analysis previously expected from this type of filmmaking is distilled into an opposition of corrupt materialism versus stripped-down authenticity. These positions are personified by the two male leads; John, the 'yuppie' lawyer, and Graham, the student-like, unemployed drifter. This opposition is not just to do with money and objects, it is also applied to relationships between characters, such as in John's 'ownership' of Ann (in fact, Ann's situation as a suburban housewife convinced by her husband that she can't cope with the world is reminiscent of 1970s feminist popular fiction). The lack of an explicit political or social context, beyond the 1980s iconography of business success, is one area of criticism of the film as well as an indicator of the future direction of independent cinema.[2]

The character of Graham (whose anxiety about having more than one key on his key-ring as it is a sign of owning too much is incomprehensible to John) is a counter to the world of Reaganomics and the belief that 'greed is good'. Graham is a new kind of representation of masculinity in American cinema; sensitive, analytical, passive (in fact, impotent) and therefore feminized. He is, though, also heterosexual and the focus of desire for the two female characters. Graham because of, rather than despite, his hobby of filming women talking about their sexual experiences, is the masculine 'ideal', a precursor of the 1990s 'new man' phenomenon.

The film's form – narrative structure and film language – reveals the way the film organizes these themes and creates meaning for the audience. The organization of events is highly schematic using repetitions of setting (characters' homes, the bar and John's office), action and events (a succession of visits between characters and the repeated giving of gifts – often plants). The most explicit example of repetition is the series of conversations which constitute the world of the film and tend to be closer to interviews due to their stylized form. These culminate in Graham's interviews with the women which make up his video collection.

Ann's narrative journey is also signified by interviews as she moves from being the interviewee to the interviewer, from being scrutinized to using film to examine the motives of others. The first shot of Ann is an extreme close-up (in a film dominated by mid-shots certain characters are privileged through the use of close-up) in her psychiatrist's office. Her face is open, defenceless and questioning, and the close-up allows the audience to study her, much as the psychiatrist and then Graham do, in a way that could be described as voyeuristic. The emphasis on Ann as the central character is reinforced through the use of omniscient narration; a way in which the filmmaker controls narrative information to allow the audience to know more than the character does. In the opening minutes the audience is told, through a variety of explicit and implicit techniques, that Ann's husband is having an affair (with her sister), that their marriage will end and that she will form a bond with the stranger (Graham) whose visit she is dreading. This way of addressing the audience creates identification with Ann; we feel sympathy for her as her ignorance makes her appear vulnerable.[3] The omniscient narration continues throughout. Sometimes the audience's extra knowledge is short-lived; we only solve the enigma of the videotapes minutes before Ann (although this is long enough for us to feel protective of her). Other examples last nearly the length of the film; Ann's discovery of her betrayal by her sister and husband comes only at the climax of the narrative. By the end, though, when she uses the video-camera to interview Graham, rather than being the object of the audience's (and the character's) gaze, she has equal knowledge with the audience.

The interview in the psychiatrist's office is followed by the first actual meeting between Graham and Ann (although for the viewer the two have already 'met' through the use of cross-cutting). Graham's first appearance shows him washing in the men's room of a gas station and changing from one black shirt to an identical one. This immediately signifies him as someone who has rid himself of extraneous objects; he is an answer to Ann's question about what to do with all the garbage. The new setting reveals another form of repetition – Ann's living room is a mirror image of the psychiatrist's office with Graham in the doctor's chair.[4] Ann is sitting on the edge of the sofa, looking at the floor, framed at an extreme angle in contrast to the previous straight ahead, open shot; suggesting she is more nervous in her own home than the psychiatrist's office. This meeting between the two lead characters is crucial in further telling the audience about their compatibility. This is achieved partly through the awkward, but also intimate, speech but particularly through the shots and editing. The sequence is filmed conventionally for a conversation using continuity editing – specifically shot–reverse shot – but within this it reflects the relationship between the two. The shots signify equality between the characters with both being given close-ups and similar shot duration. It initially seems that the camera remains static but in fact it does move and the slowness and brevity of the movement make it charged with meaning. As Ann struggles to explain why she likes being married to John, the shot cuts away from her to Graham, the camera then tracks back almost imperceptibly away from her and towards him. This suggests the dominance Graham has in this conversation but also gives a visual representation of the way Ann is drawn to him. This movement is then repeated, this time moving away from a close-up of Ann to create an empty space next to her, signifying the reality of her experience and undercutting her words about her happy marriage. This is reinforced in the final image of the scene, a high-angled shot of the living room showing her alone and isolated.

The way the camera moves in this scene, the way it travels towards and then draws back from the characters, evokes the atmosphere of desire in the film. This is also apparent in the composition and choreography of shots; when Ann helps Graham go house-hunting, they continually move around the house, they are never in the same part of the frame and are kept physically separate by a partition. Immediately after this they are at a restaurant, now on either side of the table with the camera repeating its movement away from the characters. This tentativeness of *mise-en-scène* and mise-en-shot in representing Ann and Graham is in direct contrast to the depiction of John and Cynthia. The style provokes in the audience a feeling of tenderness towards the main characters, a hope for their happiness which is fulfilled in the final shot of the film; a calm, contemplative framing of the two sitting close together, arms touching. The recognition of this style is also to be aware of the filmmaker's presence as an artist and organizing influence on the audience's beliefs and responses.

Notes

1 For a detailed account of Miramax's distribution of *sex, lies, and videotape*, see Biskind (2004).
2 Although the central theme of the film – the importance of desire rather than consummation – can be read in the context of AIDS.
3 This also creates much of the humour: Ann's comment about the state of her and John's sex-life ('Lately, I've been curious at how things have slacked off ... ') plays over a scene of John and Cynthia engaged in energetic sex.
4 The motif of 'reflections' is also clear in the casting: John and Cynthia are mirror images of each other.

Further reading

Peter Biskind, *Down and Dirty Pictures: Miramax, Sundance and the Rise of Independent Film*, London, Bloomsbury, 2004.
Anthony Kaufman (ed.), *Steven Soderbergh: Interviews*, Jackson, University Press of Mississippi Press, 2002.
Steven Soderbergh, *Further Adventures of the Luckiest Bastard You Ever Saw*, London, Faber and Faber, 1991.
Steven Soderbergh, *sex, lies, and videotape*, London, Faber and Faber, 1990.

SARAH CASEY BENYAHIA

DO THE RIGHT THING (1989)

[Production Company: A Forty Acres and a Mule Filmworks Production. Director: Spike Lee. Producer: Spike Lee. Co-producer: Monty Ross. Screenwriter: Spike Lee. Cinematographer: Ernest Dickerson. Editor: Barry Alexander Brown. Music: Bill Lee, featuring Branford Marsalis. Cast: Danny Aiello (Sal), Ossie Davis (Da Mayor), Ruby Dee (Mother Sister), Richard Edson (Vito), Giancarlo Esposito (Buggin' Out), Spike Lee (Mookie), Bill Nunn (Radio Raheem), John Turturro (Pino), Paul Benjamin (ML), Frankie Faison (Coconut Sid), Robin Harris (Sweet Dick Willie), Joie Lee (Jade), Miguel Sandoval (Officer Ponte), Rick Aiello (Officer Long), John Savage (Clifton), Samuel L. Jackson (Mister Señor Love Daddy), Rosie Perez (Tina), Roger Guenveur Smith (Smiley), Steve White (Ahmad), Martin Lawrence (Cee), Leonard Thomas (Punchy), Christa Rivers (Ella), Frank Vincent (Charlie).]

Do The Right Thing opens to the strains of a soprano saxophone rendition of James Weldon Johnson's 'Lift Every Voice and Sing'. The song ends screen black and the title sequence begins with Public Enemy's 'Fight The Power' and cut to a stage. Evoking the conceit of the film musical's opening number, the sequence features the hiphop dance of Rosie Perez in different costumes against a changing backdrop of Brooklyn photographs backlit by an array of color schemes. This opening montage is cut to match the movements of Perez's dance, a dance of militancy and popping contractions with a face that never smiles.

Based on a poem by James Weldon Johnson, 'Lift Every Voice and Sing' debuted in 1900 and was dubbed the 'The Negro National Anthem' by the National Association for the Advancement of Colored People (NAACP) in 1919. The NAACP promoted the use of the song as a celebration of the black lifeworld and expressive culture, and also as an important anthem for the struggle against anti-black racism. Moreover, the use of the song during the Civil Rights Movement and its eventual retitling ('The Black National Anthem') continued the valuable purposing of the song as emblem of black culture and protest. Public Enemy offers an alltogether different anthem, clearly less reconciled to the Christian doctrine of social protest and non-violence. While the first song offers the perseverance of faith and belief in inalienable rights, the latter demonstrates a cultural nationalist tact, a more highly politicized sense of culture and the black lifeworld. Cultural nationalism shifts the hermeneutics of race from the realm of the biological and experiential to a culture of action that framed anti-hegemonic struggle against anti-black racism and whiteness as the fundamental terms for the embodiment of black personhood. Moreover, the distance between the poles is made plainer with the modal of hiphop modernism and not that of the sacred verse of gospel. 'Fight the Power' offers a sobering and artful discontent from streets far removed from Birmingham, Alabama, but a relation nonetheless.

The opening sequence of the film functions as *Do The Right Thing*'s dialectical claim of a political art inflected by multiple black historiographies of struggle. Anti-realist in its stance, the film positions itself in the matrixing contest of black representation. Significantly, the film employs the conceit of a 24-hour period on the hottest day of the year in the Brooklyn neighbourhood of Bedford-Stuyvesant ('Bed-Stuy'). This plotting amplifies the masterful way the film functions as a discrete representational system. This affect of the seamless accounting of the day on the block through continuity editing is facilitated by such things as Mister Señor Love Daddy's radio broadcast, color, physical movements, emblematic framing, an intricate orchestration of ensemble casting in the depth of field, and sound bridges. Through the deliberateness of the film structure, one learns to watch the film and recognize the spatiality of the setting. Eventually, one recognizes that at one end of the block are Mookie and Jade's building, Mother Sister's brownstone, the Korean-run grocery, and across the street against the red wall are the corner crew (Sweet Dick Willie, ML, and Coconut Sid). At the other end of the block, starting across from the grocery are Sal's Famous Pizzeria, the stoop where the Puerto Ricans sit, the station home for 108FM 'We Love Radio', and the brownstone owned by the Celtics fan.

The cohesiveness of this spatial conceit does not comply with the empty platitudes of Our Town, USA. The film proves that the most rewarding consequence of America as 'The Melting Pot' is that the analogy does not work. We the people are not the same, we have different cultures and systems of belief. Our differences represent at times collateral interests but never truly identical ones. In this way, the interethnic conflicts that circulate throughout the block are but a red herring. The film evinces a great deal of investment in complicating the matter of the continued imagineering of America. In this way, *Do The Right Thing* vitally avoids the classical tact of the social problem film to present the problem of differences in such a way that these problems never appear systemic or fundamentally a result of the idea of America itself. This means that these staged eruptions of conflict are resolved and contained with a tacit framing of our spectatorship in terms of an analyst/analysand and dynamic and enacted cures. As Michael Rogin writes,

> Hollywood, inheriting and universalizing blackface in the black-face musical, celebrated itself as the institutional locus of American identity. In the social problem film it allied itself with the therapeutic society. Generic overlap suggests institutional overlap; Hollywood was not just Hortense Powdermaker's dream factory, but also the American interpreter of dreams, employing roleplaying as national mass therapy.[1]

Social problem films with race as an object usually enact a limited and circumspect sense of social problem-solving. In particular, the way these films are saddled with the extra-diegetic responsibilities of reconciliation between the races promotes a dangerously ridiculous sense of film as social policy. After all, what James Baldwin called the 'price of the ticket' should mean more than matinee admission. *Do The Right Thing* poignantly demands that spectatorship entail a recognition of our respective subject positions and/or complicities in a very productively non-patronizing way.

The central conflict of *Do The Right Thing* cycles around the issue of *How come they ain't no brothas on the wall?* Buggin' Out is outraged by the absence of black representation on the pizzeria wall. The boycott he organizes against Sal's develops over the 'Wall of Fame', a collage of photographs devoted to Italian Americans. The call for economic sanctions echoes the use of these strategies throughout the twentieth century by churches, unions, and civic leaders as a way of challenging the economic disenfranchisement of anti-black racism. This call of representation is emblematic of a diacritical sense of value. First, there is the value suggested by economic empowerment of a raced consumer-citizen. Second, there is the measure of culture as value; as significa-tion. In this way the central conflict that accrues over the course of the film becomes that of the political and cultural value of blackness.

However, the ensemble vessel for this amalgamation of civil dis-obedience and cultural nationalism is far from sound. Buggin' Out does not represent a clear political programme or plan of black eco-nomic development. His persona is that of empty cultural nationalist rhetoric; more hothead than firebrand. Radio Raheem lumbers and speaks like a heroic throwback from the mind of Jack Kirby. A laco-nic giant, his voice is of course embodied in 'Fight the Power' that constantly blares from his boombox. His 'Love vs. Hate' direct address constitutes the most that he ever speaks. At once it is a gesture to the absurd holy roller ways of Robert Mitchum's itinerant honeymoon killer in *Night of the Hunter* (Charles Laughton, 1955). Yet, this sense of latent struggles of good and evil *ad infinitum*, coupled with Raheem's devotion to the gospel of Public Enemy frame him as a complicatedly textured figure. He wanders throughout Bed-Stuy spreading the word, battling any and all windmills along the way. Every interaction is a contest and exclamation of his being. Finally, closing out the rebel band is Smiley. Semi-retarded and physically spastic, Smiley's speech is as indecipherable as the irreconcilable coupling of Malcolm X and Martin Luther King Jr. in the photograph postcards he peddles. Stumbling through the film, Smiley marker tags his cherished wares with a crudely imitative, Basquiat flair.[2]

This crisis of representation, emblematic of this rebel ensemble, embodies and enacts the necessary tensions surrounding the political question of black representation and film as an art practice. Specifically, what is the purpose of the term 'black film'? Does it represent an entirely foreign film practice? Is it merely a reflection of black people; not art but simply black existential dictation? In this way, it is vital to keep in mind that the 'black' of black film should not be thought of as an absolute indexical tie to the social category of race. Fundamentally, if you need to see yourself, look in a mirror and not at a screen. The 'black' of black film is a term for the art of film that enacts the visual and expressive culture of blackness, a critical term of aesthetics, epistemology, and the signification of race. Even from the first few minutes of the film, this rich complication is evident as the film addresses and provokes the tensions between politics and aesthetics, as well as the social category of race and art as creative political interpretation. The film demonstrates an acute sense of blackness as an epistemological art.

This alienation effect of the film plays out most poignantly with the final sequence of Radio Raheem's murder by the police. The broken band of rebels storm the pizzeria and what becomes canted and absurd becomes accelerated. Sal begins a nigger litany and the bat signals Howard Beach and kills the anthem of 'Fight the Power' roaring from Raheem's box.[3] Yes, the film resonates with prejudices and interethnic conflict but it also shows an affection for the idea of communities constituted by ambivalences. Regardless, the confusion of this confrontation signals a shattering break. Things have gone too far and as Radio Raheem strangles Sal, pulling him over the counter, it spills into the street. The fight draws a crowd and eventually the police arrive. The hold is administered and Raheem is raised and lynched as his kicks wind down. Radio Raheem is dead.

A void appears in the quick exit of the police with a corpse and Buggin' in tow. There is the mournful calm of what has happened and how it has come to this. *Mookie they killed him. They killed Radio Raheem.* A divide appears, with Mookie, Sal, Pino, and Vito on one side and the witnesses from the neighbourhood frozen still, growing angrier in the street. Everyone is a stranger; everyone is revealed. *Murder. They did it again. Just like Michael Stewart. Murder. Eleanor Bumpers. Murder.*[4] The extradiegetic victims of murder at the hands of the police (not persons unknown) now have Raheem among their ranks. Mookie walks away before returning into this breach, throwing a garbage can through the plate-glass window. Fireman and police readied in riot gear arrive and the historical rupture is complete. Even in the absence of Birmingham's finest with German Shepherds at hand, Sweet Dick Willie makes it plain: *Yo where's Bull Connor?*[5] Smiley begins a new Wall of Fame in the wreckage, finally some brothers are on the wall. But, was this really what it was all about? Smiley with his ever-delirious and goofy visage appears to be the only one to have solved the mystery and claimed a victory.

The awkward final meeting of Mookie and Sal and the endorsement of David Dinkins by Love Daddy is met by the closing citations of King and X.[6] The offering of these two contrasting political positions as the closing bookend is one of the major reasons that the film continues to haunt, inspire, and provoke. For only there on the screen does their proximity hint at some kind of dialectical resolve or compatibility. Regardless, *Do The Right Thing* is a question masquerading in the form of a call to action. In other words, the film functions in a way too irresolute to be thought of as merely provocative protest. If the film is troubling, so be it. Killing the messenger has always been convenient, but it never truly disavows that a message was sent. *Always do the right thing. That's it? That's it. I got it, I'm gone.*

Notes

1 Michael Rogin, *Blackface, White Noise: Jewish Immigrants in the Hollywood Melting Pot*, Berkeley, CA, University of California Press, 1998, p. 221.

2 The photograph was taken on March 26, 1964, in the halls of the United States Capitol Building during Senate debates on the Civil Rights Bill. It documents the only meeting between the two men. A meeting that lasted only a few minutes.

3 On the evening of December 19, 1986, a group of black men entered a pizzeria in the Queens neighbourhood of Howard Beach seeking help after their car broke down a few miles away. Upon leaving, the men were confronted by a group of Italian Americans from the neighbourhood

armed with baseball bats. Attempting to escape from a continued beating by the mob, Michael Griffith was struck and killed by a car on the highway.

4 Michael Stewart was a New York City graffiti artist killed while in the custody of New York transit police (1983). Eleanor Bumpers was a black, mentally-ill senior citizen killed by NYPD officers aiding in her eviction from her home (1984).

5 Eugene 'Bull' Connor served as Public Safety Commissioner of Birmingham, Alabama, during the significant period of the Civil Rights Movement. A rabid white supremacist, Connor was responsible for the more brutal and violent responses to the desegregation campaigns spearheaded by the Southern Christian Leadership Conference.

6 David Dinkins would eventually become New York City's first black mayor (1990–93).

Further reading

Darby English, *How to See a Work of Art in Total Darkness*, Boston, MIT Press, 2007.

Ed Guerrero, *Do The Right Thing*, London, BFI Publishing, 2001.

Spike Lee with Lisa Jones, *Do the Right Thing*, New York, Fireside, 1989.

Paula Massood (ed.), *The Spike Lee Reader*, Philadelphia, PA, Temple University Press, 2007.

W.J.T. Mitchell, 'The Violence of Public Art: Do the Right Thing', *Critical Inquiry*, Vol. 16, No. 4, Summer, 1990, pp. 880–99.

MICHAEL B. GILLESPIE

THELMA AND LOUISE (1991)

[Production Company: Metro-Goldwyn-Mayer. Director: Ridley Scott. Screenwriter: Callie Khouri. Cinematographer: Adrian Biddle. Music: Hans Zimmer. Editor: Thom Noble. Cast: Susan Sarandon (Louise Elizabeth Sawyer), Geena Davis (Thelma Yvonne Dickinson), Harvey Keitel (Hal Slocumb), Brad Pitt (J.D.), Timothy Carhart (Harlan).]

Released in 1991, *Thelma and Louise* cost MGM a modest $16.5 million and was a rather unlikely bet for a mainstream Hollywood film. Callie Khouri's first screenplay, it was prompted by dissatisfaction with the way women were portrayed in Hollywood film:

> I wanted to write about two normal women ... I wanted to write something with strong women in it. ... that's another one of the things I've never seen dealt with in a film, the anger women feel about the way they're talked to.[1]

It was also inspired by an incident which resonates within the film's narrative:

> I was walking down the street, when this old guy in a car starts talking to me ... I'm ignoring him, which is what you're supposed to do in that situation ... Then he said, 'I'd like to see you suck my dick', and I just lost it for a second ... I walked over to the car and said, 'I'd like to shoot you in the fucking face.'[2]

In the pragmatic business world of Hollywood, the script stood no chance without an accredited director behind it. Ridley Scott had power in Hollywood due to the success of *Alien* (1979) and *Blade Runner* (1982) and his decision to direct the film made it a viable proposition. He recalls that 'the script ... had floated around for ages and fallen through the net ... You'd be amazed how many directors turned it down.'[3] Two strong female leads, an array of unattractive male characters, a generic mix of western and road movie which were generally considered 'male' genres and were not in fashion, plus a downbeat ending – certainly not reassuring ingredients for box office success. Scott was aware the subject matter needed careful handling if it was to succeed with a mainstream audience: 'I thought it should be really humorous and then you didn't ostracize two thirds of the audience.'[4] While this suggests Scott 'watered down' the script's feminist credentials to secure a mainstream audience, Khouri herself has commented that, if anything, he made the male characters less sympathetic than her originals:

> When you read the script you'll see that in *Thelma and Louise*, the male characters were portrayed in a way that was more caricatured on the screen than on the page. And that was a decision made by the male director and the male actors who played them.[5]

She is also ambivalent about the film's status as a feminist text: 'the issues surrounding the film are feminist. But the film itself is not.'[6]

Considering all these factors, the film's reception was surprising. An immediate hit with audiences, it made $45 million in the US and £4 million in the UK. Critical acclaim followed with an Oscar and a Golden Globe for the screenplay, and three further Oscar nominations.[7] The American popular press were equally fascinated by the film: *Time* magazine carried the headline, 'Why *Thelma and Louise* strikes a nerve'.[8] Subsequent critical debate even found its genre contentious: road movie, buddy movie, screwball comedy, rape-revenge narrative, western? This strange generic mix, the unlikely pairing of Khouri and Scott, and the 'feminist' issues mapped onto a mainstream Hollywood film, provide a framework for understanding the para-doxical and controversial response to the film.

The opening shot of the desert road stretching ahead to the hills is iconic of both the road movie and the western and encourages par-ticular generic expectations. It connotes not just the wide open spaces of the American West, but the freedom and self-determination coded into the myth of 'the West' and popularized by Hollywood. The first sequence (Thelma being bullied by Darryl in her dimly lit kitchen, and Louise waiting tables in a diner) resonates with ideas of entrap-ment because of its juxtaposition with the opening shot. The sense of forbidden territory is increased by the fact that to an audience familiar with Hollywood films such spaces are gendered: in both the road movie and the western, this is a predominately 'male' space.

Encounters along the road with a series of men are used to explore, as Hal Slocumb trenchantly puts it, all the ways women can be 'fucked over'. The road movie and the western are genres which explore the relationship between the individual and society, and related issues of freedom and justice. Here this is inflected specifically towards issues of power and gender. Each incident shows how men exert power over women: with brute physical force (Harlan), bullying and belittling (Darryl), emotional abuse (Jimmy), financial exploitation (JD), sexual harassment (the truck driver) and, in a more complex way, under the guise of fatherly protection (Hal, who betrays them to the FBI). The laws of society are portrayed as 'some tricky shit' and do not protect the women from abuse.

So far, so radical; but also present in the opening sequence are comic elements creating audience expectations which temper the seriousness of this message. The narrative structure and iconography of the road movie (long shots of the road, shots of the road through the rear-view mirror, the 'T-bird') mixed with western (mesas, desert scenery, the flight to Mexico, outlaws, Stetsons, bandanas, guns, the law) are undercut by the element of 'feminine' screwball comedy, evidenced by the appearance of the two women at the beginning of the film (Thelma's incompetent packing, their names, their witty badinage). This mix of genres complicates the ways in which we read the film. The very image of Thelma and Louise against the typical scenery of the western constantly reminds audiences that they are out of place, and the dialogue underlines this. The 'feminine' nature of their discourse juxtaposed against the setting and 'masculine' narrative in which they find themselves produces humour: comments such as

'Thelma, don't you litter!' and 'Would you do that to your mother or your sister?' are staples of motherly discourse but their displacement onto the narrative of the western/road movie (shootings, flight from the law, hold-ups) make them comically ludicrous, and paradoxically remind us these women are not *really* the outlaws the narrative seems to make them. This makes the female representations oxymoronic in ways which may reflect more truly the ambivalent position of women in society.

Scott's decision to emphasize the humour, pushing the male characters further towards caricature, is another way in which meanings are destabilized. The sharpness of the critique of male power is lessened and the audience can react to the encounters along the road with enjoyment, untroubled by the depressing lack of power which got the women into these situations or the dubious morality of their responses. Darryl stepping into his pizza, his exaggerated comic gestures on the phone to Thelma, the traffic cop's finger wiggling impotently through the bullet hole in his car, and the truck driver shaking his fists against the backdrop of his exploded vehicle ensure humour predominates and the very male power the narrative is criticizing is stripped of threat. The strongly cathartic element in some of the incidents: the shooting of Harlan, the blowing-up of the tanker and the 'Nazi' traffic cop reduced to an impotently weeping shadow of his former self, invert the usual power balance. This has an obvious appeal to women all too familiar with the status quo but the element of comedy enables the appeal to transcend gender. This combination of elements makes the film a heady and exhilarating mix: a powerful evocation of 'busting out of your life'.[9]

The attempted rape at the Silver Bullet is the only sequence devoid of a comic element. Here the film's exploration of gender and power is at its most bleak and literal. Positioned to share Thelma's distress, the powerlessness of women is at its most apparent. The appearance of the gun, as if by magic in the top right-hand side of the frame, stops the attack. Much controversy was aroused by the women's appropriation of that quintessentially male symbol, but this is the only point where the gun is used to kill. A symbol of power in the film, it is used primarily to question just how much power it bestows. Here it can stop the rape but it cannot change the attitude that led to it. Some critics felt that for women to use the gun to exert power was a pyrrhic victory for feminism, but the meanings which cluster around the image of the gun are more complex.

Although the attempted rape and the unspoken story of what happened to Louise in Texas are used to highlight the injustice of the law, it is what happens after the attack which really interests Khouri: even armed with a gun Louise is not taken seriously by Harlan and he continues to insult her. She shoots him because of this contempt ('I should have gone ahead and fucked her') and her final comment ('You watch your mouth, buddy') reflects this. This becomes a central and contradictory metaphor in the film: women may appropriate all the trappings of male power but they will never overturn the power balance. Part of the force of the film can be explained by the complexity of this one moment: it is at one and the same time a depressing acceptance of powerlessness, a fairytale ending to an ugly all too common female experience, the start of an adventure which make Thelma and Louise unlikely outlaws, and the beginning of Thelma's growth to self-knowledge, discovering 'her calling' and feeling more 'wide awake' then she ever has in her life.

Subsequent encounters along the road can be read as comic replays of the rape sequence. Each balances a recapturing of the 'feel-good' element with restating the stark fact that women have no real power. Thelma and Louise's attempt to get an apology from the male characters – the word echoes through the film, starting with Harlan ('You say you're sorry, or I'm going to make you sorry.') and ending with the truck driver ('We think you should apologize') – reasserts their femininity; they remain essentially 'nice' women, feminine in their demeanour, apologizing profusely as they go. They are parody mothers, on a mission to improve the manners of the men ('We think you have really bad manners'), but the fact is they have no power to make any of the men apologize, not even at gunpoint.

This makes their choice at the end a fitting conclusion: there is no place for them in this society. The law, represented by the hyperbolic display of male power facing them on the edge of the Grand Canyon, is uninterested in justice. However, to anyone who has seen the film this potentially depressing reading doesn't ring true to the experience of *watching* the film. The ambivalence of the ending with its tension between the essentially depressing representation of female powerlessness and its fairytale happy ending where the women 'just keep going' (emphasized by the use of the freeze-frame and the reprise of shots from earlier in the film) are in keeping with the rest of the film. The slow motion image of Hal, arm outstretched, forever trying to catch the women and forever doomed to fail, underlines their ultimate escape from male power and allows the audience to leave the cinema feeling uplifted rather than outraged. A great part of this film's power is to achieve the seemingly incompatible aims of both presenting a stark reality and providing an enjoyable escape from it.

Notes

1 Callie Khouri interviewed by David Konow, www.creativescreenwriting. com, accessed 2 February 2007.
2 'The Art of Visual Storytelling: Callie Khouri on Creating Character in *Thelma and Louise*', www.sydfield.com, accessed 2 February 2007.
3 'Ridley Scott Uncut', *Times Online*, timesonline.co.uk, accessed 2 February 2007.
4 Ibid.
5 Marita Sturken, *Thelma and Louise*, London, BFI, 2000, p. 20.
6 Ibid, p. 8.
7 Data from the Internet Movie Database (IMDb), accessed 9 May 2007.
8 Sturken, 2000, p. 20.
9 Ibid, p. 16

JEAN WELSH

DAUGHTERS OF THE DUST (1991)

[Production Company: Geechee Girls/American Playhouse. Director: Julie Dash. Producer: Julie Dash. Screenwriter: Julie Dash. Cinematographer: Arthur Jafa. Editors: Joseph Burton and Amy Carey. Music: John Barnes. Cast: Cora Lee Day (Nana Peazant), Alva Rogers (Eula Peazant), Barbara O (Yellow Mary), Trula Hoosier (Trula), Umar Abdurrahamn (Bilal Muhammad), Adisa Anderson (Eli Peazant), Kaycee Moore (Haagar Peazant), Bahni Turpin (Iona Peazant), Cheryl Lynn Bruce (Viola Peazant), Tommy Redmond Hicks (Mr Snead), Malik Farrakhan (Daddy Mack Peazant), Vertamae Grosvenor (Hair Braider).]

Daughters of the Dust, 'a lovely visual ballad about Sea Island blacks in 1902' is the first feature film by an African American woman to gain major theatrical distribution in the United States (Kauffman 1992). As an impressionistic narrative about a little-known Black linguistic community called the Gullah, *Daughters* could be seen as not merely an art film, but as a 'foreign language film' due to the characters' Gullah patois and Dash's unique film language. Dash said, 'We took an Afrocentric approach to everything: from the set design to the costumes, from the hair to the way the make-up was put on' (Boyd 1991). Further, Dash uses a style, which filmmaker Yvonne Welbon calls 'cinematic jazz'. It resonates with the fragmentary cultural forms associated with the use of collage (i.e. Romare Bearden, quilting traditions) in the African Diaspora. Such aesthetic choices typically run counter to normative American film practices, which are more likely to favour coherence and a trajectory of transformation. For example, classic Hollywood films tend to be characterized by close focus on a single leading white man, who faces clearly defined obstacles that he overcomes due to transformations in his character. By contrast, Dash uses a wide lens to capture many characters in long takes, emphasizing their relationships to each other and to cinematic space rather than exclusively showing them in action. In the film, there are 'no white people – that alone can be disturbing for some' (Jones 1992). Then, *Daughters'* editing pattern is marked by simultaneity-over-continuity, which is effected through the use of scenic tableaux. They show what characters are doing in different spaces at the same time, though not necessarily with the same implications of parallel editing where two lines of action are shown together in order to create dramatic tension. Finally, 'It was shot on super 35mm film so it would look better. And of course we used Agfa-Gevaert film instead of Kodak because black people look better on Agfa' (Boyd 1991). The prestige *Daughters* has gained since its 1991 release represents a significant achievement for Dash, African American film and culture, as well as American independent filmmaking in terms of both form and content.

Daughters concerns the fictional Peazant family, who are part of an actual ethnic community located among the Sea Islands, a region composed of barrier islands that extend along the Eastern coastline from South Carolina to Georgia. Most of the characters in the film are Gullah, a group that has been studied and celebrated for their unique African American culture. In terms of language, religion, and cuisine, the Gullah are said to have retained a greater degree of continuity with West African cultures than did the slaves on the mainland, due to their relative geographical isolation on the islands during slavery. Thus, *Daughters* is an essential African American text about key issues of migration and cultural retention. The film seeks both historical authority and poetic expressivity on questions of identity and location within black American culture, especially where they intersect with formations of black womanhood.

The film opens on a somewhat didactic note with opening titles that introduce viewers to the Gullah. By contrast, the sequence that follows mystifies acts of ritual and religion as well as fragments of family history through disjointed tableaux in which the viewer sees an unnamed fully clothed figure bathing in an undistinguishable body of water and a pair of hands releasing dust into the air. These poetic images, which represent the Gullah's 'old ways' are later explained through dialogue but initially they lend the film an exotic and mysterious impression. Subsequent sequences focus on the domestic. For all the visual richness and emotional intensity, the actual content is simple: the extended Peazant family makes preparations for a supper to mark the eve of their migration to the mainland. On this day of both crisis and celebration, introspection and confrontation, family members of different generations question each other about what will be lost and gained personally and culturally when they leave the islands. These narrative themes are analogous to the issues of identity and location that have preoccupied African American intellectual history in works such as W. E. B. DuBois's *The Souls of Black Folk* (1903). Dash condenses these broad concerns into the intimacy of family drama. The ambivalence the Peazants feel about the old ways and what new ways await them on the mainland permeates every scene. One of the ways this tension manifests is in the presence of visual technologies in the film.

The significant and repeated appearances of three visual devices constitute a motif, which embodies the film's reflexivity: the kaleidoscope, the still camera, and the stereoscope. The fact that these devices arrive from the mainland suggest a range of possible meanings from anxieties over documenting the self, the intrusion of observing eyes outside the community and the lure of new worldly pleasures on the mainland. In the film, the kaleidoscope acts as a metonym of *Daughters'* style. Mr Snead, who is the family photographer, introduces the kaleidoscope early in the film, describing it as a blend of science and imagination. Through point of view shots, spectators see the ways in which the kaleidoscope creates abstractions of shape, colour, and movement and they are aligned with the characters' delight in such formalist experimentation. These kaleidoscopic images refer to the film's impressionistic, fragmentary structure, which is composed of semi-discrete tableaux arranged in an elliptical or spiral pattern where images and themes return but not to the exact same place. These images contrast with the documentary function and style of Mr Snead's family portraits.

Meanwhile, the stereoscope, no less a device of the imagination, is used to introduce footage fragments possibly orphaned from a larger newsreel or ethnographic work. Whereas a man of science and the family documentarian introduces the kaleidoscope into the film, it is the mystical character of the Unborn Child (Kai-Lynn Warren) who uses the stereoscope. 'Sent by the ancestors to restore her father's faith in the old ways', this character is Eli and Eula's yet-to-be-born daughter, except that she appears from the future when she is about 8 years old; invisible to the other characters, only Mr Snead and the spectators can see her when he looks through his camera (Jones 1992). The Unborn Child transforms the use of the stereoscope. It was a late nineteenth-century entertainment used to create the illusion of a three-dimensional image, however, in *Daughters* it is an imaginative pathway for animating postcards into motion pictures, which perhaps represent the future that awaits the family when they migrate.

Started on a budget of $200,000, *Daughters* took ten years to complete, and finished with $800,000. In Dash's book *Daughters of the Dust: The Making of An African American Woman's Film*, she explains that her film took so long to complete in part because its structure, themes, and characters nonplussed industry representatives from whom she sought financing. Once *Daughters* was released, however, the film found its audiences and went on to receive a number of significant awards. Shot by Arthur Jafa, *Daughters* won best cinematography at the Sundance Film Festival (1991). The Black Filmmakers Hall of Fame recognized it as Best Film (1992) and that same year it received the Maya Deren Award from the American Film Institute. Dash's achievements and tenacity as independent director, writer and producer earned her the Oscar Micheaux Award from the Black Filmmakers Hall of Fame (1991). In 2004, *Daughters* was placed on the prestigious National Film Registry of the National Film Preservation Board. Defined by Dash as a black woman's film, *Daughters'* awards mark its status within intersecting independent, African American, American, and female audiences and facilitates further the reaches of Dash's visionary work.

While the film's recognition is based on its uniqueness, *Daughters of the Dust* is embedded within the history of black independent films through its financing and aesthetics as well as through its casting. Many of the film's key roles are played by actors who would be familiar to audiences of black independent films: Cora Lee Day (Nana Peazant) played Oshun, a deity in Yoruba spiritual cosmology, in Larry Clark's *Passing Through* (1977) and Molly in Haile Gerima's *Bush Mama* (1979). Opposite Day in the Gerima film was Barbara O. Jones in the role of Dorothy. Jones appeared in *Child of Resistance* (1972) by Gerima, in *Diary of an African Nun* (1977) by Dash, and in *A Powerful Thang* (1991) by Zeinabu Irene Davis. Trula Hoosier (Trula, Yellow Mary's companion) appeared in *Sidewalk Stories* (1989) by Charles Lane and Adisa Anderson (Eli Peazant) worked in *A Different Image* (1982) by Alile Sharon Larkin. Kaycee Moore (Haagar Peazant) appeared in Charles Burnett's *Killer of Sheep* (1977/2007) and in Billy Woodberry's *Bless Their Little Hearts* (1984), which Burnett wrote. Tommy Hicks (Mr Snead) had been seen in Spike Lee's early films *Joe's Bed-Stuy Barbershop: We Cut Heads* (1983) and *She's Gotta Have It* (1986). Significantly, these actors' prominence and the complex characters they created in *Daughters of the Dust* did not cross over to mainstream films. Their careers tend toward prominent roles in black independent films but minor roles in television or mainstream films. In using actors from the black independent film world, Dash established the film's aesthetic lineage and its target audiences outside the territory of Hollywood and dominant formations of celebrity.

Daughters is further linked with feature films by black women, which would include French director Euzahn Palcy's *Sugar Cane Alley* (1983) and American director Kathleen Collins's *Losing Ground* (1982) among others. Later films such as Cheryl Dunye's *The Watermelon Woman* (1996) and Kasi Lemmons's *Eve's Bayou* (1997) share *Daughters'* thematic concerns with memory, history, identity and visual storytelling. Further, the 1980s and 1990s saw film and literature sharing discursive concerns. Novelists such as Alice Walker (*The Color Purple*, 1983) and Toni Morrison (*Beloved*, 1987) explored black women's identity and African American memory through stories that focused on family dynamics and women's friendships. The circulation of black women's novels doubtless influenced the creation and reception of *Daughters*, which began its life as a novel, and the film helped to articulate black feminist and womanist frameworks cinematically. Dash has said that she wanted to 'make films for and about black women, to redefine African-American women' (Chan 1990). In *Making of An African American Woman's Film*, Dash gives the following hierarchy of desired or expected audiences: black women, the black community and white women. Dash hopes black women will be the film's main audience, advocates and consumers because it intervenes specifically in the history of black female invisibility and misrepresentation in the cinema.

While *Daughters* is a black woman's film, it is still part of the long history of American independent and experimental filmmaking by men and white women that pushes against received traditions and industry standards. For instance, *Daughters* has much in common aesthetically with films such as Shirley Clarke's *The Cool World* (1964), John Cassevettes's *Shadows* (1959), and William Greaves's *Symbiopsychotaxiplasm* (1968). These semi-documentary and jazz-influenced films depart from dominant presentations of black identities and, each in its own way, experimented with merging film's formal, poetic expressivity and its social status as a bearer of objective visual evidence. *Cool World* and *Shadows* both depicted African

American urban subcultures, teenagers and jazz musicians, respectively, while *Daughters* focused on rural communities. However, all three works avoid the black–white paradigm, in which the presentation or formation of Black identity in the film would be limited to its opposition to whiteness within adversarial American race relations – not that the effects of American racism are entirely avoided. *Daughters*, as the title of Dash's post-production book about the film indicates, was strongly motivated by the director's desire to bring African American women's stories to the screen. However, the film's aesthetics link it with significant independent films that are not explicitly concerned with black women. All these films take on broader themes of identity, location, and film form.

Certainly, the success of Steven Spielberg's black women-centred film adaptation *The Color Purple* (1985) opened up possibilities for a film like *Daughters* as it likely did for *Waiting to Exhale* (Forest Whitaker, 1995). Yet *Color* and *Waiting* followed the traditional narrative arc used in mainstream films while *Daughters* has a more languid, diffuse narrative structure. *Daughters* shares some content with *The Color Purple* or *Waiting to Exhale* but since it is done in a very different cinematic style, these films may not appeal to or reach the same audiences. *The Color Purple* was released widely and played in mainstream multiplexes while *Daughters of the Dust*'s release was limited and it counts New York City's art house theatre Film Forum as one of its early venues. *Daughters of the Dust* and the black independent films that it references through the cast share the conundrum of reaching out to black audiences through their content but being embraced by mostly white audiences who view these films in the art house settings to which their forms and perceptions of their inaccessibility have segregated them. Meanwhile, Dash calls for various film audiences and industry professionals to recognize the universe within black women's stories and identify with black female characters. She says,

> There's just a wide array of different characters and people and types and professions that have never before been depicted on the screen. You know, unfortunately Hollywood relies on the old standard stereotypes that are a bit worn and frayed around the edges at this point. But black women are everything and they do everything, and they have a whole lot of different concerns that are just not paying the rent, having babies, worrying about the next fix or the next john. I mean, there's a whole world in here.
> (Chan 1990)

Further reading

Jacqueline Bobo (ed.), *Black Women Film and Video Artists*, New York, Routledge, 1998.

Valerie Boyd, 'Daughters of the Dust', *American Visions*, February 1991, pp. 46–9.

Vera Chan, 'The Dust of History', *Mother Jones*, November/Dececember 1990, p. 60.

Patricia Hill Collins, *Black Feminist Thought: Knowledge, Consciousness and the Politics of Empowerment,* New York, Routledge, 2000.

Julie Dash, *Daughters of the Dust: The Making of an African American Woman's Film*, New York, New Press, 1992.

Jacquie Jones, 'Film Review', *Cineaste*, December 1992, p. 68.

Stanley Kauffman, 'Films Worth Seeing', *New Republic*, 30 March 1992, p. 26.

Jacqueline Stewart, 'Negroes Laughing at Themselves? Black Spectatorship and the Performance of Urban Modernity', *Critical Inquiry*, Vol. 29, No. 4, 2003, pp. 650–77.

Winston-Dixon Wheeler and Gwendolyn Audrey Foster (eds), *Experimental Cinema: The Film Reader*, London, Routledge, 2002.

TERRI FRANCIS

SHORT CUTS (1993)

[Production Company: Fine Line Features. Director: Robert Altman. Screenplay: Robert Altman and Frank Barhydt, based on the stories by Robert Carver. Producer: Cary Brokaw. Cinematography: Walt Lloyd. Editors: Suzy Elmiger, Geraldine Peroni. Cast: Lily Tomlin (Doreen Piggot), Tom Waits (Earl Piggot), Andie MacDowell (Ann Finnigan), Bruce Davison (Howard Finnigan), Jack Lemmon (Paul Finnigan), Zany Cassidy (Casey Finnigan), Julianne Moore (Marian Wyman), Matthew Modine (Dr Ralph Wyman), Madeleine Stowe (Sherri Shepard), Tim Robbins (Gene Shepard), Anne Archer (Claire Kane), Fred Ward (Stuart Kane), Jennifer Jason Leigh (Lois Kaiser), Chris Penn (Jerry Kaiser), Lily Taylor (Honey Bush), Robert Downey Jr (Bill Bush), Frances McDormand (Betty Weathers), Peter Gallagher (Stormy Weathers), Annie Ross (Tess Trainer), Lori Singer (Zoe Trainer).]

At the heart of *Short Cuts* is an accident: when driving through a fancy neighbourhood in Los Angeles, Doreen Piggot (Lily Tomlin), a waitress living in a trailer park, hits Casey Finnigan (Zany Cassidy), a little boy late for school who runs across the street without looking. There are many other 'accidents' in the film: 'Accidents happen every day', a television voice proclaims. 'I wish it hadn't happened but it did', Marian (Julianne Moore) explains to her husband who cannot get over her affair with a painter. 'If they'd had a gate, that would have changed things', Paul Finnigan (Jack Lemmon) muses, implying that his life would have taken a different course. Accidents can be chance. Accidents kill people. Accidents bring people together. As the thread that holds together a disconnected populace, weaving a tapestry of the complexity of social relations across a spectrum of class differences in white Los Angeles, accidents are full of potential and problems. And by the end of the film, we no longer really know what an 'accident' – and a world based on 'accidents' – is.

Accidents define the late twentieth-century megacity of Los Angeles, a city defined in the film by medfly plagues and earthquakes. Los Angeles has often been seen as symptomatic of a 'postmodern geography' (in Edward Soja's phrase), a geography defined by highways and (sub)urban sprawl, with no real centre (no scene in the film is set in Downtown Los Angeles), a geography that expresses (and precipitates) the fragmentation of the social fabric, a geography where social inequality takes on increasingly stark contours as different neighbourhoods are not only distinct from each other but are unequally served by governmental, economic, social and cultural institutions. Sprawling space requires a sprawling narrative, Altman seems to say, connecting his vignettes tenuously, though graphic motives, such as a milk glass, or chance encounters, such the Wymans and the Kanes' meeting at a concert. Social contexts here have the ability to affect aesthetic form, or rather, changing social circumstances ask for a different aesthetic form. Not that *Short Cuts* is aesthetically that experimental. But the widescreen frame seems especially appropriate to Los Angeles, and the lateral pan and tracking shots, where people and objects move in and out of frame, without us being able to anticipate their full movements, are trademarks of the film, not only in the final credits when the camera pans over a Los Angeles map one neighbourhood at a time, never managing to capture the city in its totality.

At the same time, *Short Cuts* is much smaller and much bigger than Los Angeles. Much smaller, because the Los Angeles of the film is a curiously white Los Angeles, an issue that *Crash* (Paul Haggis, 2004), a film much indebted to *Short Cuts* made a point of addressing. To be sure, race nibbles at all the margins of the film's frames, but African American characters never fully enter the storylines and Latinos seem entirely absent: the middle-class black couple leaves town during the first scene of Lily and Bill Bush's story. Zoe repeatedly plays basketball with a number of non-white teenagers. An African American family looks on as Gene Shepard, Betty and Chad Weathers celebrate her birthday in a diner. Paul Finnigan befriends an interracial couple at the hospital. Tess Trainer – in a storyline not found in Carver's original stories – sings at a jazz club where 'it's all black people', as Jerry Kaiser says, before getting himself into a racially loaded altercation with another customer. Letting these characters enter the frame but not the stories, the film both evokes and resists cultural stereotypes.

Despite the film's demographic specificity, critics have often seen the world depicted as typical of the nation. *Short Cuts* provides a 'vast, tragicomic portrait of America' (Heller 1993: 172); it deals with 'feelings of *oppression* ... unnameable events – loss, separation, tragedy – in the suburban malls and fast-food joints of plastic America' (Conley 1994: 332); characters 'embody some half droll and half miserable facet of our national life. Or rather, they *would* embody a national life, taken together, if only they could recognize in each other something more than an occasion for blame' (Klawans 1993: 542). Part of the reason for this thinking must have to do with the fact that Altman had the status of an *auteur* in 1970s Hollywood – before falling from grace in the 1980s – making acclaimed and political films such as *M*A*S*H* (1970), set during the Korean War but widely understood as a critique of the US war in Vietnam, and *Nashville* (1975), another multi-protagonist film that is locally set but acquires a national dimension as it unfolds before the backdrop of a presidential campaign. By contrast, *Short Cuts'* focus is 'domestic and intimate' (Smith 1993: 37). Gone are the rallies and public spectacles. The climactic earthquake replaces the assassination that ends *Nashville*, natural catastrophe succeeds political violence. As if in the larger scope of things, public issues have been replaced with more narrowly private concerns – what some would diagnose as the withering away of the political sphere. No one in *Short Cuts*, Stuart Klawans noted, 'talks politics'.

Part of this absence of politics, this impoverishment of public debate that the film registers, has to do with the way it frames a discussion about the function of media in contemporary life. In fact, not only politics, but Hollywood is curiously absent from this film about Los Angeles – especially since right before *Short Cuts,* Altman had made *The Player* (1992), an acerbic film about the Hollywood film industry (though in *Short Cuts* Hollywood is looming just off-frame, as film crew signs suggest). In fact, the question of how new media change our ways of life, our relationships and our politics are omnipresent in a film where televisions are everywhere. And other media – for instance, phones and photographs – become crucial agents in the film. The baker makes threatening phone calls. Jerry watches a fake suicide as he talks on the phone to Bill, the make-up artist in training. Stuart and his friends take pictures of a real corpse on their fishing trip; Bill takes pictures of a fake corpse. Lois, the housewife making a living through phone sex, has a conversation about 'virtual reality', the 'really real'. Her husband, who ends up killing a young woman, an act that never becomes 'real' to the extent that it never makes it into the media (or the police records), cannot deal with the conflation between the real and the fake. And we might wonder if the more 'serious' media – music and painting – offer any solutions to the conundrum of having to live in a world where the fake and the real increasingly mingle. For Annie, believing Zoe's suicide attempts to be fake, fails to anticipate – and prevent – her real suicide. And Marian, who thinks her art is about the 'responsibility of seeing' only angers her husband: 'What do you think you are, one of your goddamn paintings?' One wonders then, what the function is of the make-believe at the very end – the acting out of conflicts in clown costumes.

What happens to human relationships in such a mediatized, accidental world that has lost a public dimension that might give it cohesion? That's one of the key questions that *Short Cuts* asks, and a fitting one at that for a film so driven by actors' superb performances. The film is full of relationships that exhibit various degrees of dysfunction: Stormy Weathers, the ex-husband who destroys his ex-wife's apartment (but in a supremely surreal touch has the carpet shampooed); Annie who lives with but has lost touch with her grown-up daughter; Ralph and Marian, whose marriage is haunted by an old, accidental affair. The social fragmentation and withering of communication often seem to lead to violence and death: the shooting on the highway, the rape and murder of Caroline Avery, the killing of Nancy, the suicide of Zoe. The film wants to talk about the numbing of emotions and the effects of social performance, but the effects are not always the same. Claire the clown is appalled by her husband's willingness to continue fishing after they found a corpse in the water, but in the end says 'that's really not bad, one person' when listening to the earthquake's death toll announced on television. A father calls Dr Wyman a 'miracle worker', right before something goes horribly wrong with Casey, another of Dr Wyman's patients. About social performance, Claire says: 'I can change but I can always come back to me.' The latter statement prompts Ralph to ask his wife: 'What do you have underneath, Marian?' 'You know,

Ralph, nothing', she responds, in yet another act of performance. We are left with characters whose 'inner lives remain undisclosed' (ibid.: 36).

Within this context of personal relations, the question of gender and sexuality has prompted more specific comment and disagreement. Ever since Laura Mulvey's classic statement on 'Visual Pleasure and Narrative Cinema', that explored how classical Hollywood always seems to either fetishize or investigate the female body from a male point of view in order to contain the threat women supposedly present to men, we have at least become somewhat more aware of the difficulty of representing women on film. *Short Cuts* abounds with naked female bodies. Terrible mothers who say mean things about their ex-husbands to their children. Men who threaten, observe and assault women. Women who discuss sex freely in ways men don't seem to be able to. It may be no coincidence, then, that the film opens itself up to charges of sexism (however defined). And yet, as Klawans has poignantly pointed out, female nakedness – Zoe naked in the pool, observed by Jerry; Sherri posing nude for her sister as Ralph accidentally walks in; Marian taking off her skirt revealing she's not wearing panties; maybe even the naked body in the water – rarely seems to function as a 'visual come-on'. Instead, the film is driven by 'the mutual misrecognition of female despair and baffled male lechery' (ibid.: 542).

For Altman, as we have seen, the ensemble film, the film with multi-strand, non-linear narrative was not new. While earlier films like *Citizen Kane* had experimented with non-linear narrative, in 1970s Hollywood Altman helped consolidate and elaborate the form. In the wake of Hollywood's move to a different business model in the late 1970s – the blockbuster and high-concept cinema – there was little room for a filmmaker like Altman, if only because ensemble films are difficult to reduce to one idea and thus difficult to market. But Altman experienced a resurgence in the 1990s, testament to the importance of the 1970s *auteurs* to the development of commercial film in the nineties. Part of this development had to do with the mainstreaming of independent cinema – witness the success of *Pulp Fiction* (Quentin Tarantino, 1994), or consider that even a film like *Gangs of New York* (Martin Scorsese, 2002) is technically an independently produced film. *Short Cuts* was bankrolled by New Line Cinema subsidiary Fine Line Features, which, along with Miramax, became one of the most successful independent production companies in the 1990s. In 1993, Miramax was bought by Disney and New Line merged with the Turner Broadcasting Corporation (see Wyatt

1996). While many may lament the fact that independent film is now often indistinguishable from mainstream cinema, the confluence also allowed for a change in film aesthetics and film narrative. Nonlinear narrative films, such as in *Pulp Fiction* and *Memento* (Christopher Nolan, 2000), could suddenly become commercial successes. Multistrand narrative films, such as Steven Soderbergh's *Traffic* (2000), Paul Haggis' *Crash* (2005) and Alejandro González Iñárritu's *Babel* (2006), are certainly different from each other, but also became a trend at the beginning of the twenty-first century. In many ways, these changes in narrative style appear to reflect and negotiate contemporary life, characterized by global and digital cultures, where narrative causality and (male) character agency (which so much defined 'classical' Hollywood) no longer seem appropriate or possible, where we need to find new ways of making sense of the world we live in. At the very least, *Short Cuts* – as well as other Robert Altman films – experimented with narrative storytelling that made this larger development possible.

Further reading

Tom Conley, 'Short Cuts', *Psychoanalytic Review*, Vol. 81, No. 2, Summer 1994, pp. 331–6.
Zoë Heller, 'Hollywood's Last Angry Man', *Vanity Fair*, October 1993, pp. 170–80.
Geoff King, *American Independent Cinema*, London, I. B. Tauris, 2005.
Stuart Klawans, 'Short Cuts', *The Nation,* 8 November 1993, pp. 541–4.
Laura Mulvey, *Visual and Other Pleasures,* Bloomington, IN, Indiana University Press, 1989.
Gavin Smith, 'Faultlines of a Daydream Nation', *Film Comment*, Vol. 29, No. 5, September 1993, pp. 36–7.
Edward Soja, *Postmodern Geographies: The Reassertion of Space in Critical Social Theory,* New York, Verso, 1989.
Justin Wyatt, 'Economic Constraints/Economic Opportunities: Robert Altman as Auteur', *The Velvet Light Trap*, Vol. 38, Fall 1996, pp. 52–67.

SABINE HAENNI

PULP FICTION (1994)

[Production Company: A Band Apart and Miramax Films. Director: Quentin Tarantino. Screenwriter: Quentin Tarantino (stories: Tarantino and Roger Avery). Cinematographer: Andzrej Sekula. Editor: Sally Menke. Cast: John Travolta (Vincent Vega), Samuel L. Jackson (Jules

Winnfield), Uma Thurman (Mia Wallace), Ving Rhames (Marsellus Wallace), Bruce Willis (Butch Coolidge), Tim Roth (Pumpkin), Amanda Plummer (Honey Bunny).]

It is difficult to think of another contemporary film which has created a similar impact to *Pulp Fiction*. Others have been as controversial (e.g. *The Last Temptation of Christ* [Martin Scorsese, 1988], *Natural Born Killers* [Oliver Stone, 1994]) but *Pulp Fiction* is different in the way that its reception affected not only the industry and audiences but also pressure groups and academics, resulting in an argument about the morality of the film and the future of filmmaking. *Pulp Fiction* was an event film in the context of mid-1990s postmodern culture and the cinematic trend of 'cool violence', already linked with Tarantino's previous film *Reservoir Dogs* (1992). Tarantino himself became a star and selling point for the film. The divided reactions to *Pulp Fiction* have to be read through the debate around postmodernism itself as being either a mainstream or an oppositional mode. In other words, is it a stylish but superficial imitation of existing texts, or a reinterpretation and re-assessment of cultural forms?

The success of *Pulp Fiction* challenged (particularly in the US) the boundaries between art-house, independent and mainstream cinema. *Pulp Fiction* was the first fully formed incarnation of the 'independent major'; an increasingly pejorative term for a film which has conventions associated with independent cinema (i.e. unconventional style and structure, character rather than action led) but which is coded to appeal to a more mainstream audience because of demands on the producer/distributor as an affiliate of a media conglomerate. This style of filmmaking was embodied – perhaps invented – by Miramax in the mid-to-late 1990s. The Hollywood agent Rick Hess described the way *Pulp Fiction* amalgamated art-house and Hollywood styles; 'Yes it had an unusual timeline totally non-linear in every way, but it had sex and drugs and rock 'n' roll, and violence, and that's something that every studio would have gone for' (Biskind 2004: 169). Miramax, although owned by Disney in 1994, had developed a marketing brand as an independent, small-scale producer battling against the power of Hollywood (a narrative repeated in the persona of Tarantino as the outsider). They had had a relatively successful period distributing independent American and European films before the incredible commercial success of *Pulp Fiction*. The estimated budget for the film was $8.5m which represented minimal risk to Miramax as they had sold the worldwide rights for $11m before filming began. The film went on to gross over $100m at the US box office – the first time an independent film had achieved this. The effect of this success on the independent film sector is debatable. For some filmmakers, *Pulp Fiction* created economic opportunities and an interest in new filmmakers which hadn't existed before. Others were concerned about the phenomenon of 'indiewood' – independent films now carried the kind of financial expectations more usually associated with Hollywood films.

The mixing of Hollywood genres and European cinema styles which made this film so appealing to the emerging independent majors can be also read as an example of postmodernism (which continues to be evident in Tarantino's more recent work, *Kill Bill* [2003] and *Grindhouse* [2007]). The discussion of postmodernism as an aesthetic is itself controversial with some critics arguing the post-modern is a period rather than a style (Jameson 1983). However, there are characteristics which have become accepted as signifying a postmodern text – and which are particularly applicable to film. This categorization relies on the interrelated concepts of simulation, bricolage and intertextuality. All these concepts emphasize the 'ready-made' nature of postmodern culture – the assembly of new texts from existing ones. It is this stylistic tendency which has led to readings of postmodernism as ahistorical. This interpretation argues that the lack of any history or context beyond the reference to other texts in the postmodern aesthetic results in a loss of meaning and analytical possibilities.

Postmodern characteristics are apparent in *Pulp Fiction* in the acknowledgement of film history through references to and recycling of genres, narratives and visual styles. Intertextuality is evident in the construction of the plot, where narrative 'old chestnuts' (gang member takes out the boss's wife and must not fall for her, a boxer past his best is bribed to throw a fight, hit-men on a mission) of B-movie history are re-told. Genre iconography from the 1940s – guns, black suits, briefcases, cigarette smoke, crimson red lipstick and nail polish – appear throughout the film but don't signify that the film belongs to a specific genre. The concept of recycling is also evident in the use of stars; specifically John Travolta whose back catalogue (*Saturday Night Fever* [1977] rather than *Look Who's Talking* [1989]) allows his turn on the dance floor to be read as iconic (rather than merely nostalgic or poignant).

Individual characters are also linked to a specific genre or film style, even though the rest of the cast may not co-exist within it. Mia (the wife of the boss, Marsellus Wallace) is introduced as a femme fatale, her entrance imitating Barbara Stanwyck's in *Double Indemnity* (1947). She is represented in black and white fragments – black hair, trouser legs, ankles, mouth – we don't see her face until the car pulls up at Jack Rabbit Slims. Her role as the untouchable but irresistible wife also echoes the triangular set up of 1940s film noir. Mia is a failed TV actress whose cancelled pilot *Fox Force Five* is an example of Tarantino's references to invented cultural signs (Jack Rabbit Slims, the Big Kahuna Burger) which are intertwined with examples of real popular culture and people (*Modesty Blaize*, Douglas Sirk). Mia's ability to affect the film stock itself – she draws a square on the screen to illustrate 'Don't be a square' – points to the increasingly slippery distinctions between reality and representation highlighted by post-modernism. Mia is a character constructed from the fragments of other imaginary characters whose back story is an invented (but real in the film) TV pilot for a series which never existed (in any context). These levels of referencing and quotation within a single character are reminiscent of *A bout de souffle* (Jean-Luc Godard, 1959) and the way in which Godard constructs the character of Michel Poiccard (Jean Paul Belmondo) as a 'would-be gangster' who imitates Humphrey Bogart.

The difficulty of defining postmodern style is evident in the dif-fering claims for it as either oppositional to or part of mainstream culture; parody or pastiche. The mainstream tendency is pastiche – a visually exciting imitation of existing styles which remains superficial because it is divorced from wider contexts (often dismissed as form over content). The oppositional mode – parody – is also imitative but aims to evaluate and subvert the original codes or meanings associated with the imitated form. The oppositional tendency questions and challenges, attempting to construct new meaning through placing existing cultural styles and movements in new contexts. In post-modern cinema this could refer to the way the intertextual mixing of genres (e.g. blaxploitation, gangster and musical) changes the meaning of the original representations (e.g. race and gender). The mainstream mode is merely an imitation or copy with nothing new to say. Whether a text is parody or pastiche, it will share characteristics of style, form and content but it will operate within either the opposi-tional or mainstream mode. Predictably, the categorization of texts in these terms is open to debate.

This debate is particularly pertinent to the main areas of con-troversy around *Pulp Fiction*; the representation of violence and race. The sudden shifts and contrasts in tone which continually move from suspense and violence to comedy and the banal is another important borrowing from Godard – and the French New Wave. In 'The Bonnie Situation' Vince accidentally shoots Marvin, the student whom he and Jules specifically did not kill in interrogating Brad and his partners. The impact of the violence is undercut by humour – the gun unexpectedly goes off – and irony, as at that moment Vince is asking Marvin whether he believes that God controls people's actions. After the death in the car, Jules is more upset about the mess Vince has made in Jimmie's bathroom, more fearful about his reaction than the death of a young man. The most sustained period of suspense, verging on horror, is during 'The Gold Watch' when Butch and Marsellus are tortured in a pawn shop basement by the owner and a corrupt sheriff – both of whom are drawn as stereotypical hillbillies reminiscent of *Deliverance* (1972). Even when the two men are gagged, bound, covered in petrol and blood, and while the threat of rape is clear but unspoken, the use of film language provokes comedy. This is achieved through the long takes – so long that they have the effect of the uncomfortable silence referred to earlier by Mia – someone in the audience will have to break it, quite likely through nervous laughter. As the sheriff plays 'Eenie Meenie' between the two men to select his victim, the camera remains on their faces capturing their intense concentration on the game and the moment of hope in Marcellus' eyes when he thinks he isn't 'it'. The contrast between the children's game – and the gravity given to it – and the grown, sadistic men becomes absurd and is part of the representation of masculinity in the film; the men are often childlike and bewildered. It is characteristic of Tarantino's style of this period that the actual violence takes place off screen; behind closed doors or just out of frame. This technique allows greater manipulation of the audience whether through the anticipation created in the period before the violence or through the unguarded reaction (often laughter) to the unpredictable. It is in this context that the violence initially made the film so controversial and led to calls for censorship. This tone is not new in American cinema – *Bonnie and Clyde* (1967) also deliberately copied this technique from European films – but in *Pulp Fiction* it is allied to an explicitness that was not previously possible.

Perhaps the more lasting and divisive controversy of the film though is that of the representation of race, particularly in the use of racially taboo words. The effect on the audience is similar to the effect of the unexpected violence – shock and laughter. That it is the director himself speaking the words (as Jimmie) means an aura of 'cool', of being daring and transgressive, is also attached. For some critics (see Hill 1998), the use of postmodern style in Hollywood films operates at a conservative level, smuggling in traditional ideologies (of, for example, race and gender) beneath the experimental style

The film opens, like so many of Jarmusch's, with a journey; a train ride taking naïve accountant Bill Blake (Johnny Depp at his most luminously opaque) towards an inevitably reneged-on promise of a job at the end of the line. A 15-minute sequence virtually devoid of dialogue, this opening is almost a silent movie short in itself, punctuated by Jarmusch's signature blank screen followed by intermittent bursts of sound from the train's wheels and brief melancholic chords from Neil Young's guitar. A series of mid-shots direct to camera show Bill, an uneasy traveller in his interview suit, as an object of curiosity for the other passengers, who are ranged against him in groups or inter-cut in lingering shots. Close-ups detailing faces do nothing to lessen the effect of his rather distanced discomfiture, while the view from the window, far from a release from the stifling carriage, frames images of wrecks: first wagons, followed by Indian settlements, deserted landscapes between looming mountains and forests. Eventually the silence is broken by the fireman, increasing Bill's unease by questioning why he has come 'all the way out here, all the way to Hell', offering the opinion that 'you're just as likely to find your own grave'.

As if prompted by these words a gunshot by Bill's head announces the first moment of action; a group of passengers fire at buffalo through the windows, while Bill's companion tells him the government has sponsored the killing ('a million of them last year alone'). Arriving at last, the train, like so many of Jarmusch's characters, crosses into the frame from one edge, suggesting a pre-existing world into which we, like Bill, have inadvertently and probably misguidedly wandered: the town of Machine dominated by the looming building of Bill's destination. His walk towards it along the length of the single street is reminiscent of the iconic western hero's climactic walk towards a final shootout; here its climax is already undercut by images of townsfolk in an environment shot through with skeletons. A mother and child sit in a doorway beside a wooden trolley full of bones, animal skull trophies line a wall and men are busy loading coffins, followed by the notorious shot of a woman performing a blow job at gun-point – the gun prophetically turned on Bill as he stares.[3] By the time he finally walks through an arch proclaiming 'Dickinson's Metalworks' the viewer is in no doubt that, like Dante's Hell, it may as well proclaim that all hope should be abandoned here.

But this extended preamble to the action, if the events of this laconic film can be so described, does more than simply prepare us for a bad outcome. The unmistakable iconography of the western genre is already fatally disturbed, undercutting even the possibility of heroics, by prefiguring Bill's death – and indeed most of the rest of the film consists of his journeyings while protractedly dying. Far from opening up frontiers for any kind of American Dream, the inhabitants of these territories seem already terminally in decline; perhaps a reflection of that aspect of the genre which, through its narratives of the past, broods on the current state of the country.

Fans of Jarmusch who might have been dismayed to find him working with a traditional genre at all can be swiftly reassured by the early reassertion of his characteristic signatures. The tale may be rooted in death, but the ironic tone is Jarmuschesquely set at the outset through a quotation, here by Henri Michaux, which under-states 'It is better not to travel with a dead man.' This tone extends to the expected deadpan humour of two-shot short exchanges; it also extends to a 'hero' who stumbles over his words, gets his first shot wound by proxy and takes three shots to retaliate against a jealous rival. By misfortune, this rival turns out to be the son of the metal-works' boss, Dickinson (a magnificently irascible cameo by Robert Mitchum), who sets a motley threesome of hired killers on Bill's trail, and also offers a reward, setting up the rather leisurely manhunt which comprises the rest of the narrative. So, his transformation into the archetypal legendary wanted man is characteristically by mistake, just as the gun-toting turns out to be more absurd than heroic. Yet, the film's tone is simultaneously serious, with a documentary-like lingering on shots of townspeople and the Indian tribes, while back-ground events are carefully based on authenticity.[4] The detachment and downplayed tone disguise the seriousness of a refusal from the outset to reproduce the hegemony of 'how the West was won' as anything other than a bloodbath bordering on genocide; a theme of displacement which becomes a key element of the film, thereby, some might consider, introducing a more political edge to Jarmusch's usual free-wheeling style.[5] This is increased with the appearance of Bill's counterpoint character, an Indian calling himself 'Nobody' (played with both humour and gravitas by Gary Farmer), his insub-stantial name prompting ironic dialogue which points up the ever-present shadowland of the spirits ('Who are you travelling with?' 'Nobody'). In the company of Nobody, the film becomes, like all of Jarmusch's, at once a road movie and a buddy film.

If Depp's Blake shows impassivity echoed by several of Jarmusch's more recent characters, Nobody embodies a level of cultural mix and displacement perhaps greater than any of the director's many strangers and outsiders. Yet, this very mix functions to deliver a groundedness of cultural stability in a world of destruction and sudden death. Again, this is rooted in names, as Bill has never heard of the eighteenth-century poet William Blake; whereas Nobody is familiar with his work, and continually quotes it, due to his having been captured and displayed in Europe by white men, and he persists in the belief that Bill is William Blake's re-incarnation. So, snatches of Blake's poetry form a further level of refrain through events.

Rejected by his tribes, Nobody is displaced but far from rootless, as witnessed by his concern to guide the dying Blake over the 'mirror' of the horizon on his last spiritual journey. The film becomes a series of contrasting episodes, alternating pairs of horsemen engaged in desultory conversation, which trails in and out of sequences as voice-over to a blank screen, followed by campfire incidents. One of these campfires shows a skewed version of frontier family values, presided over by a too disturbing to be comic Iggy Pop in a shabby dress. Sally's presence echoes the gender role displacement, evident also in the passively lingering close-up shots on the exquisite Depp face, here verbalized by Sally and her rival companion, as they paw over him ('Your hair's soft like a girl's'), and so forming a further layer of comment on the predominantly male white frontier culture. This is splendidly offset by a diatribe (un-translated, as all the Indian dialogue is) delivered by Nobody's self-possessed and vocal Indian mate when Bill interrupts their love-making.

The cultural contrasts finally elide when, after a canoe journey pursued by Cole[6] and flanked by images of burnt-out settlements, Nobody takes Bill, by then doubly shot and almost comatose, into an Indian compound to acquire the canoe necessary to take him over the 'mirror'. The point of view is almost exclusively the hallucinatory one of Bill as native and totem faces swirl around him, harking back to previous peyote-induced super-impositions when Nobody had seen Bill's face as a skeleton. Eventually, cast up on the shore, Bill's by now prone profile echoes the prow of the sea-canoe provided to make his last journey, in a headdress fully Indian but also echoing the 'religious icon'-like skull crushed underfoot earlier by Cole. As Nobody pushes the canoe towards open water, the beat of the music intensifies, and Bill's head is raised just enough to see the final cartoon 'western' encounter rendered poignant as the Indian and Cole exchange shots, simultaneously stagger, and fall. An extended long shot of sea, sky and drum beat follows the small speck of the boat into oblivion beneath the darkening clouds. A final blank screen gives to apparently uncharacteristic closure the openness of simply another episode on William Blake's journey.

Jarmusch's indie credentials are here intensified by a film which might have been expected to scupper them given its genre base, an array of star cameos, and a more fully extended narrative to frame his usual series of episodes. Yet, these only serve to show how fully the king of the cool slacker pace and tone integrates his use of more conventional elements to point up his risks and departures. Robby Muller's 'art-house' black and white cinematography[7] is beautiful as well as bleak, spectacular without cliché. Jarmusch's early experiments with a static camera[8] are echoed by a lingering hold on composed scenes, extending Jarmusch's long-term homages to the rhythmic stillness of Japanese director Yasujiro Ozu.[9] This contrasts a tranquillity of pace to the overheads and hand-held restless journeyings, and the insubstantiality of a disturbing propensity of shots to recede away from the viewer. The musical score, composed to a rough cut of the film by Neil Young, interposes at key points to hold together the episodic and improvised method[10] with a remarkable emotive force, as this darker take on Jarmusch's style elides into a poetically hallucinatory formality. The director's own scepticism about the usefulness of the 'indie' label, and its current use as a marketing tool,[11] belies his longevity as a director whose collaborative methods contrast with a refusal to exchange control of content or edit for financial backing; the ironic plays and light touch similarly belie a layered weight of meaning, a giving of space for both the slacker and the poet.

Notes

1 See, for example, Mike Atkinson, 'American Indie, That's Entertainment', *Sight and Sound*, Vol. 17, No. 4, April 2007, pp. 18–22.
2 Dead Man Press Conference 1995, http://jimjarmusch.tripod.com/cannes95.htm, accessed 27 June 2007.
3 This shot caused the film to be banned in Australia on its release, to the bemusement of the director. Geoff Andrew, (Jim Jarmusch Interview, in Hertzberg 2001: 195).
4 Such as the statistics of buffalo deaths, and the manner of their killing, also the deliberate infection of blankets sold to Indians – see Jonathan Rosenbaum, 'A Gun Up Your Ass', in Hertzberg (2001: 158).
5 Though this is not the view of the director, whose response to the suggestion is that everything can be analyzed as political (Rosenbaum, in Hertzberg 2001: 161).
6 In shots reminiscent of a similar journey by another group of men on the run in *Down By Law* (Jarmusch, 1986).
7 Based on the grey tone and feel of Mizoguchi's films: Scott Macaulay, 'End of the Road', in Hertzberg (2001: 150).
8 Notably in *Stranger than Paradise* (Jarmusch, 1984).

9 For example, the 'Ozu shot': Cathleen McGuigan, 'Shot by Shot Mystery Train', in Hertzberg (2001: 102).
10 With no use of storyboard or shot list in advance to encourage immediacy (Macaulay in Hertzberg 2001: 150); though with some script concessions to the legendary Mitchum (Andrew in Hertzberg 2001: 190).
11 Macaulay in Hertzberg (2001: 151–3).

Further reading

Ludovig Hertzberg (ed.), *Jim Jarmusch Interviews*, Jackson, University Press of Mississippi, 2001.
Gregg Rickman, 'The Western Under Erasure: *Dead Man*', in Jim Kitses and Gregg Rickman (eds), *The Western Reader*, New York, Limelight Editions, 1998.
Jessica Winter, *The Rough Guide to American Independent Film*, New York, Penguin, 2006.

LYNDA TOWNSEND

SE7EN (1995)

[Production Company: New Line Cinema. Director: David Fincher. Screenwriter: Andrew Kevin Walker. Cinematographer: Darius Khondji. Music: Howard Shore. Editor: Richard Francis-Bruce. Cast: Brad Pitt (Detective David Mills); Morgan Freeman (Detective Lt. William Somerset); Gwyneth Paltrow (Tracey Mills); Kevin Spacey (John Doe).]

Representations of the city have been a staple aspect of Western art and literature stretching back into antiquity. *Se7en* is underpinned by this cultural heritage and in particular by a strand of thought back to the Biblical story of Sodom and Gomorrah[1] that has seen the city as a place of human degradation and sin.

In relation to the specific medium of film, the city in *Se7en* is the bleak world of film noir where the central protagonists find themselves enmeshed in a nightmare world; but it is also the dark place of the horror genre (and the serial killer sub-genre) where evil lurks in human form, the foreboding place of perpetual rain found in a modern sci-fi such as *Blade Runner* where identity is uncertain and nobody is to be trusted, and the place of unrelenting tension amidst elaborate plot twists that features in the psychological thriller. Genres and their overlapping thematic concerns entwine, coming together in the underpinning concept of tragedy.

When as an audience we view the opening credits, like Dante in the opening to the third canto of *The Inferno*, we are in the position of being about to pass into 'the city full of woe' and find ourselves among 'the lost souls'.[2] To be fully prepared for what is to come we should know that Dante begins Canto I of *The Inferno* by saying he 'came to in a gloomy wood' as if awaking into a nightmare place, and that the best-known words of Dante's work constitute the final phrase over the gate of Hell: 'All hope abandon, ye who go through me.' If we know Gustave Dore's opening engraving to Dante's text we might also usefully recall the image of the lone figure in the wood at night with the very roots of trees and tendrils of bushes seemingly alive and reaching out to ensnare him.[3]

The continual murky gloom and rain of the city allied to the dark central thematic idea of the Seven Deadly Sins confirms this film's noir heritage. Outside, we are frequently positioned in such a way as to be surrounded by bleak, grey city buildings that tower over us, or we see things from behind fences or wire mesh that seem to cage and enclose. Inside, we find ourselves in dark corridors and box-like rooms, and always the relentlessly intrusive sounds of the city remain inescapable. The urban space we are given displays modern life as a labyrinthine hell.

In this world, young people believe they can make a difference, that things can be changed for the better: older people know they can change nothing, that the world is destined to continue as a place of sin. These contrasting perspectives and the resulting tensions are embodied in the central relationship between Detective Lt. Somerset (Morgan Freeman) and Detective Mills (Brad Pitt).[4]

The city is this terrifying place where Tracey (Gwyneth Paltrow), the embodiment of innocence,[5] shudders at the thought of bringing up a young child and where even the perverse logic of the serial killer, John Doe, contains a horrifying element of both logic and ultimate truth.[6] In this place, even the calm, ordered, learned and apparently highly civilized Somerset has his midnight habit of throwing a switchblade at a dartboard. Doe (Kevin Spacey) is sometimes shown dressed in a similar way to Somerset, a shadowy character in a dark hat and long cloak-like coat. The implied connection between the two complicates any notions of characters embodying good and evil in any simple way. If Mills is Somerset's younger self with a belief that with others he can contribute towards bringing about change, then Doe is Somerset's alter ego, an other self whose thinking as a result of his own world-weary cynicism he is able only too fully to understand.

Anything good cannot live in this world of darkness and so the fate of Tracey and her unborn baby, as with Ophelia in Shakespeare's *Hamlet*, is entirely to be expected. It is not simply the death of a 'good' character that is at stake but the death of goodness itself. The evening meal scene, during which we come to identify with Tracey, also presents her relationship with Mills as an idealized high school romance. In their 'young love' they are the embodiment of 'the American Dream' and this is what is also therefore destroyed in the resolution phase. The woman here is not the femme fatale of classic post-war film noirs but much more like the embodiment of inno-cence that in movies back to *Nosferatu* (F. W. Murnau, 1922) has had to give itself willingly as a sacrifice to save others, except this time the sacrifice is pointless and fails to defeat evil.

As the audience, we are taken on a tour of 'the dark side' during which we are positioned in such a way as to be powerless to escape the experience. In the brothel scene, in which Somerset and Mills investigate the 'lust' murder, we descend from the dark, chaotic streets above following the detectives into the red hell-like depths of tight rooms and narrow corridors. We are confused by the back-ground noise, which makes it difficult to distinguish exactly what is being said, and by the editing that works to further disorientate us as we struggle to get our bearings. The overall feeling is one of being enclosed in claustrophobic tunnel-like spaces, which is not relieved when we enter the dark boxed space of the room in which the murder took place. Here we are placed in such a position as to be unable to make out exactly what has happened, our view is blocked and we are left only with further uncertainty and confusion. Only gradually in the interview session that follows are we permitted to piece together the gruesome details. This scene is built around lengthy close-ups of the male visitor to the brothel who has been forced to carry out the murder, compelling us to confront in his face the full extent of the horror. The blank grey background and the white blanket framing his face only serve to make doubly sure we concentrate on the actor's performance. The editing that acted to confuse and disorientate in the previous scene is now minimal and unobtrusive. In the grey, box-like space of this police interview room we again feel we are trapped within a confined space. The actor, trapped between the wall and the 'in-his-face' camera, delivers his lines directly to us in close-up, denying us any opportunity to look away. Each movement of the facial muscles is intimately linked to movements of the eyes and to the carefully timed rising and falling voice pattern.

Performance is crucial to our experience of this film but it is performance that is enhanced by careful use of *mise-en-scène*, cinematography, editing and sound. Early on, in the face of opposition from Freeman's character, Pitt as Mills asks the police chief to be allowed to take over the whole case himself. Both his language and his gestures are brash and expansive and this air of confidence is reinforced by the use of low angle camera shots. By contrast, when next morning, Mills is given his own case involving the murder of a district attorney we see someone who is nervous and uncertain of his abilities. Pitt folds his arm across the top of his head to reveal an almost childlike vulnerability, the gesture highlighted for us by the use of a close-up. And our interpretation of performance is further aided by point of view of sound, which is used to give a sense of the isolation Pitt's character feels as he enters the building. We hear the snippets of conversation and muffled exchanges as he would and sense the pressure he feels he is under. Our understanding of this character as someone who displays confidence but is in reality much more fragile and vulnerable is achieved through Pitt's performance allied to camerawork, editing and sound (and the juxtaposition of these two contrasting scenes).

The conclusion to the film confirms the bleak note of the whole, Doe's master plan has been fulfilled on his terms; he has achieved his goal. By contrast, the 'heroes' have been defeated; and their demise would have been all the more complete if we had cut to a black screen after Mills had unloaded his weapon and the compromise ending with Somerset quoting from Hemingway's *For Whom the Bell Tolls* had not been employed to mitigate our confrontation with the tragedy.[7]

Somerset's earlier doom-laden words, 'This is not going to have a happy ending', may be spoken to Mills before they venture into the wasteland beneath the spider's web of overhead power cables, but the warning could just as easily be meant for us. His final voiceover narration restores some sense of equilibrium but only in the limited sense that Laertes' speech might achieve the same at the end of *Hamlet*.

Hollywood narrative focuses almost exclusively on the psychological causes for actions or events that take place, for the decisions or choices that are made, and for individual character traits that are revealed. In *Se7en*, we are continually being asked to understand events in terms of the psychology of our three central characters, the naïve young rookie cop who idealistically believes in attempting to act as a force for good, the cynical older cop who has lost any belief he may have had in the possibility of bringing about change, and the insane yet coldly calculating, even intellectual, psychopathic killer. Little or no concession is made to the possibility that social forces might be at work in creating the city in the image of hell, that there might be more at work than the incomprehensible and inevitable struggle between good and evil. And yet, without ever seemingly setting out to achieve this, what we have here is an ending that is entirely appropriate for a superpower that increasingly finds itself unable to understand the world around it.

Notes

1 Genesis xviii–xix.
2 Dante Alighieri, *The Inferno of Dante Alighieri*, trans. C. Carson, London and New York, Granta, 2002.
3 Dante actually deals with the deadly sins (each representing a weakness of human nature – pride, envy, wrath, sloth, avarice, gluttony and lust) in his book Purgatory rather than Hell, suggesting that these sins are not to be finally and irredeemably connected with hell.
4 This is the classic detective genre combination of the older, hard-bitten professional and the younger, less cynical prodigy; in essence, a relationship often used in other genres such as the western. It allows for confrontation but also some sense of reconciliation between age and youth, experience of life and enthusiasm for life. And it is also a representation of the father–son relationship; an opportunity for the working out of the tensions and joys of that relationship. (Furthermore, we have the now often favoured Hollywood combination of lead actors: black and white.)
5 Exploring the male focus of the text we might not only see Paltrow's role as undeveloped and peripheral but also observe the way in which other female characters are brutalized at every opportunity. The victim of the 'lust' murder is not the person practising lust but the objectified 'person' offering man the possibility for the performance of lust.
6 The irony of Doe quoting the lines from *Paradise Lost, Book II* ('Long is the way/ And hard, that out of hell leads up to the light') is that these words occur as Satan and his fallen Angels are deciding whether one of them can find their way out of hell to the newly created Earth in order to conquer that realm, that is to persuade Adam and Eve to follow their path away from grace with God. The lines are not, therefore, a call to move towards goodness but evil.
7 Even facing death, Hemingway's character, an American professor fighting with the Loyalists in the Spanish Civil War, maintains the importance of struggling for a better world. The words immediately following what Somerset says are 'and I hate very much to leave it'.

Further reading

Richard Dyer, *Se7en*, London, BFI, 1999.
Nick Lacey, *Se7en*, London, Longman, 2001.

James Swallow, *Dark Eye: the Films of David Fincher*, Richmond, Reynolds and Hearn, 2003.

JOHN WHITE

THE INCREDIBLES (2004)

[Production Company: Pixar Animation Studios. Director: Brad Bird. Cinematographers: Andrew Jimenez, Patrick Lin, Janet Lucroy. Music: Michael Giacchino. Editor: Stephen Schaffer. Cast (voices): Craig T. Nelson (Bob Parr/Mr Incredible), Holly Hunter (Ellen Parr/Elastigirl), Samuel L. Jackson (Lucius Best/Frozone), Jason Lee (Buddy Pine/Syndrome), Spencer Fox (Dash Parr), Sarah Vowell (Violet Parr), Elizabeth Peña (Mirage), Brad Bird (Edna Mode).]

Bob Parr's Incredibile is the ideal sports car for the bachelor superhero, featuring a hidden GPS system, a police scanner, a gear shift with settings like 'Hover Mode' and 'Hydro Pursuit', an apparatus for applying Mr Incredible's uniform (including gloves!) while the vehicle drives itself, an ejector seat for irritating stowaways, and a jet engine with rear-mounted rocket booster, activated with that old standby, the red push-button. In this single graphic conceit, *The Incredibles* announces its dual propensities toward avid futurism and cheeky reminiscence and, from an animation standpoint, its twin affections for strong, clean lines and rapid, suggestive detail.

Nevertheless, after the first five minutes of the movie, plus one four-second comic encore as Bob, aka 'Mr Incredible', pulls up to the church where he marries Helen (née Elastigirl), the Incredibile never returns. Worse, flashing forward 15 years to the cubicled, time-clocking, home-making era of the Incredible family's saga, Bob's anhedonia is indexed by his squat two-door sedan, mired in dull grey traffic, barely accommodating the top-heavy and bleary-eyed motorist. This downward trade from the first vehicle to the second – to include, centrally, the deliberate freefall in aesthetic excitement – marks an early frame of reference by which *The Incredibles* establishes its theme of midlife compromise, a primary lode of meaning in the film and a major inroad for audience identification. Certainly, in mining humour and grief from American middle-class experience, *The Incredibles* distinguishes itself profoundly from the vast majority of mainstream animation, though not, importantly, from Pixar's own corpus. *Toy Story* (1995) and *Toy Story 2* (1999) leaven their joyful nostalgia with portents of even the favourite toys' obsolescence.

A Bug's Life (1998) follows an ant named Flik whose colony is coerced by a thuggish grasshopper into producing a double-quota of food. *Monsters, Inc.* (2001) explicitly braids these threads of childhood's evanescence and corporate soullessness, as two aging bogeymen lose their playroom calling and serve as scapegoats for upper-management megalomania. Thus, against the usual folkloric tide of orphans and abandoned children, Pixar often focalizes characters abandoned *by* children. Moreover, these films trace direct links between the dispossession of their heroes and the perversions of capitalism and commodity fetishism: consider the Al's Toy Barn sequences of *Toy Story 2* and the broad protest against rapacious development and regional homogenization in *Cars* (2006). Even *Finding Nemo* (2003), the very biggest of Pixar's hits, and the one least like a capitalist allegory in its Disneyish tale of a stranded clownfish, nonetheless asks the tykes in the audience to empathize for half of the film with the distress not of Nemo but of his panicked and self-critical father.

The emotional weight of *The Incredibles* tilts even more toward parents over offspring. Bob and Helen's gloomy, self-effacing daughter Violet (as in 'shrinking') and their high-octane son Dash disappear for long stretches of the narrative, especially in those sequences that follow Bob to the island laboratory operated by Syndrome – formerly the irksome young fan whom Bob booted from the Incredibile, now a full-blown arch-enemy. Thus, *The Incredibles* risks sidelining the kids, even as the plot pivots on the dangers of alienating children. Only in the last third of the movie, as Helen, Violet, and Dash rescue Bob from his island prison and together vanquish Syndrome does *The Incredibles* galvanize the whole family at the centre of the action. Still, this promotion of the children as agents within the action entails unexpected costs. Violet learns, with familiar and surprisingly regressive overtones, to wipe her bangs away from her eyes and wear brighter colours, thereby snagging a glance from a boy in her school. Wardrobe is destiny for Dash as well, constraining the boy's superheroic potential. Sporting a #2 on his jersey, he deliberately falls behind in a sprint competition, then keeps himself entertained by speeding to a second-place finish.

Copious reviews and editorials at the time of *The Incredibles'* release underscored the film's exceptionalist ethic, some relishing and some balking at the script's perceived elitism, others finding the film complicit with that conservative shift in middle-class sensibilities that surfaced in the 2004 US Presidential and Congressional elections, only three days before *The Incredibles* bowed (see Broder 2004; Howell

2004). Fans and critics alike invariably cited Bob's perturbed pronouncement that 'they keep creating new ways to celebrate medioc-
rity'. The archvillain, Syndrome, raises the stakes of this lament,
weaving the recurrent Pixar anxiety about dubious commodities into
his full-frontal assault on the gifted and talented: 'When I'm old and
I've had my fun, I'll sell my inventions so that everyone can have
powers! Everyone can be super! And when everyone's "super", no
one is!'

In fact, the trajectory of Dash, who intuits this same contradiction
earlier in the film, challenges a pure-exceptionalist reading of *The
Incredibles*. His family simultaneously cheers, micromanages, and confuses him on his way to the silver medal, and in his last line in the
movie, indeed the last line spoken by any Incredible, he admits to his
beaming Dad and Mom, 'I didn't know what the heck you wanted
me to do!' At this instant, the Underminer, the last in the movie's
series of villains, crashes through the asphalt of the stadium parking
lot. As the Parrs apply their superhero masks, the movie lays their
images over the Underminer's stentorian threats: 'I hereby declare
war on peace and happiness! Soon all will tremble before me!' Does
the family's collective recommitment, then, to their extraordinary
abilities entail its own kind of 'war on peace and happiness', the very
sort of pandemonium which prompted the outlawing of superheroes
in the prologue? Is the superfamily as threatening to social order as the
outcast or resurgent antagonist? In that sense, do the Underminer's
endowments of evil genius and wit ('I am always beneath you, but
nothing is beneath me!') invite comparison with the Incredibles' gifts
for public crusading? The dizzying layers of nuance embedded across
the film – right through these final, paradoxical tropes of violent
eruption and reclaimed identity, ironized here as *masked* identity –
trouble the stakes of exceptional self-realization, even as the movie
appears to promote that principle.

These levels of shading and ambivalence, rendered at such high
velocity and in the trademark pitch of Pixar comedy, surely occa-
sioned A.O. Scott's giddy expostulation, 'At last, a computer-animated
family picture worth arguing with, and about!' Again, though, *The
Incredibles* is only a 'family picture' in a highly idiosyncratic way, for
tonal as well as generic reasons. The movie delivers as an action-
adventure, a comedy, and a fantasy film spanning multiple timeframes
and physical worlds. It embodies and revises, too, Stanley Cavell's
famous genus of the 'comedy of remarriage', not only because Mr
Incredible and Elastigirl must recalibrate their relationship in their
new personas as Bob and Helen Parr, but because Helen's moral

authority and, in every sense, her *flexibility* strike a definitive link between 'the new creation of a woman' and the 'new creation of the human' (Cavell 1981: 16).

These strata within *The Incredibles*, confronting adult burdens without fleeing into adolescence, limning spiritual epiphany with elements of risk and threat, and capturing the dismay of the father (in narrative as in design) while signalling the superior pliability of the mother (in wisdom as in derring-do), also set the movie apart from that other genre it otherwise invokes, the male midlife-crisis drama. Many such films assuage the flailing patriarchal ego through harsh parodies of the feminine, like Annette Bening in *American Beauty* (1999) or June Squibb and Kathy Bates in *About Schmidt* (2002), or else filter their primary epiphanies through sons (*Life as a House*, 2001) or male chums (*Sideways*, 2004). Most also take the easy route of telegraphing spiritual malaise through dreary visuals, as in *Little Miss Sunshine* (2006), another dramedic referendum on the state of the middle-class American family. If young Olive's exuberant fiasco in the *Sunshine* finale rhymes somewhat with Dash's indecision about whether to go for the gold or revel privately in his uniqueness, the filmmaking tips its scales decidedly in favour of modesty. By contrast, the stylistic brio and surreal flourishes of *The Incredibles* preach the virtues of setting (and reaching) extraordinary standards, even when the script appears to muffle that message.

This general distribution of sensory vivacity and creativity must be taken as central to everything *The Incredibles* is 'about', especially insofar as these formal hallmarks reiterate the film's and indeed the studio's pervasive valuation of collectivities and potentials over autocrats and rules. Notwithstanding the important graphic and thematic threads one can trace between *The Incredibles* and writer-director Brad Bird's other films, *The Iron Giant* (1999) and, for Pixar, *Ratatouille* (2007), the feature-animation format and *The Incredibles* in particular pose formidable challenges to auteurist readings. With delegated leaders placed in charge of different characters, sequences, environments, and technical conundrums – such as muscle movement, lighting effects, and background-foreground relationships – animation on this scale necessitates the choreography of a massive creative team (see Daalder 2005). An industrial context thereby emerges around Pixar's recurrent vilification of dictators and oligarchies, and also around the widespread reports of the company's struggle to secede from the oppressive parentage of Disney.

If market-watchers have thus cast Pixar in the same David-against-Goliath role as Flik in *A Bug's Life* or Mike and Sulley in *Monsters,*

Inc., arts journalists have cast the company in a more Incredible light: possessed of uncanny strengths, anxious about growth and senescence, competing more than anything with its own Herculean legacy. 'Can Pixar Keep Up the Magic?' a *Business Week* editorial asked as early as 1998, before the studio's second movie had even arrived in multiplexes (Burrows and Grover 1998). With every technological breakthrough and box-office conquest, such as the creation of fully functioning skeletal and muscular systems for each of the Incredibles, or the 8 million copies of *Finding Nemo* that surged off retail shelves in the first *day* of the DVD's release (Linzmayer 2004: 224), the stakes of Pixar's investors and the pressures upon their creative prospects continue to skyrocket.

Finally, though, the appeal of *The Incredibles* as an iconic text for its producing studio has less to do with stratospheric ticket sales or glowing reviews than with its cornucopial outpourings of stylistic daring, visual and sonic density, verbal sophistication, and intellectual nourishment. The Incredibile, the sedan, and the airborne Winnebago (with the Dalí-like accent of Helen's thin-stretched body as parasail) land three different punchlines in three different registers in three short scenes, compared to the static and repeated bleat and grind of *Little Miss Sunshine*'s Volkswagen van. This delicious trio of visions – among hundreds to relish within *The Incredibles*' script, *mise-en-scène*, and Oscar-winning soundtrack – evokes not only the pleasures of this text but the 'To Infinity, and Beyond!' potential of the animated-feature format. 'The superhero can do all these marvellous things, but no one wants him to', Bird says of Bob Parr. 'To me that's the medium of film. It can do all these great things, and yet so many times it isn't allowed to' (Daalder 2005: 93). Here, full permission is finally granted. Every scene is special, which is another way of saying that all of them are.

Further reading

John M. Broder, '*The Incredibles* Tussle with Truth, Justice, and the Middle-American Way', *The New York Times,* 20 Oct 2004, late edn, p. E1.

Peter Burrows and Ronald Grover, 'Can Pixar Keep Up the Magic?' *Business Week*, 16 February 1998, p. 115.

John Canemaker, 'Part Human, Part Cartoon: A New Species', *The New York Times*, Sunday edn, 3 Oct 2004, Sec 2, p. 13.

Stanley Cavell, *Pursuits of Happiness: The Hollywood Comedy of Remarriage*, Cambridge, MA, Harvard University Press, 1981.

Rene Daalder, 'Pixar Perfect: Does the Computer Make Cinema More Real?' *Modern Painters*, November 2005, pp. 90–93.

Peter Howell, 'Pixar Dazzles with Tale for Adults', *Toronto Star,* 5 November 2004, p. F01.

Owen W. Linzmayer, *Apple Confidential 2.0: The Definitive History of the World's Most Colorful Company,* San Francisco, No Starch Press, 2004.

A.O. Scott, 'Being Super in Suburbia Is No Picnic', *The New York Times,* 5 November 2004, late edn, p. E1.

Mark Cotta Vaz, *The Art of the Incredibles,* San Francisco, Chronicle Books, 2004.

NICK DAVIS

BROKEBACK MOUNTAIN (2005)

[Production Company: Focus Features. Director: Ang Lee. Screenwriters: Larry McMurtry and Diana Ossana, based on the story by Annie Proulx. Cinematography: Rodrigo Prieto. Music: Gustavo Santaolalla. Editors: Geraldine Peroni, Dylan Tichenor. Cast: Heath Ledger (Ennis Del Mar), Jake Gyllenhaal (Jack Twist), Michelle Williams (Alma), Anne Hathaway (Lureen Newsome), Randy Quaid (Joe Aguirre), Linda Cardellini (Cassie), Kate Mara (Alma Jr, age 19).]

Brokeback Mountain is something old and something new, a threnody for outlawed ideals and felled amour, for Western grandeur and sublime loneliness, so romantic (indeed, Romantic) in its images and so elemental in its montage that D.W. Griffith could, with one momentous exception, have made it. That the eulogized lovers of this American pastoral are two male sheep-herders, Ennis del Mar (Heath Ledger) and Jack Twist (Jake Gyllenhaal), patently distinguishes *Brokeback Mountain* as a contemporary artifact. Then again, after more than a century of American cinema, the idea of homosexuality as an impossible love, an impossible *life,* particularly beneath the wide-brimmed hats and cerulean skies of the mythologized West, feels trans-historically familiar, a pure form of what the popular cinema has never embraced. By giving rich, spectacular life to such a romance, while maintaining the rule of a tragic trajectory – even today, few closets brim with as many skeletons as the celluloid closet does – *Brokeback Mountain* rehearses Platonic visions of majestic nature, of the aloof rancher and solitary rider, of the passion least likely to survive the political and thematic mandates of American movies, even as the film rejects the platonic in its small-p connotations of sexless disavowal. The film tells an old story (star-crossed lovers) in a new idiom ('gay cowboys'), or else a new story (men in loving bliss with men) in an old idiom (tombs and tears).

Thus, this film, with its penchant for aphorism and its unexpected preoccupation with hetero marriage and bridal desires, is also something borrowed and something blue. Borrowed, yes, from the pages of Annie Proulx's short story, softening her robust evocations of poverty and her hardscrabble spondees ('sleep-clogged', 'broke-dick', 'clothes-pole', 'dick-clipped') with shimmering landscapes and gliding edits, but also from the long lines of antique weepies and queer doomsdays that prepare American film audiences for this otherwise *sui generis* drama. 'Blue' not just in its resplendent vistas and sun-dappled lakes – 'boneless blue' in Proulx's words, another *Big Eden* in the lingo of modern gay film – but also, increasingly, in its emotional temperature and acoustic moods. In more Freudian terms, which the story's ghastly primal scenes and the film's associative edits often invite, *Brokeback Mountain* excavates the unarticulated melancholia of the Western and the romantic drama, crossing the border between these genres and newly idealizing gay desire in both. From that point, the film resublimates these ideals as a ritual of conscious, copious mourning. Vito Russo, one imagines, would not have been appeased. Indeed, many critics and filmgoers who hoped for a flouting of morbid convention, or at least for a rebellion against middlebrow aesthetics, were nonplussed at best by *Brokeback Mountain*. Then again, for many audiences as for Freudians, the difference between mourning and melancholia made for all the difference in the world, and *Brokeback* amassed a box-office tally and a raft of prizes almost as remarkable as the sheer fact of the film's having been made at all and marketed as a mainstream entertainment.

Unprecedented and oddly self-fossilizing, then, a breakout hit sheathed in its own beautiful amber, *Brokeback Mountain* has none of the restive rhetorical fervour of Mel Gibson's *The Passion of the Christ* (2004) or Michael Moore's *Fahrenheit 9/11* (2004), two equally improbable and comparably inflammatory blockbusters of the pre-*Brokeback* year. Nor, at the formal level, does the film challenge the limits of *mise-en-scène* or montage to the outlandish and paranoid levels that the Gibson and Moore films respectively do. *Brokeback Mountain* is a different kind of Op/Ed flashpoint, a film perhaps more newsworthy in concept than in execution, more in its being than in its saying, except insofar as, extending the film's long train of para-doxes, its ostentatiously reticent craftsmanship served both to quell anxieties (it's 'well-made') and to stoke them (what ever happened to New Queer Cinema?).

The first wave of scholarly responses imply that, in large part, queer academics find the furore as predictably contoured as many of them find the film itself. Scott Herring prefaces a *GLQ* roundtable about what he calls 'the *Brokeback Mountain* noncontroversy of 2005 and 2006' with a sharp remark about the film's 'prosthetic politicization' as 'a socially conscious "issue" film that invites nothing but pure escapism' (2006: 94). Ara Osterweil (2007) likens the film's emotionally ripe close-ups, its ideologies of thwarted romance, even its dialogue, as terse and mannered as intertitles, to those of Griffith's 'yellowface' melodrama *Broken Blossoms* (1919), an analogy that Ang Lee, the Taiwanese director of *Brokeback Mountain*, could only take as rebarbative. D.A. Miller finds even more infuriating these recurrent ambiguities and anachronisms in the film's politics of form and characterization:

> Male homosexuality in *Brokeback Mountain* is massively contradictory: it is, by turns, depending on which opinion is up for flattery, irresponsible and committed, casual and deeply felt, shocking and perfectly natural. In one scene, the Homosexual appears as the declared enemy of the family; but in another, he rises nobly to its defense; he hates women, of course – at least when he is not shown loving and caring for them; and though the film implicitly affirms his right to social recognition, it also dooms him, inexorably, to suffer more than social death.
>
> (2007: 51)

However specific and persuasive a case Miller makes for the ideological dodges and self-insulations of *Brokeback Mountain*, the polyvocality he describes help to certify the film as art rather than lobbyism. Moreover, while Miller reads the abundance of *Brokeback*'s ingrained interpretive possibilities as nothing but a cynical proliferation of media hooks and profit potentials, the film astutely nourishes and invites those forms of collective, caucus-style deliberation that characterize modern reception. *Brokeback*, crafted as a throwback to the days of the nickelodeon, and seemingly invested in the pathos if not the ethos of the abject loner, nonetheless encourages and rewards the democratic structures of the critical roundtable (as in special issues of *Film Quarterly* and *GLQ*), the call-in show, the conference panel, and the blogosphere, with all of its proliferating links and concatenated reader comments.

Compounding these layers of discourse, further afterlives and accidents have already gauzed the film in even more layers of myth. Commercial success vindicated *Brokeback*'s centrist champions while ratifying the scepticisms of anti-mainstream detractors. The surprise loss of the Best Picture Oscar to Paul Haggis' *Crash* (2005) conscripted the film into the annals of famous Academy affronts, and into a spurious feud between anti-racism and anti-homophobia among Oscar trackers, muffling the liberal effusions one might have expected on the occasion of a non-white filmmaker finally winning Best Director. The abrupt and nonsensical death of Heath Ledger, barely two years after *Brokeback*'s world premiere, has again shifted the framework of cultural memory, recharging the film's atmosphere of portent and loss, detaching Ledger from the persistent Brando comparisons of the initial reviews and re-affiliating him as well as the film with the fragile, unresolved agons of James Dean and his 1950s triptych.

More generic models of critical reframing will also, no doubt, unfold. Devoted auteurists, for example, may seize the occasion of *Brokeback* to resuscitate the popular standing of *Ride with the Devil* (1999), Lee's overlooked epic about Confederate vigilantes during the Civil War, and therefore his other major exercise in American political and regional revisionism. Lee followed *Brokeback* with the Chinese-language, World War II espionage drama *Lust, Caution* (2007), rated NC-17 in the United States for the extended, acrobatic sex scenes between its mainland-born spy (Tang Wei) and her brutal, collaborationist quarry (Tony Leung Chiu Wai). These frank sequences call into question the concision and visual obliquity of *Brokeback*'s erotic exchanges between Ennis and Jack, especially for viewers who interpreted these demurrals of framing and editing as inevitable extensions of the tactful introversion that typified earlier Lee films like *The Wedding Banquet* (1993), *Eat Drink Man Woman* (1994), *Sense and Sensibility* (1995), and *The Ice Storm* (1997). Meanwhile, Focus Features, which had so recently consolidated itself when it produced and distributed *Brokeback Mountain* – and which therefore took a major risk, as a new brand and a nascent mini-studio, on a film with such impalpable commercial appeal – imposes its own set of associations. Lee's film, however stylistically disparate, strengthens its credentials as revisionist queer historiography when situated among the series of other Focus projects about sexual dissidence and complex modes of representation, including Todd Haynes' *Far from Heaven* (2002) and Gus Van Sant's *Milk* (2008). Then again, the Focus imprimatur has also affixed itself to films like *The Motorcycle Diaries* (2004) and *Atonement* (2007) that sparked *Brokeback*-style misgivings about the dubious effects of beatific aesthetics applied to seemingly anti-nostalgic material.

Of course, every film evolves and mutates, as historical artifact, as critical touchstone, as artistic achievement. Beyond, however, the sheer volume of ideological debates, generic turf wars, scholarly investments, pre- and post-production narratives, burgeoning and truncated star trajectories, and liberal-political disquiets about 'positive' representations that encircle *Brokeback Mountain*, beyond the film's inevitable embroilment in speculations about the future of cinema (or of particular storylines and niche markets), *Brokeback Mountain* ironizes and enriches all of these discussions because the film itself is so intensely structured by the trope of original, inscrutable meanings and moments that years of retrospection and discourse finally overwhelm. Readings of the movie unanimously privilege the sequences of Ennis and Jack's initial and sublime acquaintance, toward which the rest of the movie indeed points, even as the frames grow tighter and the palette more subdued. Yet we diminish our sense of the film if we read its second hour in terms only of subtraction and not of melancholic accumulation. Consider the sedimenting of characters, many of them absent from or only implied within the story, who here inhabit important passages of story and time; the geographic spread, to Texas and Mexico; a gathering focalization on Ennis' daughter Alma Jr (Kate Mara) and her imminent wedding; the narrowing of mountaintop reveries to quick, subjective flashes, a pattern that eventually describes the film's whole, confounded vantage on Jack. *Brokeback Mountain* lays general but also specific sheets of time and distance over its initial rush of spontaneity and feeling, itself left inarticulate by the film as well as its characters.

The key tension in the film lies between the abrupt stunting of possibility (the performative assertion 'You know I ain't queer', the expulsion from Brokeback, Alma's mid-coital refusal to bear more children, the divorce, the break-ups, the diegetic disappearance of Ennis' other daughter, the rejection of Jack's plan for happy togetherness, the end of Jack's life) and the open, infinite, textual and contextual accretion of years, meanings, regrets, legibilities and illegibilities. 'If you can't fix it, Jack, you gotta stand it', Ennis advises. Jack's apropos response: 'For how long?' Indeed, what needs fixing, and what ain't broke(back)? What is 'it' we gotta fix and stand? After all of our readings, quarrels, and interventions, what is left standing in *Brokeback Mountain*, and for whom or what does it stand? The open/shut dialectic indexes itself in the final shot, after Lee has shrunk and displaced the regality of the mountain to the azure flatness of a postcard – reversing, in the process, the famous melodramatic pivot in Douglas Sirk's *Magnificent Obsession* (1954) as a postcard of Italy springs to life. Ennis shuts the door where the postcard hangs, together with the iconic shirt-within-a-shirt (again, layers within layers). But as he

INDEX

Cinema Studies: The Key Concepts
(Third Edition)

Susan Hayward

Ranging from Bollywood superstar Amitabh Bachchan to Quentin Tarantino, from auteur theory to the Hollywood blockbuster, *Cinema Studies: The Key Concepts* has firmly established itself as the essential guide for anyone interested in film. Now fully revised and updated for its third edition, the book includes new topical entries such as:

- Action movies
- Art direction
- Blockbusters
- Bollywood
- Exploitation cinema
- Female masquerade.

Providing accessible and authoritative coverage of a comprehensive range of genres, movements, theories and production terms, this is a must-have guide to a fascinating are of study and arguably the greatest art form of modern times.

ISBN 978-0-415-36782-0

Available at all good bookshops
For ordering and further information please visit www.routledge.com

Communication, Cultural and Media Studies: The Key Concepts
(Third Edition)

John Hartley

Communication, Cultural and Media Studies: The Key Concepts is a book to help you come to terms with terms, compiled by a leading figure in the field. The third edition of this classic text forms an up-to-date, multi-disciplinary glossary of the concepts you are most likely to encounter in the study of communication, culture and media, from 'anti-globalization' to 'reality tv', from 'celebrity' to 'tech-wreck'.

This latest edition includes:

- over 70 new entries
- most entries revised, rewritten and updated
- coverage of recent developments in the field
- an extensive bibliography to aid further study.

ISBN 978-0-415-26889-9

Available at all good bookshops
For ordering and further information please visit www.routledge.com

Cultural Theory: The Key Concepts
(Second Edition)

Edited by Andrew Edgar and Peter Sedgwick

"Thorough, well-written and accessible, this text should be an indispensable part of every library"

Professor Douglas Kellner, *University of California at Los Angeles*

Now in its second edition, *Cultural Theory: The Key Concepts* is an up-to-date and comprehensive survey of over 350 of the key terms central to cultural theory today. This latest edition includes new entries on:

- Colonialism
- Cyberspace
- Globalisation
- Terrorism
- Visual Culture

Providing clear and succinct introductions to a wide range of subjects, from feminism to postmodernism, *Cultural Theory: The Key Concepts* continues to be an essential resource for students of literature, sociology, philosophy and media, and anyone wrestling with contemporary cultural theory.

ISBN 978-0-415-39939-5

Available at all good bookshops
For ordering and further information please visit www.routledge.com

Fifty Contemporary Filmmakers

Edited by Yvonne Tasker

Fifty Contemporary Filmmakers examines the work of some of the most popular, original and influential cinematic voices. Each entry offers both an overview and a critique of its subject's career and works, looking at the genres in which they work and their relationships to other films and filmmakers. It covers figures drawn from diverse cinematic traditions from around the world and includes:

- Luc Besson
- Spike Lee
- Joel and Ethan Coen
- David Lynch
- Martin Scorsese
- John Woo
- Mira Nair
- Wim Wenders

Each entry is supplemented by a filmography, references and suggestions for further reading, making *Fifty Contemporary Filmmakers* an indispensible guide for anyone interested in contemporary film.

ISBN 978-0-415-18974-3

Available at all good bookshops
For ordering and further information please visit www.routledge.com

Film Studies: The Basics

Amy Villarejo

Whether it's *The Matrix* or *A Fistful of Dollars* that's brought you to film studies, this is a lively and thorough introduction to exactly what you will be studying during your course. *Film Studies: The Basics* will tell you all you need to know about:

- the movie industry, from Hollywood to Bollywood
- who does what on a film set
- the history, the technology and the art of cinema
- theories of stardom, genre and film-making.

Including illustrations and examples from an international range of films drawn from over a century of movie making and a glossary of terms for ease of reference, *Film Studies: The Basics* is a must-have guide for any film student or fan.

ISBN 978-0-415-36139-2

Available at all good bookshops
For ordering and further information please visit www.routledge.com

Fifty Key British Films

Edited by John White and Sabine Haenni

"I feel this book will become a standard classroom text and I would heartily recommend it to all students and teachers of British films"

Professor James Chapman, *University of Leicester*

This book provides a chance to delve into fifty British films considered a true reflection of the times. With case studies from the 1930s heyday of cinema right up to the present day, this chronologically ordered volume includes coverage of:

- The Ladykillers
- The 39 Steps
- A Hard Day's Night
- The Full Monty
- A Clockwork Orange
- The Wicker Man.

In *Fifty Key British Films*, Britain's best known talent, such as Loach, Hitchcock, Powell, Reed and Kubrick are scrutinised for their outstanding ability to articulate the issues of the time from key standpoints. This is essential reading for anyone interested in film and the increasing relevance of the British film industry on the international scene.

ISBN 978-0-415-43330-3